14 95/X

COGNITION IN PRACTICE

COGNITION IN PRACTICE

*Mind, mathematics and culture
in everyday life*

JEAN LAVE

University of California, Irvine

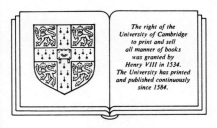

The right of the
University of Cambridge
to print and sell
all manner of books
was granted by
Henry VIII in 1534.
The University has printed
and published continuously
since 1584.

CAMBRIDGE UNIVERSITY PRESS
CAMBRIDGE
NEW YORK   PORT CHESTER
MELBOURNE   SYDNEY

Published by the Press Syndicate of the University of Cambridge
The Pitt Building, Trumpington Street, Cambridge CB2 1RP
40 West 20th Street, New York, NY 10011, USA
10 Stamford Road, Oakleigh, Melbourne 3166, Australia

First published 1988
Reprinted 1989

Printed in Great Britain at the University Press, Cambridge

British Library cataloguing in publication data

Lave, Jean
Cognition in practice: mind, mathematics
and culture in everyday life.
1. Cognition
I. Title
153.4   BF311

Library of Congress cataloguing in publication data

Lave, Jean.
Cognition in practice: mind, mathematics, and culture in everyday
life / Jean Lave.
    p.   cm.
Bibliography.
Includes index.
ISBN 0-521-35015-8
1. Cognition.   2. Psychology, Applied.   I. Title.
BF311.L29   1988
153.4 – dc19   87-23289 CIP

ISBN 0 521 35015 8 hard covers
ISBN 0 521 35734 9 paperback

This book is dedicated to my mother and father
Elizabeth DeWees Carter and Herbert Edmund Carter

CONTENTS

FIGURES

TABLES

TABLES

PREFACE

It seems impossible to analyze education – in schooling, craft apprentice-ship, or any other form – without considering its relations with the world for which it ostensibly prepares people. But further, these relations cannot be addressed within the social sciences today without re-examining the role of cognitive theory in explaining the effect of education on everyday activity. This book begins with a general question about the connections between cognitive theory, educational forms, and everyday practice – specifically, the manner in which their complex interactions have shaped the historical and cultural character of each. In order to consider this question, orthodox explanations of cognitive processes, and the assumptions underlying them, are explored anew. This excursion, which will lead us through diverse empirical investigations, ends with suggestions that transform our conceptions of culture, cognition, and activity in the lived-in world.

I have pursued these general issues in several contexts over the years, beginning with a study of the learning and use of math among Vai and Gola apprentice tailors in Liberia (1973–78). At that time, differences between schooling and other instructional forms were couched in terms of "formal" and "informal" education. Apprenticeship was assumed to exemplify concrete, situation-specific learning. Yet experiments de-signed to explore the transfer of arithmetic knowledge from apprentice-ship and schooling to unfamiliar problems showed that the effect was trivial. A later study by Mary Brenner (1985) also called into question the common belief that schooling is a font of transferable abilities. She found that Vai school children invented, and progressively improved, their skill at a syncretic form of math drawn from both everyday practice and concepts taught formally. This syncretic math was learned – but not taught – in school, and did not seem to be used elsewhere. Further ethnographic research among Vai tailors provided strong evidence that routine calculations in the tailor shops were quite different from those evoked in experiments, whether or not the tailors had attended school. Existing theoretical perspectives on problem solving and the effects of schooling threw little analytic light on all this. Quite the opposite: the Liberian research challenged the importance of learning transfer as a source of knowledge and skill across situations, raised doubts about experimental methods of investigating cognition, and made plain the need for an alternative analytic framework with which to approach the study of everyday practice.

Since these doubts ran to the very heart of cognitive anthropology and psychology, it seemed important to pursue the discoveries of the Liberian project in a comparative study of everyday mathematics in the US; even more urgent, clearly, was the need to find a theoretical framework that would account for the specifically situated structuring of cognitive activity, including mathematical activity, in different contexts. The Adult Math Project was born of these concerns. It was designed to investigate arithmetic use *in situ*, following the same individuals across varied settings in the course of their daily lives. At the same time, during a sabbatical year (1981–82) spent at the Center for Human Information Processing at the University of California, San Diego, I began a critical review of the literature of cognitive theory itself. This, for reasons that will become apparent, led me to consider theories of practice as an alternative basis for characterizing everyday mathematical use, educational processes – and, yes, cognitive theory. The ethnographic and experimental materials of the AMP became the testing ground for an enterprise far more comprehensive than first intended. In the end, these developments took precedence over the study of craft apprenticeship. The present book is, in fact, the second in a series, of which the first (*Tailored learning: apprenticeship and everyday practice among craftsmen in West Africa*) has yet to be completed.

The Adult Math Project was supported by the National Institute of Education (Grants NIE-G-078-0194 and G-081-0092). The Institute for Research on Learning, Palo Alto, California provided support for the preparation of the manuscript. Two close collaborators contributed deeply, creatively and with sustained hard work to the realization of the project: Michael Murtaugh and Olivia de la Rocha. When pronouns shift from I to we in the text it reflects their direct involvement in the collection of the data and its analysis, as well as in the evolving theoretical position presented here. In particular, we worked out and wrote up much of the analysis of arithmetic in the supermarket in Lave,

Murtaugh and de la Rocha 1984. (An expanded version appears in chapter 7 here.) Michael Migalaski and Katherine Faust collected and analyzed parts of the data exceedingly skillfully. Hugh Gladwin and Mary Brenner have contributed ideas and support with great generosity. John Comaroff has been a deep source of knowledge and encouragement throughout. The work of Kurt Danziger, Steinar Kvale and Sylvia Scribner had special impact at turning points in the development of the argument. Aaron Cicourel, Benjamin N. Colby, Michael Cole, Anthony Giddens, Dorothy Holland, Edwin Hutchins, Willett Kempton, Bruno Latour, Ray McDermott, Andrea Petitto, Douglas Price-Williams, Barbara Rogoff and John Thompson read various versions and parts of the manuscript. I am glad for this opportunity to acknowledge publically my thanks to each one for their thoughtful, critical contributions to the project.

Very special thanks and cheers to my daughter Rebecca.

1
INTRODUCTION: PSYCHOLOGY AND ANTHROPOLOGY I

The problem is to invent what has recently been nicknamed "outdoor psychology" (Geertz 1983). The book is an inquiry into conditions that would make this possible. The conclusion: that contemporary theorizing about social practice offers a means of exit from a theoretical perspective that depends upon a claustrophobic view of cognition from inside the laboratory and school. The project is a "social anthropology of cognition" rather than a "psychology" because there is reason to suspect that what we call cognition is in fact a complex social phenomenon. The point is not so much that arrangements of knowledge in the head correspond in a complicated way to the social world outside the head, but that they are socially organized in such a fashion as to be indivisible. "Cognition" observed in everyday practice is distributed — stretched over, not divided among — mind, body, activity and culturally organized settings (which include other actors). Empirical support for this proposal has emerged recently from research exploring the practice of mathematics in a variety of common settings. These studies converge towards a view that math "activity" (to propose a term for a distributed form of cognition) takes form differently in different situations. The specificity of arithmetic practice within a situation, and discontinuities between situations, constitute a provisional basis for pursuing explanations of cognition as a nexus of relations between the mind at work and the world in which it works.

The problem and the project

The Adult Math Project (AMP), an observational and experimental investigation of everyday arithmetic practices in different settings, has provided a basis for the analytic and theoretical development of such an

1

argument. It began several years ago with simple descriptive questions about arithmetic practice: How does arithmetic unfold in action in everyday settings? Does it matter whether it is a major or minor aspect of ongoing activity? Are there differences in arithmetic procedures between situations in school (e.g. taking a math test) and situations far removed from school scenarios (in the kitchen or supermarket)? To search for answers we undertook a number of closely related studies: of "best-buy" arithmetic calculations in the course of grocery shopping in the supermarket; a simulation experiment on these same calculations; an extensive set of arithmetic tests; and observations across time, settings and activities of dieting cooks in their kitchens; and of people managing the flow of money through their households.

More general questions focused on relations between arithmetic use and its sociocultural locus in time and space. Success at problem solving, the procedures employed, and the problems themselves, varied for the same people in different contexts. For example, a teacher in an arithmetic lesson might pose a word problem for the children: "Becca has four apples and Maritza has five apples, how many apples in all?" The answer to this "apple" problem and another observed in the supermarket is "nine." But here is the problem as it appeared in the market, observed during a grocery-shopping expedition. The shopper was standing in front of a produce display. As she spoke she put apples, one at a time, into a bag. She put the bag in the cart as she finished talking:

> There's only about three or four [apples] at home, and I have four kids, so you figure at least two apiece in the next three days. These are the kinds of things I have to resupply. I only have a certain amount of storage space in the refrigerator, so I can't load it up totally . . . Now that I'm home in the summertime, this is a good snack food. And I like an apple sometimes at lunchtime when I come home.
>
> *(Murtaugh 1985b: 188)*

This is a problem in several senses other than those posed by a conventional math "word problem." There are several plausible answers — 9, 13, 21. It appears that the problem was defined by the answer at the same time an answer developed during the problem, and that both took form *in action* in a particular, culturally structured setting, the supermarket. We also observed this shopper's math practices in other settings, one of which was a test-like format borrowed from school arithmetic. A week after the grocery-shopping expedition she worked out a large number of math problems during a comprehensive survey of her knowledge of school arithmetic (e.g. integer, fraction, decimal and negative number arithmetic). Her activity in this setting offered little useful information about her success at math in the supermarket, about the kinds of problems encountered there, or about the procedures she devised for resolving them.

The AMP investigated arithmetic practices in a variety of settings to gain a different perspective on problem solving from that found in school or laboratory. The research focused on adults in situations not customarily considered part of the academic hinterland, for no one took cooking and shopping to be school subjects or considered them relevant to educational credentials or professional success. AMP "experts" were grocery shoppers rather than physicists and none of the novice learners beginning a new dieting program was a college sophomore. In order to observe variation in (still ordinary) cognitive activity the 35 participants were chosen to reflect broad differences in schooling, age, time since schooling was completed, family size and income. We began with participant observation, analysis of the settings for their activities, and description of the organization of the activities within which we hoped to catch glimpses of arithmetic in process. All were interviewed, observed in action, and asked occasionally to vary their everyday activities in specified ways. And we asked them to endure our experimental and test-like attempts to learn about their current knowledge of school and other arithmetic procedures.

Several years of exploration of arithmetic as cognitive practice in everyday contexts had led to a kernal observation from which the argument follows. The same people differ in their arithmetic activities in different settings in ways that challenge theoretical boundaries between activity and its settings, between cognitive, bodily, and social forms of activity, between information and value, between problems and solutions.

The empirical and theoretical characterization of situationally specific cognitive activity – what it is, and why – is, therefore, the central project of the book. This subsumes a number of analytic questions. Is the absence of school-problem formations in everyday math activity to be interpreted as "the absence of school mathematics," the construction of some other mathematics, the inadequate or incomplete use of school arithmetic? How does schooling shape arithmetic activity in everyday situations? What model might best capture the unfolding character of problem-solving processes *in situ*? What constitutes an adequate, general theoretical formulation of situationally specific cognitive activity, of mundane settings, and of activity in such settings? Resolutions to these questions will be pursued throughout the book.

It may seem odd that the work has been concentrated on participants and activities rather far removed from school and laboratory, and yet focused on arithmetic – school subject and exemplar of beliefs about the rational, scientific mind. Both the sites and content of the research reflected our assumptions about the cultural construction and distribution of mathematical knowledge. It seemed crucial to take into account the web of relations among academic cognitive theory, the organization of schooling, the socialization experiences of people in school, and their theories (as alumni) of cognition, schooling, and "proper" arithmetic practice. This seemed especially important because research on the ongoing activities of AMP participants suggested that our understanding was entangled with institutions and dilemmas which, for purposes of cognitive research, are usually treated as if they had no direct bearing on each other.

One example of these intricate ties is a widely shared belief that "scientific thought" is a proper yardstick with which to measure, diagnose and prescribe remedies for the "everyday thought" observed in experiments and schooling. This belief has long historical roots (see chapter 4) that have influenced cognitive theory, the institutional form of schooling, and folk theories alike. Further, Western culture links science, schooling, and everyday practice in a hierarchical ordering of the kinds of thinking and knowledge supposed to be characteristic, respectively, of professional experts, "laypersons" (a term that should give pause), and "just plain folks" (jpfs).[1] There are influential networks of communication between academic psychology, the school establishment that educates both laypersons and scientists, and the alumni of these institutions. These networks ensure that psychological theories affect, though not reliably, both educational theories and educational practice, which in turn shape and are shaped by the beliefs of students. Alumni of schooling are the objects whose after-(school)-life is theorized about by psychologists and educators, who at the same time *are* the theorists, the teachers, and the parents of children in school.

At the center of this cultural web lies the concept of learning transfer, reflecting widely shared assumptions about the cognitive basis of continuity of activity across settings. Conventional academic and folk theory assumes that arithmetic is learned in school in the normative fashion in which it is taught, and is then literally carried away from school to be applied at will in any situation that calls for calculation. There are conventional opinions about how well this works: "most kids fail to learn in school so the world must be made up of un-numerate people who cannot multiply or divide," or "school arithmetic algorithms are used routinely in the everyday lives of school alumni (there is no other kind of math to use)." The most common view distinguishes successful alumni from the unsuccessful, attributing constant and skilled use of school knowledge to the former, and rare, often erroneous, use to the latter. None of these propositions is given support by AMP research. Nor would one expect them to be if arithmetic practice were in any serious sense constructed *in situ*.

All of this suggests that schooling is implicated in any analysis of arithmetic activities in everyday practice. But there is a further implication: to the extent that the interconnections among cognitive theory, schooling and everyday practice are not taken into account as such, they form a major impediment to penetrating a cultural edifice whose monumental character has, arguably, prevented anything *but* confirmation of conventional, socially and culturally organized beliefs about cognition. One remedy for this state of affairs is to focus studies of cognition on situations as far removed from school and laboratory as possible, not in order to achieve the impossible feat of neutralizing their influence on practice, but to refract it from a different angle while keeping relations with schooling continually in view. The other is to approach and analyze *cognitive theory* as a routine, unexceptional aspect of Western culture.

There is still pending the question of why arithmetic is the subject matter of these studies. In earlier research on relations among educational forms, cognitive theory and everyday practice, with Vai and Gola tailors' apprentices in Liberia (Lave 1977, 1982, in preparation: Reed and Lave 1979), the focus on arithmetic was initially motivated by methodological concerns. Math provided a basis for comparison, since both apprentices and school children learned and used it in their everyday educational activities. But the longer I have pursued the matter, the richer the reasons for continuing to do so. Briefly, arithmetic is an accepted topic for research within cognitive psychology, hence observational research in settings other than laboratories offers opportunities to compare results and raise questions about the ecological validity of experimental studies. Arithmetic is a sympathetic "medium" for the researcher who wishes to study activity in open-ended situations, for it has a highly structured and incorrigible lexicon, easily recognizable in the course of ongoing activity. For the same reason it is more easily analyzed in the absence of complete process data. And it allows us to focus on activity whose specific presence in the web of relations among academic psychology, school organization and folk models, was as explicitly available for examination as possible.

Another, powerful, reason for focusing on math lies in relations between practices attributed to "lay" cognition, the practices of academicians interested in cognition, and the theory behind the practices behind the attributed cognitive characteristics. The participants of the AMP inhabit a world conventionally presumed to be populated by faulty mathematicians – a world in which the importance and ubiquity of math has not been assessed but is never questioned. Yet experimental tasks call for mathematical and logical problem solving as a central, ongoing activity. In this context the central theoretical metaphor is a computational one in which the mind is supposed to reflect, represent and hypothetically to operate on, rather than interact with, the world (de la Rocha 1986, especially chapter 2). Arithmetic practice in everyday life is of interest beyond its immediate scope and value to practitioners because of these relations between theory, practice and the attribution to subjects' practice of a common set of principles. One way to rethink models of mind is to reexamine cognitive processes that have been infused with a specific theoretical meaning by contemporary cognitive theory, as has mathematics. In short, a different description of the phenomenon may provide grounds for pursuing a different problematic of cognition altogether.

A dilemma of shared dilemmas

Cognitive psychology and cognitive anthropology have elaborated the study of how people think on the basis of, among other things, fundamental assumption about the nature of culture, the social world, and their relations with cognition. There may be no reason to review these assumptions unless the main task, the investigation of cognition, is hampered by their conventional formulations. The latter situation has developed in the last 15 years, as some psychologists have begun to doubt the ecological validity of experimental findings and to ask what thinking is like in the pervasive contexts of people's lives (Bronfenbrenner and Mahoney 1975; Neisser 1976; Cole, Hood, and McDermott 1978; Bronfenbrenner 1979). For their part, cognitive anthropologists have long expressed concerns about the psychological validity of their analyses of cultural category systems (e.g. Burling 1964; Romney and D'Andrade 1964), and more recently have questioned the conventional uses of linguistic models for cognitive anthropology in general (Dougherty and Keller 1982). Assumptions about cultural and cognitive uniformity have been questioned as well.

In the mid-1970s, faced with these difficulties, cognitive and educational anthropologists began to look to cognitive science, which offered increasingly sophisticated formal models of language, logic and problem solving (Quinn 1982), while cognitive scientists recognized that anthropologists employed a method which could lead to detailed knowledge of "real life" activities and situations. Given increasingly cordial suggestions that each might contribute to solutions of the problems of the other, there is reason to examine critically the degree to which either discipline is in a position to illuminate those complementary concerns. I take a skeptical view, given the difficulty of challenging an entrenched division of labor.[2] However more importantly, those who have worked within the culture and cognition paradigm, and within cognitive psychology and cognitive anthropology more broadly, *share* assumptions about culture, cognition and their relations too strongly to offer each other solutions to the dilemmas they face. It appears, indeed, that major dilemmas as well as assumptions are common to both.

The shared position (assumptions, forms of explanation, and even, in broad terms, method) is a functionalist one:[3] very briefly, society is characterized as a set of macrostructures in place, a *fait accompli* to be internalized by individuals born into it. Consensus – shared norms, values and culture more generally – is the foundation of social order. Degrees of consensus define social boundaries of different levels of inclusiveness. Cultural transmission, or socialization, is clearly central to achieving such consensus, and is the crucial relation between society and the individual. A duality of the person is inherent in this view. Articulated plainly by Durkheim (1915; Durkheim and Mauss 1963) and Levy-Bruhl (1910), it is implicit in the logic of cognitive studies today. Thus, thinking is said to have an emotional component, social in origin, and a cognitive–rational, individual one; their weighting in the person is a reflection of the degree to which collective life dominates the individual. On the face of it this proposition may not be immediately recognizable as a feature of cognitive theorizing, perhaps because its corollaries are more salient than the original proposition. Today, for example, it is likely to be assumed that if ongoing activity consists of problem solving – "individual, rational, cognitive" – it is not necessary to address the possibilities that it is culturally and socially structured, primarily expressive of feelings, or part of socially contextualized experience in ways that require theorizing, empirical description, or analysis. The experiment as a form of investigation customarily reflects these assumptions as does the very category "information processing."[4]

More specifically, functional theory treats processes of socialization (including learning in school) as passive, and culture as a pool of information transmitted from one generation to the next, accurately, with verisimilitude, a position that has created difficulties for cognitive psychology as well as anthropology. Neither discipline appears to be theoretically equipped to elaborate a theory of active social actors, located in time and space, reflexively and recursively acting upon the world in which they live and which they fashion at the same time.

Functional theory underlies the web of relations between academic, novice and jpf "worlds." In this theory, duality of the person translates into a division of (intellectual) labor between academics and "the rest" that puts primitive, lower class, (school) children's, female, and everyday thought in a single structural position *vis-à-vis* rational scientific thought (see chapter 4). Functional theory arose in the early nineteenth century as an argument of the new industrial bourgeoisie against aristocratic privilege in Great Britain (Cooter 1979), an argument that if all individuals were given equal opportunities to advance in life, those who were superior physically, mentally and morally would naturally rise to the top. Those who lacked these qualities would stay where they justly belonged. Schooling, and relations that are assumed to hold between schooling, the academy, and the world of work, reflect this belief in a meritocracy. Functional theory permeates rationales, explanations, and the organization of schooling in American society, and imbues much of anthropological, educational, and psychological theory with its particular logic (cf. McDermott and Goldman 1983; Apple 1979). In particular, it is enacted in schools by their claim to treat all children alike (cf. Varenne and Kelly 1976; Bourdieu 1973) and its view that unequal ranking is an epiphenomenon of differential merit.

The functionalist sociology of education has been elucidated too thoroughly to require rehearsal here. But it may not be as well understood that the functionalist position contains a theory of learning: in particular, that children can be taught general cognitive skills (e.g. reading, writing, mathematics, logic, critical thinking) *if* these "skills" are disembedded from the routine contexts of their use. Extraction of knowledge from the particulars of experience, of activity from its context, is the condition for making knowledge available for *general* application in all situations. Schooling reflects these ideas at a broad organizational level, as it separates children from the contexts of their own and their families' daily lives. At a more specific level, classroom tests put the principle to work: they serve as the measure of individual, "out of context" success, for the test-taker must rely on memory alone and may not use books, classmates, or other resources for information. Arguably examinations are also condensed, symbolic, ritual ordeals which inculate the essence of the theory.

Cognitive psychology accounts for stability and continuity of cognitive activity across settings through the psychological mechanism of learning transfer. That is, knowledge acquired in "context-free" circumstances is supposed to be available for general application in all contexts, widely transportable but relatively impervious to change in the course, and by the process, of travel and use. The central role of learning transfer reflects the functionalist assumption of literal culture transmission that informs broad conceptions of socialization and more specifically, the conceptualization of relations between school and everyday practice. In sum, even this short survey of the general functional model of cognition, culture, continuity and the social world confirms that there are strong, common theoretical assumptions in cognitive studies in psychology and anthropology. A discussion of their contemporary dilemmas will also show common patterns of concern across disciplines.

Cognitive anthropology has traditionally applied linguistic models, notably classical formal semantics, to classificatory paradigms of general cultural knowledge (e.g. kinship, plant, and color terminologies), an interest with direct roots in early twentieth-century functionalism. This theory came under critical analysis when cognitive anthropologists raised questions about relations between cultural knowledge and actors' cultural practice, one aspect of the problem of intracultural variation. Pelto and Pelto (1975) argued that:

> the predominant tendency in anthropological . . . theory-building continues to be made up of constructions reflecting fundamental assumptions of cognitive homo-geneity and behavioral sharing.   *(1975: 6)*

They suggest that the use of quasi-linguistic models, "based on a mentalistic meta-theory of human behavior" (1975: 7) has contributed to uniformist views and a strong penchant for treating culture in the same terms as language, concluding that:

> the monolithic view of behavioral causation that makes culture the cause of culture – with perpetuation of cultural patterns neatly through the generations by means of child training and other socialization – must be discarded.   *(1975: 10)*

Cognitive psychologists have also espoused simplifying assumptions of cultural uniformity. Anthony Giddens, a social theorist who persistently raises issues about conventional conceptions of social actors and their relations with action, structure and social systems, has pointed out that:

> It is clear that much work on the psychological development of the individual is deficient as an account of socialization, in so far as the overriding focus is upon the differentiation of personality within an undifferentiated "society." This is true also in some considerable degree of the theory that has long dominated child psychology in respect of cognitive development: that associated with Piaget.   *(1979: 129)*

The Laboratory of Comparative Human Cognition (LCHC 1981) has made the same point in relation to cross-cultural research on cognitive style.[5] But they are exceptional in a field not known for its self-critical views (see also Bronfenbrenner 1979: 258), perhaps because the problems raised by such critics are so easily avoided merely by honoring conventional limitations on subject matter.

The concept of cultural uniformity reflects functionalist assumptions about society as a consensual order, and cultural transmission as a process of homogeneous cultural reproduction across generations. It has served as a mandate to treat culture in cognitive studies as if it were a constant, as if nothing essential about thinking would be disturbed if its effects were controlled experimentally. This is surely one means by which cognitive psychology has kept within the bounds of the division of labor between the study of the individual and anthropological studies of culture and social organization. For such a strategy legislates away major questions about social diversity, inequality, conflict, complementarity, cooperation and differences of power and knowledge, and the means by which they are socially produced, reproduced and transformed in laboratory, school and other everyday settings. (These same questions are more difficult to avoid when the arena of investigation is the lived-in world.) It is worth keeping in mind that the specific character of this division of labor strongly influences theoretical speculation about the sources of continuity of activity, as well as methodological questions about the ecological validity of experimentation.

Indeed, validity is another of those issues that has been raised in both cognitive anthropology and psychology, though in slightly different guises. In the late 1960s, cognitive anthropologists began to worry about the psychological validity of their componential analyses of semantic categories. The problem is closely related to the question of intracultural variation, for it depends on recognition that people within a single culture have various means for classifying the same things (e.g. Wallace and Atkins 1960; Burling 1964, Romney and D'Andrade 1964, Wexler and Romney 1972). Responses within cognitive anthropology included sophisticated attempts to model processes of choice and decision making (Gladwin and Gladwin 1971; Gladwin 1975; Quinn 1976) and statistical modeling of variation (e.g. Romney, Shepard, and Nerlove 1972; Shepard, Romney, and Nerlove 1972). There have also been explorations of richer and more-sophisticated theories of semantics (notably Quinn on the concept of marriage 1982) and logic (Hutchins 1980; D'Andrade 1982), reflecting the seriousness with which cognitive anthropologists have queried cognitive science for new theoretical perspectives. The psychologists' version of the problem concerns ecological validity, a critique of laboratory experimentation as a basis for generalizing about cognitive activity in other settings, especially those of everyday life (Bartlett 1932; Barker 1963a, 1968; and especially Cole, Hood and McDermott 1978). But though the problem is widely recognized within the discipline, psychologists themselves have been critical of what they fear are only *pro forma* efforts to rethink experimental methods. Neisser has pointed out the exasperatingly programmatic character of many quick pitches for ecological validity – "Like so many admonitions to virtue, it emphasizes the superior righteousness of the moralizer without giving much guidance to the moralizee" (1976: 33–34; see also Siegel 1977: 192).

The question has been given impetus by difficulties in exporting laboratory experimental paradigms to cross-cultural research situations (e.g. Cole, Gay, Glick and Sharp 1971; Scribner 1977; Lave 1980). The cognition-and-culture psychologists have been critical of claims that laboratory experimentation is a sufficient basis for generalizing about cognitive attributes of individuals. Bartlett (1932) provided a historical charter for the enterprise, characteristic also of more recent work (Cole, Hood and McDermott 1978; Scribner and Cole 1981; Bronfenbrenner 1979). These critiques have two dimensions. Bartlett (1932, chapter 1) argued that generalizing about "how people think" on the basis of what transpires in laboratory experiments is a contradiction in terms. For if experimental situations are sufficiently similar to each other, and consistently different from the situations whose cognitive activities they attempt to model, then the validity of generalizations of experimental results must surely be questioned. He proposed that observation of everyday activities in context should form the basis for the design of experiments. Experimental findings would, in turn, inform further observation. Secondly, critics have focused on laboratory experiments as a class of activities in and of themselves, as socially and culturally structured events (LCHC 1981; Bronfenbrenner 1979: 123; Lave 1980 and in preparation).

The responses within both anthropology and psychology to uniformist dilemmas and those of research validity have been mildly reformist, at best. In part this represents a withdrawal from issues that are easy to identify but difficult to resolve. In part it reflects beliefs that modest modification of existing practices is all that should be required. But if the pervading theoretical position is the source of dilemmas which have assumed substantial significance, and these are intractible even when explicitly delineated, tactical change may not be sufficient. A different logic seems more appropriate, and indeed, timely, for there appears to be a growing legitimacy for alternatives to a functionalist/positivist theoretical position. There are numerous general critiques of functionalist theory (e.g. Giddens 1976, 1979; Jarvie 1968; Warren 1984) and a growing body of serious critiques of cognitive theory (e.g. Dannefer 1984; Danziger 1979; Dreyfus 1979; Samelson 1974; Sampson 1977; Henriques, Hollway, Urwin, Venn, and Walkerdine 1984). The critical literature on functionalist sociology of education is notable: (e.g. Apple 1979; Bourdieu 1973; Bowles and Gintis 1976; Collins 1979; Giroux 1981; Hurn 1978; Willis 1977). Others have argued against isolating theorizing about cognition from analysis of the activity of which it is a part, in the social world of which it is also a part (e.g. Bourdieu 1977; Minick 1985; Mehan in press). In short, a virtual functionalist consensus in the social sciences 20 years ago has dispersed (though notably less in cognitive studies than in many other arenas in the social sciences). While elsewhere in anthropology and sociology variations on the questions raised in the present discussion are to be found within the epistemological perspectives of (post)structuralists, Marxists, and phenomenologists as well as functionalists. The natural attitude, *praxis*, activity, cultural practice, *habitus*, dispositions and practical consciousness are embedded in a diverse spectrum of theoretical formulations of the social and cultural character of human thought and action, and in different conceptions of culture, structure, knowledge, self and body, not to mention the nature of theory and method.

While there are clearly burgeoning opportunites for reconceptualizing common concerns, one *caveat* is in order before we proceed. These rich theoretical possibilities must create a new generation of problems for cross-disciplinary relations. Collaboration between cognitive anthropology and cognitive psychology, never a simple matter, becomes

more complicated in the face of increasingly varied theoretical possibilities. For either of these disciplines to look to the central formulations
within the other for theoretical inspiration is not likely to help, since it
is at their centers that they have the most in common including the
limitations and drawbacks which have sent them prospecting outside
their normal academic boundaries in the first place. While to cobble
together a theory of cognition and a theory of culture, or "a
psychology" and "an anthropology," requires specification of *what*
theory of cognition and *what* theory of culture first – they are no longer
all compatible with one another.

Cognition and synthetic social theory

Where lie alternatives and how do I propose to cope with the difficulties
envisioned above? It seems useful to look to recent social theoretical
syntheses for a theory of the social actor in action in the lived-in world as
a basis for developing a more adequate model of cognition in cultural
context. The problem has not always taken a salient role in social
theoretical concerns – 20 years ago social theory was broadly concerned
with questions about the nature of social order and would not have
offered a hospitable ambience for such a discussion. But today
prominent questions include how, and if, it is possible to overcome
subject/object dualism, bridging the hiatus between material and ideal
monist theories, micro- and macro-sociologies, and thus also studies of
the individual and studies of society. Theoretical syntheses such as
Giddens' (1979; 1984) argue that integrating social action with social
structure (individual/society; subject/object) is the key problem.[6] Other
major discussions of synthetic possibilities (e.g. Sahlins, 1976, 1981;
Comaroff and Roberts 1981; Comaroff 1982 and in preparation) locate
crucial divisions to be transcended in relations between structure and
history, and materialist and idealist dialectics, respectively. It should be
obvious that any such theoretical synthesis implicates relations between
individuals and the society in which they live and also assigns varying
theoretical characterizations to concepts such as "cognition" and
"culture." In the process they challenge the Durkheimian separation of
individual from collective aspects of cognition which has supported
strategies of cognitive research for so long.
 I am encouraged to conceive of a social anthropology of cognition as a
theory of practice by recent developments within social anthropology in

addition to the syntheses fermenting in social theory generally. Ortner has proposed that theories of practice offer a central unifying concept for contemporary research in anthropology. The approach I propose to take here, especially the focus on everyday activity, and its constitution in relations between social system and individual experience, falls within theoretical debates about the nature of social practice as they seek to explain relations between human action and the social or cultural system at the level of everyday activities in culturally organized settings.

Cultural uniformity was singled out by anthropologists as a fundamental theoretical weakness because in the end it reduces to a claim that culture reproduces culture, through socialization. Ortner suggests that anthropology has in the last two decades moved from the view that socialization is the central mechanism for the reproduction of the social system, to a view that ritual is the most powerful formative factor in maintaining social order. She goes on to suggest that both have been replaced with the view that routines of everyday living "embody within themselves, the fundamental notions of temporal, spatial and social ordering that underlie and organize the system as a whole" (1984: 154).

This has several implications for the study of cognitive activity in everyday settings. Everyday activity is, in this view, a more powerful source of socialization than intentional pedagogy. The latter bears a complex and distorted relationship with everyday practice (Bourdieu 1977). Practice theories thus challenge conventional assumptions about the impact of schooling on everyday practice. Functionalists argue that verbally transmitted, explicit, general knowledge is the main prerequisite that makes cognitive skills available for transfer across situations. Social practice proponents argue that knowledge-in-practice, constituted in the settings of practice, is the locus of the most powerful knowledgeability of people in the lived-in world. Practice theory, in short, suggests a different approach to cognition and to schooling than that embodied in functional-schooling theories, educational ideologies, and cognitive theory.

In the functionalist view the label "everyday" is heavy with negative connotations emanating from its definition in contrast to scientific thought. Its customary use encompasses the unmarked, unsung category of humble domestic activities and their associated social roles (e.g. housewives, running errands). In the version of practice theory developed here, mundane activities in domestic settings do *not* delimit the boundaries of some putative "everyday world." Nor does the term denote a division between domestic life and work, domestic and public domains, routine maintenance and productive activity, or manual routines and creative mental work. "Everyday" is not a time of day, a social role, nor a set of activities, particular social occasions, or settings for activity. Instead, the everyday world is just that: what people do in daily, weekly, monthly, ordinary cycles of activity. A schoolteacher and pupils in the classroom are engaged in "everyday activity" in the same sense as a person shopping for groceries in the supermarket after work and a scientist in the laboratory. It is the routine character of activity, rich expectations generated over time about its shape, and settings designed for those activities and organized by them, that form the class of events which constitutes an object of analysis in theories of practice.

If everyday experience is the major means by which culture impinges on individuals, and vice versa, then functionalist and social-practice theories imply different answers to questions about *what* cognitive activity is the appropriate object of analysis. In traditional cognitive experiments subjects' performance on laboratory tasks are compared to a normative model, to an ideally meritocratic performance. In practice, theory attention shifts to everyday activity, which becomes both the measure of the experimenter's ability to design generalizable experiments, and the source of explanations for varieties of performance in those experiments (chapter 5). This motivates, as we shall see, a different set of problems and questions than the study of virtuoso performance and peoples' failures to produce such performances.

Practice theory has eclectic roots in the work of Marx, Bourdieu, Sahlins, and Giddens among others, and might be described as a cluster of theories about the nature of practice which agree about the importance of a broad range of issues and levels of analysis embodied in the focal concept. This work emphasizes the dialectical character of relations fundamental to the socially constituted world – dialectics provides an obvious relational model for synthesis. And it is focused in part on experience in the lived-in world. Giddens argues:

> Social analysis must be founded neither in the consciousness or activities of the subject, nor in the characteristics of the object (society), but in the duality of structure . . . The subject/object dualism has . . . also to be overcome in the rather different form in which it appears in theories of socialisation. That is to say, we have to avoid any account of socialisation which presumes either that the subject is determined by the social object (the individual as simply 'moulded' by society); or, by contrast, which takes subjectivity for granted as an inherent characteristic of human beings, not in need of explication. *(1979: 120)*

Bourdieu, anthropologist turned sociologist, whose *Outline of a Theory of Practice* (1972; English edn 1977) has given strong impetus to synthetic theorizing, locates the enterprise in the study of everyday practice:

> We shall escape from the ritual either/or choice between objectivism and subjectivism . . . only if we are prepared to inquire into the mode of production and functioning of the practical mastery which makes possible both an objectively intelligible practice and also an objectively enchanted experience of that practice.
>
> *(1977: 4)*

This last includes:

> all that is inscribed in the relationship of familiarity with the familiar environment, the unquestioning apprehension of the social world which, by definition does not reflect on itself and excludes the question of the conditions of its own possibility.
>
> *(1977: 3)*

And, to add a third, anthropological, voice, Comaroff (Comaroff and Roberts 1981; Comaroff 1982; in preparation) proposes a dialectical theory that takes the constitution of sociocultural order and political economy as one term of a dialectical relation, and individual experience of, and action upon, the lived-in universe as the other.

> In formal terms, this dialectic has its genesis in the dualistic character of all historical systems, which exist at two analytically distinct levels. On the one hand, they consist in the social and material relations which compose the everyday lived-in world of any society, a world of appearances that represents itself, in the consciousness of experiencing individuals, in the form of substantive rules and relationships, values and interests, constraints and conflicts. On the other hand, behind this lived in world lies a constitutive order. The latter subsists simultaneously as a semiotic system, a cultural *langue*, of signs, symbolic oppositions and categorial relations, and as a set of organizational principles which structure the material and social universe, its component productive and political arrangements.   *(in preparation: 16)*

All of these social theorists are critical of functional (and also phenomenological) problematics.[7] They are notably concerned with dialectical synthesis, and assume the partially determined, partially determining character of human agency, thus emphasizing the impact of practice on structure as well as the reverse. Their work recommends the study of social practice in spatial and temporal context. For the synthetic character of these theories makes it difficult to argue for the separation of cognition and the social world, form and content, persons acting and the settings of their activity, or structure and action. Internalization is a less-important mode of contact with the world than action in the world.[8] In sum, theories of practice do offer fields for action within which to fashion a theory of everyday activity. And they are major sources of theoretical claims for the centrality of practice in the reproduction of society.

In recommending "practice" as a focal concept, Ortner has nonetheless criticized studies of social practice for their individualistic, narrowly rationalistic bent, a tendency to emphasize utilitarian interests as the motivation for human action (1984). Everyday arithmetic provides especially apt subject matter for considering the problem she has raised. AMP analysis suggests that the motivations of mundane arithmetic are varied, being far more complex and specifically constructed than they are assumed to be when reduced to the global self-interested calculation of a "rational economic man" (sexism intended). But there *is* a disturbing parallel between practice theories and existing cognitive theory, as both tend to reduce activity (or cognition) to narrowly defined rational action. Foucault provides a reminder that there have been very different historical forms of description and meaning imposed on everyday life, and that ours is but one, culturally constituted, possibility. He traces the uses and meanings of everyday life through early-Christian confession, to seventeenth- and eighteenth-century *lettres de cachet* addressed to kings (Morris and Patton 1979: 84) to a diffused, depersonalized version of "the everyday" in today's academic discourse. Instead of "disputes between neighbours, the quarrels between parents and children, the domestic misunderstandings, the excesses of wine and sex, the public bickerings and many secret passions" (quoted in Morris and Patton 1979: 86), today the everyday is addressed in research journals as a field to be colonized and improved by psychologists and educators, styled as a technological field of mental skills, rational interests and problem solving. Instead of petitioners and enforcers of royal directives, there are novices and experts whose goals, respectively, are to acquire scientific knowledge, and to engage in professional, normative science.

If the analytic concept of the individual is reduced to a self-contained, disembodied technology of cognition, knowledge is reduced to scientific "discoveries," and society to a set of actors whose lives are structured only by self-interested motives, then both the analyses and conclusions that follow must surely involve deep impoverishment and distortion of their object. It will be argued here, instead, that a more appropriate unit of analysis is the whole person in action, acting with the settings of that activity. This shifts the boundaries of activity well outside the skull and beyond the hypothetical economic actor, to persons engaged with the world for a variety of "reasons;" it also requires a different version of the everyday world.

It is within this framework that the idea of cognition as stretched across mind, body, activity and setting begins to make sense. But we have arrived at the limits of the sociological theories of practice, for they do not specify a novel theory of cognition itself. Instead, "cognition" seems to represent one limit of the field of their inquiry. Bourdieu takes cognition in its conventional sense as an unexamined primitive element of his concept of dispositions (though at the same time he blurs the distinction between mind and body by emphasizing the knowledge-ability of the body (e.g. 1977: 15ff)). Giddens uses "stocks of knowledge" stored in memory, an ethnomethodological construct, in much the same manner that a cognitive psychologist such as Simon might picture long-term memory as an encyclopedia. These views continue to relegate culture, acquisition of knowledge and memory to an internalized past, closing it to the investigator except as it "surfaces" in present action. Giddens requires actors to bring to bear "typified schemas" in everyday situations, arguing essentially for the importance of learning transfer conceived in conventional terms (1984: 22).[9] A major task of the book, then, is to work out conceptual and methodological forms that will allow us to theorize about cognition in everyday practice. But we shall also come back to the social theorists to locate practice within their more encompassing views of social order.

Answers and questions

The book is divided into two parts. The first, "Theory in practice", is a critique of the practice of cognitive research, developed in part by constructing an empirical case for the situational specificity of arithmetic activity. Chapter 2 analyzes experiments on learning transfer, since this concept specifies the conditions for general learning and continuity of activity across settings in the conventional functionalist perspective. In chapter 3 arithmetic activity in the supermarket is extracted from grocery shopping, to compare AMP participants' performances, procedures and errors in price/quantity ratio arithmetic in the supermarket with those occurring in paper and pencil arithmetic sessions. These and other analyses (e.g. the work of Carraher, Carraher, and Schliemann, and that of Scribner) provide evidence for situational discontinuities in math practices. They recommend a move away from functionalist to some form of practice theory, and from "learning transfer" as the explanation for cognitive continuity across contexts, to an analytic approach in terms of the dialectical structuring of the activity of persons-acting in setting.

The first part of the book also addresses evidence for the cultural specificity of cognitive theory. It is puzzling that learning transfer has lasted for so long as a key conceptual bridge without critical challenge. The lack of stable, robust results in learning transfer experiments as well as accumulating evidence from cross-situational research on everyday practice, raises a number of questions about the assumptions on which transfer theory is based – the nature of cognitive "skills," the "contexts" of problem-solving and "out of context" learning, the normative sources of models of good thinking and less than perfect "performances." Transfer theory may well owe its longevity to its central location in the web of relations discussed above, institutionalized in divisions between the disciplines of anthropology and psychology, in schooling, and in dichotomies between scientific and everyday thought. Basic and profoundly embedded assumptions govern the persistent loyalty to transfer and all that it stands for, and a strong break with this tradition, though costly in theoretical consensus, is a promising means for moving the study of cognition into the larger social world (chapter 4).

But establishing empirical evidence for the situated construction of arithmetic activity does not constitute an explanation of the phenomenon, nor does it offer a positive alternative. The second part of this book ("Practice in theory") addresses these issues. A comparative analysis of two experimental approaches to the study of proportional reasoning in the supermarket (chapter 5) introduces the concept of structuring resources in activity and their articulation in varying proportions across situations. A series of questions explored in chapters 6 and 7 address further the possibility that math activity takes forms not captured in school-like procedures. What constitutes "a problem" in the supermarket or kitchen? What motivates problem solving if not demands for compliance by problem-givers? To what extent is means/ends analysis an adequate description of arithmetic practice or other activity? Some answers have begun to take shape: quantitative procedures in the supermarket appear to take their character in ongoing activity rather than to imprint canonical forms of problem solving on spaces between segments of grocery shopping. People do not have a math problem unless they have a resolution shape – a sense of an answer and a process for bringing it together with its parts. Problem solvers proceed in action, often integrally engaging body, self, common sensibilities and the setting. Arithmetic relations often have closer ties to other aspects of activity than to each other. Such activity is amenable to description in dialectical terms. Impelled and given meaning by conflicts generated out of the contradictions governing social practice, "problems" are dilemmas to be resolved, rarely problems to be solved.

Analysis of money management practices, measuring devices and the measurement practices of dieting cooks, as well as arithmetic in the supermarket, suggest that arithmetic relations are underdetermined, enacted, embodied, and generated in dialectical relations with the settings with which they occur (chapters 6 and 7). New units of analysis (e.g. persons-acting, the contexts – arenas and settings – of activity, and activity as dialectically constituted by them) are proposed to reflect this theoretical position in a principled way. These chapters begin to develop an alternative to a narrow, rationalist psychology of problem solving with its progression from lower to higher cognitive functions. For the value-laden, active, integrally contextualized character of arithmetic in practice, and especially the dialectical processes by which dilemmas are resolved, are inconsistent with a model of the world that separates means from ends, or method and technology from goal and value.

The structure of activity-in-setting must be located within a broader theoretical framework, for the new units of analysis do not, by themselves, specify basic relations between culture and cognition, and individual and society. The last chapter argues that relations between culture and cognition which have defined divisions and relations between mind and society within functionalist theory dissolve into indirect, multiple, and complex relations when framed in a synthetic theory of social order. And like "rationality," the continuity of activity over contexts and occasions is located partly in persons-acting, partly in contexts, but most strongly in their relations.

The empirical research and theoretical exploration that together form the book have informed each other in a process not unlike the gap-closing arithmetic observed in the supermarket. Each has had mutually constitutive and changing effects on the other. Clearly the book does not describe a test of a theory, but rather its development. Such research is a complex and uneven process. Like the shopper putting apples in the bag, the process itself helped to shape possible answers, and with them, I hope, some interesting questions.

I
Theory in practice

2
MISSIONARIES AND CANNIBALS (INDOORS)

In the conceptual schema of cognitive psychology, cognitive transfer (or its absence) is held responsible for continuity (or discontinuity) of activity across situations. This genre of research speaks only in hypothetical voice about what cognitive activities outside school might be like, relying on the concept of transfer to provide a plausible account of relations between schooling, the workplace, and the everyday lives of jpfs. Learning transfer is assumed to be the central mechanism for bringing school-taught knowledge to bear in life after school.

Because transfer is so central, it seems logical to begin an investigation of everyday cognitive activity with a reexamination of this formulation of relations between cognition and the everyday world. These relations are reflected in the typical practices of research on learning transfer, broadly structured in sequences of laboratory experiments in which subjects are set tasks of formal problem solving. Normative models for correct solution are used to evaluate subjects' performances, and these evaluations of cognitive preparedness are extrapolated from experimental to everyday situations. I have drawn on several reports of experiments on learning transfer in order to analyze the culture of transfer research. "Culture" here includes both the cultural context within which the experimental enterprise is embedded and its customary beliefs, practices and interpretive forms. Together they help to explain the conventional conceptual boundaries which shape particular sets of meanings of "context," "culture," "knowledge," and the social world.

History, myth, and learning transfer

Learning-transfer research had its beginnings in Thorndike's critique of the doctrine of formal discipline. Any form of mental discipline was supposed to improve the minds of school pupils in a general way. This rationale, a popular defense for Latin instruction in the early 1900s, is still heard in the 1980s in defense of geometry, other branches of mathematics – and Latin.[1] In functionalist psychological theory, mind and its contents have been treated rather like a well-filled toolbox. Knowledge is conceived as a set of tools stored in memory, carried around by individuals who take the tools (e.g. "foolproof" arithmetic algorithms) out and use them, the more often and appropriately the better, after which they are stowed away again without change at any time during the process. The metaphor is especially apt given that tools are designed to resist change or destruction through the conditions of their use.

Two theories of learning transfer follow from the notion of knowledge as tool: one argues for many special purpose tools, the proper one for each task, while the other argues for a few general purpose tools to be used in the largest number of circumstances. Indeed, there have been roughly two schools of thought about the mechanisms of learning transfer. Thorndike (1913: 397) suggested that the more two situations shared specific components, such as "ideas of method and habits of procedure," the more likely the "spread of improvement" from one situation to the other. Judd (1908), a student of Wundt's, proposed that learning transfer depended upon generality of understanding: the more general the principle, the more likely the recognition that a newly encountered problem might belong to a class of problems already known. Both Thorndike and Judd reported some successes and numerous fruitless attempts to demonstrate learning transfer in laboratory and school settings.

Studies of transfer became a highly technical matter of warm-up effects and stimulus predispositions in the 1950s and 60s (Ellis 1969). But recent studies bear a closer resemblance to work early in the century. Simon, for example, in describing "new" advances in the theory of learning transfer, presents merely a conjunction of the theories of Thorndike and Judd:

> Transfer from Task A to Task B requires that some of the processes or knowledge used in Task B be essentially identical with some of the processes or knowledge that have been learned while acquiring skill in Task A . . . [And secondly] to secure substantial transfer of skills acquired in the environment of one task, learners need to be made explicitly aware of these skills, abstracted from their specific task content.
> *(1980: 82)*

This continuity with turn of the century psychology will come to light many more times in the course of the discussion, reflecting the roots of current functionalist theory in the social sciences of that time (see especially chapter 4).

The "ethnographic" exercise which follows is based on four well-known papers describing some 13 learning transfer experiments. Reed, Ernst and Banerji carried out research on river crossing problems (1974), Hayes and Simon on a version of the tower of Hanoi (1977), Gick and Holyoak (1980) on Duncker's "radiation problem" (1945), and Gentner and Gentner on models of simple electrical circuits (1983). The papers fall into a chronological sequence and the later ones take into account the results of the earlier studies. The experiments, which took place in laboratories, with high school and college students as subjects, consisted of sequences of puzzle-solving tasks. Learning transfer is inferred in several different ways, but the most common criteria are an increase in efficiency or accuracy of performance, or use of a general form of the solution to one problem in solving other problems. The cast of characters in these experiments is quite colorful – missionaries, cannibals, jealous husbands, teeming crowds, flowing water, forts and re-volutionaries and strategies for reducing tumors through radiation, as well as monsters and globes instead of the more usual pegs and rings in the tower of Hanoi problem.

Table 1 summarizes general features of the experiments, which are described in the next section. I have called this an ethnographic inquiry to suggest that the goals of analysis here are different from those of cognitive experimenters as they assess each other's work. The descriptions of experiments are intended to provide a basis for elucidating their underlying assumptions, especially those concerning relations between cognition, activity and the social world. There is the immediate question of whether the experimental evidence confirms that learning transfer is an important medium for the achievement of continuity in activity across time and situations. But there are more fundamental issues as well. First, since problem solving is ubiquitous and central to the definition of experimental tasks, there is an opportunity to look closely at the meaning of "problems" and what constitutes "problem-solving activity" in this genre. Next, whatever the conception of problem solving it must affect research strategy, especially the development of normative models of "good" or "correct" procedures and solutions, and diagnoses and proposals for the remedy of deficiencies of transfer. And since cross-situational transfer implies that situations or contexts are units of analysis, careful consideration will also be given to their role in the transfer literature.

Table 1 *Characteristics of four sets of learning transfer experiments*

Problem	Form of transfer expected	Transfer?	Rationale	Researchers	Publication date
Missionaries and cannibals	algorithm	no	understand problem solving	Reed et al.	1974
Tower of Hanoi	algorithm	(yes)[a]	understand problem solving	Hayes and Simon	1977
Radiation	analogy	(yes)	important to science	Gick and Holyoak	1980
Electric circuits	generative analogy	(yes)	important to science	Gentner et al.	1983

[a] () = a conditional answer

The everyday practice of cognitive research

(1) Reed, Ernst and Banerji set out "to study the role of analogy in transfer between problems with similar problem states" (1974: 437). They began with a formal analysis of the missionary and cannibal problem, a flow diagram showing all permissible moves for transporting pairs of people across a river in such a fashion that cannibals do not outnumber missionaries on either bank. This was paired with a formally isomorphic but slightly more complicated problem, "the jealous husbands," in which each husband-and-wife pair has a unique identity. To investigate transfer, defined as significant improvement in performance from one problem to the other, Reed *et al.* compared solution time, number of moves and number of erroneous moves for each pair of problem-solving attempts, looking for statistically significant improvement.[2] In one experiment the subjects were not told that the problems were analogous. In another they were instructed that "the easiest way to solve the [second] problem is to take advantage of your correct solution to the [first]" (1974: 440). Subjects could use objects to represent characters in the problems, their comments were recorded as they talked aloud, and measures obtained by analyzing the tapes. The results reported by the experimenters were more pessimistic than warranted by the data, since they did not control for the initial difficulty of the problems in their measures of transfer. But their negative conclusions were basically correct; when subjects were not told about the relationship between problems they failed to transfer. Moreover, there was transfer from the more complex to the simpler problem only when subjects were *directed* to do so.

(2) Hayes and Simon (1977) were concerned both with exploring the sensitivity of problem-solving activity to small differences in textual presentation of problems and with transfer of training between isomorphic problems. The tower of Hanoi, given a new disguise in terms of monsters and globes, provided the form for these problems. Half were "transfer" problems: monsters or globes moving from one place to another. The others were "change" problems: the monsters or globes changed sizes. There was a second, cross-cutting dimension. In half of the problems the monsters were agents, responsible for transforming or moving things. In the rest monsters were moved or transformed (i.e. as the object of the action, or "patient"). This produced four types of problems: transfer/agent (TA), transfer/patient (TP), change/agent (CA), change/patient (CP).

Each subject solved two problems. In the first experiment either both had active monster agents or monsters were the object of the action, while at the same time one problem involved changing the globe or monster and the other transferring it (e.g. the problem pairs included TA–CA, TP–CP, CA–TA and CP–TP). In the second experiment both were transfer or both were change problems, one of which involved the monster as agent, while in the other, the monster was both the agent and the object of the action (e.g. problem pairs TA–TP, CA–CP, TP–TA and CP–CA). In other respects these experiments were essentially identical and one example of task instructions may serve as a description of all of them.

> *The transfer/agent problem:* Three five-handed extraterrestrial monsters were holding three crystal globes. Because of the quantum-mechanical peculiarities of their neighborhood, both monsters and globes come in exactly three sizes with no others permitted: small, medium, and large. The medium-sized monster was holding the small globe; the small monster was holding the large globe; and the large monster was holding the medium-sized globe. Since this situation offended their keenly developed sense of symmetry, they proceeded to transfer globes from one monster to another so that each monster would have a globe proportionate to its own size. Monster etiquette complicated the solution of the problem since it requires that:
> 1. only one globe may be transferred at a time;
> 2. if a monster is holding two globes, only the larger of the two may be transferred;
> 3. a globe may not be transferred to a monster who is holding a larger globe.
> By what sequence of transfers could the monsters have solved this problem?
> *(Hayes and Simon 1977: 23)*

Sixty per cent of the subjects began by making a sketch of the initial situation of the monsters and the globes before going on to work out a notation scheme and the moves needed to solve the problem. Transfer problems took about 15 minutes to solve, change problems about 30 minutes, on average. References to quantum-mechanics and notation systems in the problems and instructions suggest that the subjects were, or were assumed to be, fairly sophisticated students – novices, not jpfs. Most were eventually able to solve both problems.

The central hypothesis of the paper involved a complex chain of propositions. Hayes and Simon reasoned that to derive a representation of a problem from text requires grammatical and semantic analysis; this analysis should affect how the problem is represented which in turn should affect the process of solution. Grammatical and semantic changes in text, (such as those involving transfer, change, agent, and patient) should thus lead to different analyses, representations and solution processes. They interpreted differences in initial solution times as an indication that there were differences in problem representation and solution procedures. "If [elements in two texts] . . . receive very different analyses, then the two isomorphs are likely to be represented and solved in disimilar [*sic*] ways and transfer of training will be small" (1977: 23). This, it may be noted, is not a hypothesis about learning transfer so much as a specification of limitations on transfer – quite stringent ones at that. The data provide conflicting evidence in support of this claim. There were strong solution-time differences between transfer and change problems in both experiments (it took twice as long to solve change as transfer problems). But in the first experiment there was no significant difference in solution time between the agent and patient problems (a negative finding, not identified as such in the paper), and in the second it was modestly different (F = 4.82, d.f. = 1, p < .04).

Next, they argued that if two problems are solved by the same procedures there should be strong transfer of training between the isomorphs. They compared differences in solution time when a problem was presented second, compared to when it was first. The results of the second experiment were more uniform than those of the first. When the transfer/change dimension of a pair of problems is held constant while subjects tackle one agent and one patient problem, there is in all cases a substantial reduction in solution time for the problem presented second. But this increase in speed (taken as evidence for learning transfer) disconfirms the central hypothesis, for the initial solution times for agent/patient problems were different enough that there should not have been marked transfer between these problems. In the first experiment:

> in the agent condition, transfer-of-training between transfer and change problems was quite asymmetric. Transfer from TA to CA problems was 51% on the average while transfer from CA to TA problems was only 6%. In the patient condition, the asymmetry was less marked and opposite in direction. *(1977: 27)*

The pronounced reduction in solution time when the first problem was a transfer problem and the second a change problem is worth noting because it disconfirms the original hypothesis, given the initial large difference in solution times between transfer and change problems. On the other hand, there was no difference between initial and second problem solution times in the reverse direction. This is the only evidence which confirms their hypothesis that different problem representations (thus different initial solution times) should be associated with little transfer. In the second experiment, reduction in solution times for P–A and A–P while holding transfer or change constant, is also about 50%, but this time in both directions. Given the significant (though not large) difference in initial solution times for patient and agent problems, these results also disconfirm the original hypothesis.

Given such confusing and contradictory goals and evidence it is small wonder that the experimenters sum up their results in the most concrete terms:

> We have shown that differences among the texts of isomorphic problems influence problem-solving behavior strongly in three ways:
> a. Problems involving transfer operators were solved much more quickly than problems involving change operators.
> b. Both the agent–patient variation and the transfer–change variation influence the notation which the subjects use to solve the problems.
> c. Transfer between two problems is greater when the difference between the problems is an agent–patient variation than when it is a transfer–change variation.
> *(1977: 41)*

Even these claims seem too strong. Nonetheless, this paper is cited by Gick and Holyoak as having "demonstrated positive transfer" (1980: 347).

(3) Gick and Holyoak wished to move beyond computational problems, to "the kind of ill-defined problem for which an analogy from a remote domain might trigger a creative insight." (1980: 308). They asked subjects to read a story describing a problem and its solution, and then observed how subjects used this puzzle-solving exercise analogically in solving a subsequent target problem. They constructed a propositional analysis of various stories to demonstrate the formal correspondence of relations among their elements (similar to the flow diagrams in Reed *et al.* 1974). The common problem in all their experiments was to figure out how to destroy a tumor by radiation without also destroying healthy tissue (Duncker 1945). One solution is to administer a number of small doses of radiation from different angles so that they intersect at the site of the tumor; the radiation doses to other tissue are smaller than the accumulated dose to the tumor and hence cause minimal damage to healthy tissue. Duncker found that only two out of 42 respondents gave spontaneous solutions of this kind to the radiation problem.

In the first experiment analogous stories were presented one after the other, first what they called a "base analogy" story, then the "target domain" story, Duncker's problem. Subjects were asked to think aloud as they worked, and were instructed "to try to use the first story problem as a hint in solving the second (radiation) problem" (1980: 320). The experimenters made elaborate efforts to increase the use of analogic problem solving procedures:

Subjects in the experimental conditions who at first failed to generate the analogous solution were eventually prompted to reread the instructions. If they still did not produce the analogous solution, they were then reminded to use the prior story as a hint. *(1980: 320)*

In tandem with the radiation problem subjects were given various irrelevant, complete and partly analogous stories (e.g. to move small groups of revolutionaries close to a fort they are to attack without being detected). In this experiment, as in others, subjects given analogous base stories and heavily coached, consistently made the analogic connection; those uncoached and without initial analogue stories almost never arrived at the "correct" analogue solution to Duncker's problem.

Gick and Holyoak envision analogic problem solving as a three-step process. First the subject must represent a base puzzle with its solution, and a target puzzle in propositional form, then detect a small number of correspondences between them which make it possible to assign many more. The elaborated mapping may then be used to generate a solution to the second problem parallel to the first. The central issue explored in the sequences of experiments is why people might not be able to use analogies – failures to apply them, failure to locate an analogy in memory, or failure to see its relevance to a new problem. Thus, following the initial experiment, four others were designed to counter specific competing interpretations of features of the first. One substituted written for oral instructions to eliminate the possibility that interaction with the experimenter was leading subjects to a solution, though the hints given orally in the first experiment were also included in the written instructions. In another experiment subjects generated their own solutions to the base story, instead of being told a solution. Half of them produced the experimenters' favored solution, and 40% of these solved the radiation problem analogically (20% of the group, compared to 76% in the more constrained experiments). Interpretation of this experiment was focused on the possible distracting effect of generating several solutions.

Their remaining experiments began with a critique of the first three:

In many cases of everyday problem solving in which an analogy could help, the person would have to spontaneously notice the correspondence between the target problem and some analogous problem, either of which might be stored in memory. The two experiments reported below begin to investigate the effect of such additional processing requirements on analogical problem solving. *(1980: 341)*

That is, they ignore their speculation about everyday problem solving in order to follow up the question of memory load. They concluded that:

the process of analogical problem solving is neither automatic nor invariably applied
by college students as a conscious strategy. The knowledge acquired in the context of
the story recall phase of the experiment seemed to be encapsulated in such a way that
its pertinence to the problem-solving task was not recognized . . . An important
question is whether this type of encapsulation of experience is more or less absolute . . .   *(1980: 343)*

This observation is the first indication in the studies discussed here that
situationally specific constitution of activity is a proposition that
warrants study. But they do not pursue it. Instead, they question
subjects' capacities for transfer (e.g. above), and the state of the
experimental art:

A better understanding of how analogies are retrieved and noticed is clearly essential
in order to effectively teach the use of analogies as a heuristic strategy for problem
solving.   *(1980: 350)*

There is a second issue addressed at length in this work. Gick and
Holyoak continually point out difficulties in determining the level of
generality (or specificity) at which subjects make analogies between
stories. Many of the subjects appeared not to avail themselves of detailed
correspondences or mappings of the kind anticipated by the experimenters. Instead of searching for a set of analogic correspondences
between *stories*, they simply tried to adapt their solution to the first
problem to fit the new problem. Many subjects referred to a short phrase
that occurred in all of the analogue stories (see Gick and Holyoak
Appendix III) where something "radiated outwards like spokes on a
wheel." This solution, also an apparently unintended pun on the double
meaning of "radiation," appears to have been a more salient bridge than
more elaborate mappings between the stories.

(4) Like the others, Gentner and Gentner (1983) insisted that it was
important to explore a domain in which "we can define ideal correct
understanding" (p. 107). They chose electric circuitry as their topic
partly because, being invisible, electricity invites analogic explanations.

In this research we test the Generative Analogy hypothesis that analogy is an
important source of insight by asking whether truly different inferences in a given
target domain are engendered by different analogies.   *(1983: 125)*

Their concept of analogy can be summed up rather simply and should
by now seem familiar: Given that the structure of two systems can be
decomposed into terms and relations, an analogy exists when the
relations in one system map onto relations in the other, regardless of the
magnitude or content of its elements. They give an elaborate algebraic
exposition of analogic correspondences, though it is difficult to see how

it contributes to the analysis of the experiments since subjects were only asked if they used one or another analogy. Gick and Holyoak's findings concerning the variable formulations of relations between analogous stories reinforces doubts about the exercise.

Gentner and Gentner depart a little from the procedures described in the earlier experiments. The latter treat isomorphisms between base and target problems as the ideal knowledge against which to evaluate subjects' performance. Instead, they argue that the theoretical principles of electricity provide the canonical explanation for the flow of electricity, while "no single analogy has all the correct properties, [and hence] we can compare different analogies for the same target domain" (1983: 107). They identified two analogies as partially helpful in understanding problems about the flow of electricity, comparing electrical current to flowing water or teeming crowds.

> Subjects with the flowing-water model should be more likely to see the difference between the two kinds of battery combinations. Subjects with the moving-crowd model should be more likely to see the difference between the two kinds of resistor combinations.   *(1983: 114–115)*

High school and college students who knew little physics were given problems based on diagrams of batteries and resistors wired in parallel or in series. The students were asked to indicate relative amounts of current in different parts of the circuits. They worked the problems in a booklet at the end of which was a question as to whether they used the water-flow analogy, teeming crowd analogy or "other." Of the 36 subjects, 7 consistently used the fluid flow model, 8 the crowd model. These subjects provided the data analyzed in the paper. (They do not comment on the fact that fewer than half of the subjects could be included in the analysis). As expected, "the results of the study indicate that use of different analogies leads to systematic differences in the patterns of inferences in the target domain" (1983: 118).

Their second experiment involved a short teaching session on Ohm's law, and led to less clearcut results. They discovered that many subjects employed a water-reservoir analogy they did not understand. They speculated that these results were obtained from people who were basically conservative about adopting new models. Suggesting "it is an appealing notion that analogies function as tools of thought" (1983: 124), they conclude that they have demonstrated that analogies are used generatively in inferential reasoning. But they have doubts as well, wondering whether lay people have adequate base knowledge or the creativity to use them successfully.

The culture of transfer experiments

None of these experiments led to strong evidence of transfer. Hayes and Simon attempted to demonstrate transfer of training and constraints on transfer at the same time. They succeeded in generating partial evidence for both. To the extent that the clearer result was the sensitive variation of solution procedures in the face of small differences in problem presentation, their estimation of the viability (much less ubiquity) of transfer should have been negative. By such an analysis, there would be even more erratic and unreliable transfer between, say, best-buy calculations in supermarkets where the problem solver is agent and on paper where the problem solver is the object of the exercise, than when problem representations differ very little as in their experiments. This work does not suggest a sanguine verdict for learning transfer as a major structuring feature of everyday experience.

The other experimenters also summed up their results as only partial demonstrations of transfer (Reed *et al.* 1974 negatively, and Gick and Holyoak 1980 more tentatively than Gentner and Gentner 1983). And even these equivocal conclusions were reached after research in circumstances contrived to maximize the effect – formal and distinctive problems were presented, one immediately after the other, in a single experimental session, with prompts and instructions to transfer. It surely should not require such elaborate efforts to demonstrate transfer effects if in fact it is the major mechanism for knowledge deployment in cognitive theory and Western socialization practices. But the news in this ethnographic excursion is how little transfer there is, rather than how much (see also Jeeves and Greer 1983: 88; Wagner and Sternberg 1984: 213). It really should not seem surprising: Simon comments (1980: 82) that:

> The empirical evidence for the transferability of knowledge and skills to new task situations is very mixed. The belief that students can be taught to "think logically" by offering them courses in Latin or logic was punctured by the celebrated studies of Thorndike in the 1920s.

However, he goes on to argue that Thorndike did not prove transfer impossible, only that, "certain specific kinds of instruction don't produce transfer" (1980: 82). His last remark, in the spirit of these papers generally, implies that technical modifications of conventional experiments might lead to more positive demonstrations of transfer. This is troubling, for it is just the sort of diagnosis that recommends minimal revision of experimental technique as a remedy. We shall return later to the argument that modified experimental technique will lead to improved demonstrations of transfer, for this claim may be shown to be part of the problem rather than a basis for its resolution.

All of the tasks just described involve "problem solving." A number of problem characteristics are common to all four papers and by extension to the genre more broadly. The puzzles or problems are assumed to be objective and factual. They are constructed "off-stage" by experimenters, for, not by, problem solvers. The process of their construction is therefore not relevant to problem-solving activity and not accessible to inspection. Problem solvers have no choice but to try to solve problems, and if they choose not to, or do not find the correct answer, they "fail" (as characterized in these studies, they resist, encapsulate knowledge, are conservative, or produce unanalyzable data). This interpretation of the absence of a normatively defined response as failure is so central a hallmark of experimental (and school) practice that it may be surprising to note that there are substantive alternatives in most other social situations, as we shall see.

All of the experiments were based on the idea that transfer should take place between two versions of the same story or problem. The problems seem remarkably straightforward and bounded in comparison with the apple problem in the supermarket described in the previous chapter. Even analogies were conceived in the experiments as highly formalizable mental maps or models. Solving problems was characteristically given unquestioned priority as the main activity during these experiments, and solved problems were not intended to enable any other action, or have consequences other than success or failure for the problem solver. In short, in this genre "problems" are small-scale demands for an acquiescent problem solver to operate on the information given by a problem giver using algorithms or formal inferential reasoning to match a correct or ideal answer.

Each of these characteristics of problem solving appears to be an equally apt characterization of assumptions about problem solving in school settings as well. Part of the network of relations between schooling and the study of cognition is located in their mutual influence on the choice and constitution of experimental tasks and situations, and especially in assumptions about problems and problem solving. These relations are reflected in the rationalizations offered by the experimenters for undertaking their research. Gick and Holyoak (1980) argue that noticing analogies is central to the process by which creative

scientists and mathematicians develop a new theory (see also the
introduction to Gentner and Stevens 1983 and Gentner and Gentner
1983: 99–100, 125). Simon has argued that transfer is at the heart of
educational processes and the ability of professionals to function in later
life (1980).

Transfer theory presupposes that problem-solving activities are
always a quest for truth or the "right answer" to a given problem. The
rationale in terms of scientific thinking both reflects and contributes to
this view, which is crucial not only to theories about how people solve
problems, but also to methodological formulations of research strategy.
Stevens and Gentner make explicit the pervasive conventional practice
when they argue that normative models are essential for investigating
cognition, because they make it possible to assess correct and incorrect
responses from subjects:

> Our first efforts to capture naturalistic human knowledge must necessarily center on
> the simplest possible domains. We need to choose domains for which there exists
> some normative knowledge that is relatively easy to detail explicitly. Therefore
> mental models research focuses on simple physical systems or devices. The naive
> physics of liquids, although it may seem an intimidating topic to a nonphysical
> scientist, is a considerably more tractable domain than, for example, interpersonal
> relations – it is very easy to tell an expert from a novice in a domain like Newtonian
> mechanics, and very difficult to tell the expert from the novice in a domain like
> marriage.   *(1983: 2)*

Relations between normative models and everyday practice are a
central issue to which we shall return in other chapters. But two
preliminary indications of the difficulties with this cornerstone of
cognitive research may be sketched here, one empirical, the other
theoretical. The use of normative models as the reference point for
interpreting subjects' activities stands in contrast with a recent example
(by one of the same authors) of a sustained attempt by an informant to
figure out how an unfamiliar heat exchange mechanism worked
(Williams, Hollan and Stevens 1983). They report that an informant
generated one model of the exchanger from which he inferred the
answer to an initial question. In attempting to answer another question
he recognized flaws in the first model and invented a second. This too
was flawed. The informant subsequently moved between these models,
in a process that advanced his understanding of the heat transfer
mechanism and improved the models at the same time. The two models,
and their limitations and contradictions, served as devices for generating
useful experience, though not in normative terms. Williams *et al.*
characterize their subject's activities in iterative and dialectical terms,

much like AMP descriptions of the activities of shoppers and cooks.

The second challenge to the practice of deriving experimental tasks from normative models is that they foster a static, objectified conceptualization of processes of reasoning, a transformation that occurs between their initial formulation and their incorporation into experimental procedures. It is hard to avoid the conclusion that while skills, mental maps and analogies may be conceived of as processes by the experimenters, they are treated for experimental purposes as objects. Thus, they are sometimes referred to in these papers as cognitive "tools." Subjects are on the whole expected to apply or map relations from one problem to the next. For Reed *et al.*, using analogies involves a process of *recognizing* that the current problem is analogous to a previous one and *retrieving* information about the former problem from memory (1974: 448, emphasis mine). Simon discusses the *storage* and *retrieval* of algorithms (1980). Gick and Holyoak (1980) talk about the lack of spontaneous *noticing* of analogies, and that subjects *reproduce* particular (named) solutions. Gentner and Gentner insist that analogies are used generatively in solving problems, but they too have difficulty in avoiding static, tool-like characterizations of the process. For example:

> The "objects" in terms of which a person conceptualizes a system need not be concrete tangible objects . . . Often a target system can be parsed in various ways by different individuals. . . The important point is, once the objects are determined they will be treated as objects in the mapping. *(1983: fn. 102–103)*

All of this underscores the static quality of transfer in experimental practice: it is treated as a process of taking a *given* item and applying it somewhere else.

The characterization of analogies as crystallized objects follows partly from the functional theory of transfer which treats cognition as the literal, uniform transportation of tools for thinking from one situation to the next. But its practical origins lie in the normative orientation that guides the construction of experiments. For, so long as evaluation of subjects' performances is the goal, and it is to be achieved by comparison to an ideal view of correct understanding, then the experimenter must determine what will constitute correct problem solutions (as in all the experimental studies described here). The task then becomes to get the subject to match the experimenter's expectations. In this situation the target analogy *is* a preformulated, static object, and its unmodified use by the subject is the object of the exercise. As the experiments clearly demonstrate, matching transfer expectations takes considerable effort on the part of both experimenter and subject. It may be that this matching game – rather than transfer – is the (unintended) subject of these experiments.

Gick and Holyoak offer an example as they attempt to identify the "optimal level of abstraction for representing an analogy" (1980: 349). They refer to a model of Kintsch and Van Dijk (1978) in which the latter:

> argue that the understanding process may involve the iterative application of a set of
> inference rules that generate increasingly abstract "macrostructure" representations
> of a prose passage. These macrostructures essentially correspond to summaries of the
> passage at various levels of generality.   *(Gick and Holyoak 1980: 310)*

Gick and Holyoak assume there must be an optimal level of abstraction and declare it an empirical issue, to be determined in practice. But in order to carry out their experiments they slide into a different position: "We will now consider in more detail how an analogy between two relational systems might be represented, *assuming an appropriate level of macrostructure has been derived*" (1980: 310). They carefully document the bewildering variety of levels at which subjects made connections, but were not able in this set of experiments to advance beyond a demonstration that practice does not conform to their exhaustive, normative procedure. The difficulty may be one of principle; Simon has identified as a problem a similar dilemma in simulation research (1980: 89). How closely can a normative prefabricated determination of appropriate levels of mapping address processes by which individuals generate differently pitched similarities of structure between stories and situations? The dilemma may not be resolvable, in fact, if the decision is taken to be the experimenter's. For experimental procedures that predetermine the level and kind of relations required between base and target problems and solutions, cannot address questions of how, and in what processual terms, fruitful comparisons are commonly generated.

The experimenters speculate about what is the matter when subjects do not show evidence of transfer. They agree that where there is no analogic transfer, subjects must be unaware of powerful general processes of problem solving and should be taught them (e.g. Simon 1980; Gentner and Gentner 1983). I have mentioned their suggestions (echoing economic development theorists' about "the peasants"), that subjects have erroneous folk models and that they may be reluctant to adopt and use new analogies due to their "conservatism" (Gentner and Gentner 1983: 126). Gick and Holyoak propose, similarly, that subjects may fail spontaneously to notice the pertinence of an analogy to a target problem (1980: 348) and may have difficulty in overcoming contextual barriers (1980: 349; reiterated by Gentner and Gentner 1983: 127). It should be clear that while on the one hand all are careful to emphasize how little is known about transfer, their implicit conclusion is that if the results of these experiments hold up and generalize, many jpfs must fail to use analogies in everyday life while scientists and professionals will succeed. Use of transfer mechanisms (general problem-solving algorithms, analogies) depends in this theoretical position on the explicit intentional application of correct knowledge. The recipe for ameliorating this situation is to make consciously (verbally) available techniques of transfer to those who are presumed to lack them.

In sum, there is no impatience, no hint in this work, that the meager evidence for transfer garnered from a very substantial body of work might indicate that the concept is seriously misconceived. This research genre involves school-like assumptions about the nature of problem solving and its high priority in ongoing activity. It relies on normative models of good thinking as justification, source and standard for experimental tasks and performances. This in turn has unintended consequences for the conceptualization of cognitive processes in terms that appear to pose a serious dilemma for the field. The culture of transfer experiments is, it appears, located well within the web of relations linking schooling, cognitive theory and everyday practice.

Context and motivation in the culture of transfer experiments

Whether talking about transfer across social situations (Simon 1980) or semantic domains (Gick and Holyoak 1980), all of the experimentalists operationalize the concept of setting or situation in essentially identical ways: problem content is the only "context" germain to problem-solving activity. But though operationalized similarly *across* papers, the terms "context" and "situation" are given multiple meanings at different points *within* them. Simon refers to problem states within a problem-solving process as *situations* (1980: 84, 90). In introducing the paper, however, he suggests we consider the nature of transfer across the *situations* of students' lives (1980: 81). Lest the distinction seem exaggerated, consider the uses and meanings of "context" in the following passage from Gick and Holyoak (1980: 349):

(1) The issue of how analogies are noticed is a very general one. A potential analogy may often be encoded in a very different *context* from that in which the target problem appears.

(2) Indeed, the basic problem in using an analogy between remote domains is to connect two bodies of information from disparate *semantic contexts*.

(3) More generally, successful transfer of learning generally involves *overcoming contextual barriers*. This may not be easy; for example, it is all too common for a student to fail to notice the relevance of knowledge acquired in one class to a problem encountered in another.   *(Numbering and emphasis added)*

The first occurence of "context" in this passage refers ambiguously to problem-isomorphs from a knowledge domain, or to a "social" situation. In the second, cultural systems of meaning are equated with knowledge domains. The third instance mentions a "contextual barrier," a gap between two school classes that prevents transfer.

Such ambiguous usages make it possible to equate the circumstances in which transfer is studied with the much broader circumstances in which it is supposed to infuse everyday activity with academic expertise. This may lend an aura of practical relevance to the experiments, but it obscures crucial differences between two-problem transfer in an experiment and uses of knowledge in the varied arenas of the lived-in world. Responsibility to describe and analyze the context of activity is thus confined within the boundaries of task instructions and problem content, and the resulting silence about experimental situations is then extended to unanalyzed situations outside the laboratory. I shall argue in chapter 4 that the merging of meanings of "context" grows from a particular specification of relations among knowledge, culture and socially organized groups in a cognitivist worldview.

There are other difficulties with the conceptualization of context in these experiments and more broadly in the experimental study of cognition. Transfer is characterized as occurring across unrelated, or analogically related, or remotely related situations, but never across settings complexly interrelated in activity, personnel, time, space, or their furnishings. There is an implicit assumption that each context of activity exists in virtual isolation from all others. The abstract quality of this vision is called into question by observational studies in which much of what transpires across settings interpenetrates in various ways – for example, meal planning, grocery shopping, managing money, dieting, cooking and sitting down to meals. Why the implicit assumption of isolation between contexts? It is both constructed in, and reflects, the prime institutionalized exemplar of transfer, the transportation of knowledge from school to other settings. Functional psychological theory treats school as the decontextualized (and hence privileged and powerful) site of learning that is intended for distant and future use.[3] If indeed it were possible to acquire knowledge "out of context" the school (non)context of learning would necessarily stand in an arbitrary and unspecifiable relation with all contexts-of-application. Such logic contributes to the characterization of learning transfer as occurring across unrelated situations.

At a more fundamental level, a binary opposition between "abstracted, decontextualized" knowledge and immediate, "concrete, intuitive" experience underlies experimental strategy, learning-transfer theory, and institutionalized forms of education. Bartlett has expressed the opposition eloquently:

> Memory and all the life of images and words which goes with it, are one . . . with that development of constructive imagination and constructive thought wherein at length we find the *most complete release from the narrowness of presented time and place.*
> *(1958: 199–200 emphasis added)*

Echoed in speculations about the beneficial cognitive consequences of decontextualized learning, freeing oneself from experience has been seen by Bartlett (and most other Western thinkers) as a *condition* for generalization about experience. When the question of applying a generalization arises it is by definition in situations not related to the ones in which its experiential basis was established.

Further, when "tool" is used as a metaphor for knowledge-in-use across settings, there is assumed to be no interaction between tool and situation, but only an *application* of a tool on different occasions. Since situations are not assumed to impinge on the tool itself, a theory of learning transfer does not require an account of situations, much less of relations among them. Knowledge acquisition may be considered (and organized in schools and experiments on cognition) as if the social context of activity had no critical effects on knowledge-in-use. Given this view, it is difficult to see how researchers could do anything but assume away complex relations among social situations, along with the situations themselves. It might be added that experiments, which after all are social situations, reflect and are produced by this theoretical position, for they have no multiple, well-formed, actor-generated relations with other situations and activities in the lives of their subjects.

There is little in this genre of research to hold its analyses to events in space and time, partly because, in the functionalist conception, knowledge is necessarily abstracted from experience. This belief is reflected in the common concept of "knowledge domains," a term that appears to locate knowledge-in-use in time and space without in fact doing so. Here, too, ambiguity may be the advantage which gives the concept a secure place in discussions of cognition; it provides a pseudo-space, an illusion that *knowledge* is the context of problem solving.[4] But the effect on cognitive research of "locating" problems in "knowledge domains" has been to separate the study of problem solving from analysis of the situations in which it occurs.

The lived-in world of contemporary cognitive researchers is undoubtedly furnished with phenomena that support the reification of knowledge domains – school subjects and their curricula, college majors, academic fields, textbooks, encyclopedias, and professions. But none of these would be admitted to be the root of this vision of abstract, bounded conceptual spaces, I think. I suspect that "knowledge domain" is in fact a name for a conventionally acknowledged claim by a social group (e.g. a profession or academic discipline) heavily invested in maintaining *its* boundaries. Control of a body of knowledge plays a major strategic role in such enterprises. If this view is correct, a "knowledge domain" is a socially constructed *exoticum*, that is, it lies at the intersection of the myth of decontextualized understanding and professional/academic specialization and thus is probably not the general concept sought by cognitive psychology.

Further, and also worrisome, the "knowledge domain" as a putative context of cognitive activity is an inert category of analysis. It has no interactive, generative or action-motivating properties. A major factor missing from experimental investigations of problem solving and transfer is an account of what motivates people to recognize and undertake to solve problems when not required to do so. The question need not arise when subjects have tacitly agreed to comply with an experimenter's requests, problem solving is the major ongoing activity, and problems are furnished by problem givers. But in everyday activity the presence or absence of problem solving is often not controlled by others, nor is it determined by some general eagerness or reluctance to solve problems. To analyze problem solving in everyday activity, in short, we shall need a theory of motivation. For whether to have a problem or not, and the specification of what constitutes the problem, are commonly choices made by problem solvers. And we shall need to inquire into questions of how problem-solving activity impels or gives meaning to what happens next.

There are, then, two consistent, well-structured *lacunae* in this work: serious shortcomings, I would argue. One concerns the absent social situation, the other a silence about what motivates problem solving and the transfer of knowledge from one setting to another. Both will be considered further in later chapters.

Conclusions

Learning-transfer research clearly falls in the functionalist tradition sketched in chapter 1. Its central characteristics include the separation of cognition from the social world, the separation of form and content implied in the practice of investigating isomorphic problem solving, and a strictly cognitive explanation for continuity in activity across situations. All of these *dissociate* cognition from its contexts, and help to account for the absence of theorizing about experiments as social situations and cognition as socially situated activity. The enterprise also rests on the assumption of cultural uniformity which is entailed in the concept of knowledge domains. "Knowledge" consists of coherent islands whose boundaries and internal structure exist, putatively, independently of individuals. So conceived, culture is uniform with respect to individuals, except that they may have more or less of it. This difference, in turn, may underly other typically unexamined analytic units in this research – distinctions between experts, novices and jpfs.

The learning transfer genre in cognitive studies offers little support for moving the study of activity out of the privileged and ostensibly constant setting of the laboratory. The examples discussed here provide no empirical evidence concerning problem solving as it unfolds in action in everyday settings. Confined to a tight time-frame of an hour or less of unfamiliar activity (definitely not "everyday" in the sense specified in chapter 1), where problems have been generated previously and elsewhere, they cannot speak to relations between arithmetic use and its sociocultural locus in time and space. Such an approach has nothing to say about the socially situated character of human activity, cognitive or otherwise.

This appraisal raises questions about the nature of problems and problem solving, and I would like to propose an initial conclusion: Problems of the closed, "truth or consequences" variety are a specialized cultural product, and indeed, a distorted representation of activity in everyday life, in both senses of the term – that is, they are neither common nor do they capture a good likeness of the dilemmas addressed in everyday activity. Such a culturally exotic form is more appropriate a category to *be* explained than a source of analytic terms and relations. Contrary to the spirit and practice of the experiments discussed in this chapter, "problem solving" cannot itself constitute the taken-for-granted field of analysis.

More positively, the experiments and their interpretations focus attention on questions about how people establish relations of similarity between the problems they encounter in different settings. There are very faint indications that notions of iterative and dialectical forms of problem generation and solution might be plausible relational concepts to explore. An emphasis on "iteration" would suggest the importance of repeated occasions (rather than unfamiliar situations) as effective sites of the shaping of knowledge and its uses, and "dialectical" processes would recommend the value of *in situ* investigation of relations between persons, activities and settings.

But this advances speculation beyond the current state of the project. Observations about the cultural particularities of transfer research cannot provide positive confirmation of variation in arithmetic practice across situations. This is required as a next step in exploring the situated character of everyday cognition. In the following chapters both empirical evidence and further analysis of cognitive theory provide a stronger rationale for moving into the experienced, lived-in world as the site and source of further investigations of cognitive activity.

3
LIFE AFTER SCHOOL

Drawing the investigation of arithmetic practice into the experienced, lived-in world will be a gradual process, for "problem solving" is the subject of this chapter as well as the last. The Adult Math Project did begin with a break from tradition, proceeding from Bartlett's dictum to begin experimental studies with observation of ongoing activities *in situ* (1932). We followed grocery shoppers through the supermarket and only subsequently translated certain aspects of observed activity into experimental form. Thus, the experimental tasks were not entirely based on normative models of proper cognition nor on an abstract view of proper grocery shopping. But we did search the supermarket observations for the most school-, experimental-like, aspects of shopping in order to construct the experimental tasks. Determining the best buy when comparing two similar grocery items was the central activity to emerge from this procedure. In this respect the work falls within the tradition of transfer research. But there is one further difference. The AMP gathered data on arithmetic activity by the same people in different settings. This made it possible to compare performances across situations rather than merely to extrapolate results from the laboratory to a putative everyday world. There is a fairly complex relationship then, a dialogue if you will, between conventional experimental methods and those employed here. This strongly suggests that the process of moving the enterprise into the lived-in world will require further disentangling of these alternative approaches to practice and theory at later points in the argument.

Discontinuities

Several specific questions guided the initial inquiry. Are school-learned algorithms the procedures of choice in one or all settings or are other procedures more typical? Does arithmetic prowess change over time and with age? Does more schooling lead to greater success at solving math problems, even after many years? Do differences in years of schooling have the same impact on school-like math tests as on grocery shopping math performance? The more general issue is the theoretical claim for cross-situational cognitive continuity – that ubiquitous activity such as arithmetic is relatively uniform in different settings because jpfs bring to them a durable set of cognitive tools. The analysis is directed at similarities and differences in performance by the same people in different settings. An analysis of errors provides a stronger empirical basis for the conclusions by throwing some light on problem-solving procedures.

These questions and issues reflect a definition of "learning transfer" that appears to share the fate of the "transitional" method employed in this chapter. In some respects the concept still has conventional meanings. We will begin with direct comparisons of problem-solving attempts in a single task setting. In other respects, however, "learning transfer" takes on additional, broader meaning than that so far encountered. It was possible to inquire in both test and supermarket settings about uses of school-taught arithmetic in life after school by adults of quite varied ages. Secondly, the gap over which transfer is supposed to occur was widened from two isomorphic problems in a single experimental episode to problems in different settings on differently organized occasions.

There is now quite a substantial body of research on math in practice. It started with Gay and Cole (1967). The tailors' research in Liberia and Posner's and Petitto's research on tailors, cloth merchants and farmers in the Ivory Coast began to look at math embedded in a framework of interconnected work practices (Lave in preparation; Petitto 1979; Posner 1978). More recently Scribner has carried out a complex study of math practices among blue-collar workers in a commercial dairy in Baltimore (Scribner and Fahrmeier 1982; Scribner 1984a, 1984b) and Carraher, Carraher and Schliemann have analyzed math practices of market vendor children in Brazil at work and in school (1982, 1983; Carraher and Schliemann 1982). Schliemann is currently conducting studies comparing the arithmetic practices of master carpenters with those of trade-school carpenters' apprentices, and the impact of schooling on the math practices of bookies taking street-corner bets on the Brazilian national "numbers" game (Schliemann 1985; Acioly and Schliemann 1985). And Hutchins has been following US Navy navigation teams on an aircraft carrier.

The cast of characters in these studies is almost as colorful as in the transfer experiments of the previous chapter. But in this case it is the participants, the plain folks actively engaged in a variety of everyday work activities, who provide the interest. The distinction points to a basic difference between the two approaches. In research on practice the activity to be studied is first located in the everyday activities of participants – the dairy workers, navigators, bookies, shoppers and vendors – as experimenters choose subjects who routinely do what they want to study. In the learning transfer genre experimenters construct tasks that contain a target activity and recruit subjects whose relevant experience is so general, or so meagre, that it will not "contaminate" experimental results. Participants' experience is indexed only through reports of their level of schooling.[1] Thus, everything reported about the subjects in the four articles on transfer experiments of the previous chapter easily fits in one column of Table 2. By contrast, it is only possible to indicate the number of pages, featured in each case at the beginning of the article, devoted to description of experimental problems.

The first part of the chapter lays out AMP findings concerning learning transfer, with results that are compatible with other transfer experiments. But there are some unexpected discoveries as well. These are given strong support by other research on math practice, discussed in the second part of the chapter. Results from AMP research converge with those in the work of Scribner, Carraher *et al.* and Herndon (1971), as they compare arithmetic problem solving in chore and work settings with problem solving in test and simulated everyday circumstances.

The Adult Math Project

When the project began in 1978, we were notably ignorant about the occurrence, organization and results of arithmetic practice in everyday situations. It therefore seemed useful to learn more about the lives of the jpfs with whom we worked than would be contained in a statistical profile or in the immediate specifics of their practice of arithmetic. We decided to learn about their personal histories, with special attention to their schooling, careers and work experience, family composition and household division of labor, and then more specifically about their strategies and experience with grocery shopping and dieting. It seemed important to learn about the organization of their daily lives, as part of the context of the specific organization of activities like grocery

Table 2 *Subjects and problems in reports of experimental research on cognition*

Article	Space given to general description of experimental tasks	Text about subjects (reported in full)
Reed, Ernst, and Banerji 1974	two pages	"The subjects were undergraduates enrolled in psychology courses at Case Western Reserve University. They received additional grade points for their service" (1974: 439).
Hayes and Simon 1977	three and one-half pages	No information about subjects
Gick and Holyoak 1980	six and one-half pages	"40 undergraduates enrolled in introductory psychology at the University of Michigan served as subjects as part of a required course" (1980: 320). "Subjects were 143 undergraduates tested in five introductory psychology classes" (1980: 334). "The experiment was administered to 46 students in two introductory psychology classes" (1980: 338). "Twenty-seven undergraduates from the Human Performance Center paid subject pool served as paid subjects" (1980: 342). "Forty-seven undergraduates from the Human Performance Center subject pool served as subjects" (1980: 344).
Gentner and Gentner 1983	eleven pages	"The subjects were 36 high school and college students screened to be fairly naive about physical science. They were paid for their participation" (1983: 117). "18 people . . . all either advanced high school or beginning college students from the Boston area. Subjects had little or no previous knowledge of electronics. They were paid for their participation" (1983: 120).

shopping, cooking and dieting (Murtaugh 1985a; de la Rocha 1986). We followed pilot-participants through their daily round of activities for a week. This approach turned out not to be feasible as a general research plan, for our constant presence was aggravating and participants objected. But the intensive observation was a useful source of ethnographic material. We devised a systematic observation strategy in the end that was much less ambitious; we followed participants at times when they fit shopping into their schedules (any hour of the day or night). We arrived at the house in time to observe preparations for shopping, went to the store together, shopped, and returned home to follow the process of storing groceries as the expedition ended in their kitchens.

There were a number of auxiliary forms of data collection. We tried, through interviewing only, to obtain a sense of how much and in what ways participants used math on the job. The settings – kitchens, Weight Watchers meetings, supermarkets – required description and analysis. We wondered whether new technologies, or indeed, old ones, affected the kinds and uses of arithmetic. This led to an inventory of measurement and calculational devices in the home and to interviews concerning the use of hand-held calculators and a session of problem solving with a calculator. (We did not try to address the uses of home computers. In 1978–80 they were clearly about to become a major novelty, but they had not yet become household items). The uses of math and of money are intimately connected and all of the grocery shoppers were interviewed at length about money management practices in their households. The shopping study was designed to investigate everyday practices of well-learned and routine varieties, and for purposes of contrast the Weight Watchers study investigated the learning of new arithmetic practices over a period of weeks (in a site other than school).

Work with each participant began with a lengthy general background interview, then a more specialized one on shopping or dieting routines and strategies. Observation of routine activities in their customary settings followed, either in supermarkets while shopping, or in kitchens. The latter included a tour of the kitchen and an interview about food management style, and observations while meals were prepared. Both studies involved diary keeping. Shoppers documented their uses of groceries and dieters all food items they consumed each day. Interviews on food and diet management practices were conducted with these diaries at hand, a technique that produced rich discussions

Table 3 *Participant characteristics*

	mean	range
Age	43 years	21–80 years
Schooling	13 years	6–23 years
Time since schooling completed	22 years	0–66 years
Family income	$27,000	$8,000–$100,000
Number of children in household	1.5 children	0–7
Number of persons shopped for regularly	3.2	1–9
Sex		32 females, 3 males
Use of math on job	8 kinds of routine applications	0–20 kinds of routine applications

(Murtaugh 1985a; de la Rocha 1986). Meanwhile, observations of activity in everyday settings were followed by simulation experiments. For the shoppers this was the best-buy problem session. The Weight Watchers were given small meal preparation problems each week, varied in content but formally equivalent across the six-week period, and also, for comparative purposes, cooked an elaborate Weight Watchers' meal. Next came a series of sessions exploring school-taught math procedures: a multiple choice test and a series of pencil-and-paper math problems, number and measurement facts, mental math problems and finally calculator problems. Money management interviews and the inventory of measuring and calculating devices in their homes were fit into the schedule of activities at different times for different participants.

We spent about 40 hours with each of the 35 Orange County, California women and men who took part in the project, 25 in the supermarket study, 10 in the diet study.[2] Since we knew so little about everyday cognitive activities we chose to maximize variation in the arithmetic practices observed rather than attempt a representative sample of the people using them.[3] Thus we sought participants who varied widely in age, income, family composition and size, schooling and years since schooling was completed. More detail about the backgrounds of the participants (Table 3) may be gained from analysis of material from the introductory interviews. Besides introducing the participants, the intent is to describe some of the relations among their demographic characteristics that affected decisions about whether to include such information in the analysis of arithmetic performances which follows.

We may begin with the family income of the participants, which averaged about $27,000 per year. One couple in the sample had an annual income of $100,000, the highest among the participants, while the lowest was $8,000 for a family of four. Nonetheless, it seems unlikely that the sample extended beyond the middle class. The $8,000 per year family was temporarily experiencing hard times and the wealthiest couple had achieved their current state of affluence in a relatively few years. In spite of high variance, income does not account for differences in frequency of calculation in the supermarket nor performance on arithmetic tests. This finding is of interest in itself, for it supports an argument that the role of arithmetic in grocery shopping is more one of rationalizing decisions than saving money (chapter 7). But further, it raises questions about just where in the process of managing food family income does shape decisions and activities. From interviews with shoppers it appears likely that it constrains grocery purchases at the more general level of decision making concerning where to shop and what to eat rather than at moments when shoppers debate with themselves about the value of individual purchases.[4]

In order to address questions concerning the nature of changing arithmetic performances across the life-span we attempted through sampling procedures to separate age and years since schooling was completed. The correlation between these variables is almost certainly lower than in the population at large, but they are still highly interdependent. In regression equations with math test and multiple choice test scores as dependent variables, age, schooling, and years since schooling was completed were individually significant predictors of success. When either age or schooling was held constant, however, years since schooling was completed no longer predicted test scores. Years since schooling was completed appears to reflect both age and amount of schooling, but it does not help directly in explaining variation in performances on tests.

Most of the participants were women, for among potential participants they were, much more often than men, grocery shoppers with years of experience shopping for their families, and dieters who hoped to lose substantial amounts of weight. In extensive exploration of the demographic data there was no significant statistical relationship between the gender of participants and any other variable. Though this may be a statistical artifact, it conforms with our field impressions that in the supermarket women and men engage in arithmetic activities in ways that appear indistinguishable. Reports by informants of their attitudes towards arithmetic at the time they were in school do vary between men and women in the sample, but statistical analysis shows no relationship between (reported) past attitudes and present performances.

The two schools of transfer theory discussed in chapter 2 guided AMP construction of formal arithmetic tasks for comparison with everyday math activities. There was, on the one hand, a test of general arithmetic knowledge and a multiple choice test consisting of questions from a standardized math achievement test. We also explored each participant's immediate, memorized knowledge of arithmetic facts and systems of weights and measures. The first were constructed to reflect Judd's theory of transfer, to assess a general grasp of principles of arithmetic, while the math fact exercise was closer in spirit to Thorndike's view that similarity of specific elements might promote transfer across situations. A set of ratio comparison problems formed the third element of AMP strategy for addressing conventional views of learning transfer. These problems, included in the general problem-solving session, were isomorphic with best-buy problems in the supermarket, and provided a more precise means for exploring transfer. The results of these math exercises and of observations of math activity in the supermarket formed the empirical basis for addressing questions about similarities and discontinuities in math practice between test and supermarket settings.

The specific math activities of the AMP, on which the analysis to follow is based, require a more detailed introduction, beginning with best-buy calculations in the supermarket. Two performance measures for grocery shopping arithmetic practices are relevant here. The first is the percentage of correct solutions for best-buy arithmetic problems attempted in the supermarket. The process of arriving at a base designation of best-buy calculations was fairly complicated. Of over 800 items purchased by 24 of the participants, 213 involved arithmetic problem solving, defined as "an occasion on which a shopper associated two or more numbers with one or more arithmetic operations: addition, subtraction, multiplication or division" (Murtaugh 1985b: 187). Frequency ranged from no calculations for one shopper to calculations on over half of their purchases by three shoppers. On average, 16% of all purchases involved arithmetic. Murtaugh (1985b: 137–188) reports that 85% of the 213 cases of arithmetic involved price comparison. Sixty-five cases were best-buy problems in which both prices and quantities differed. Nine of these cases have been eliminated for the present analysis because the quantity comparisons seemed trivial. The remaining 54 cases are included in the analysis. The problem, given as prices and quantities for the items compared, are listed in Appendix table 1.

The second supermarket performance variable was the frequency of calculation in the store, divided by number of items purchased, in order to compare frequencies across shoppers. This variable was drawn into the analysis as a practical matter when the properties of the first subverted the task (see below). Even so it seemed plausible that this would constitute an indirect measure of arithmetic knowledge on grounds that, all things being equal, the more people know about math the more likely they would be to calculate.

The best-buy problem-solving session was designed to explore procedures observed in the supermarket. When shoppers posed the problem of which of two or three items was the better buy, they sometimes used unit price shelf labels. But usually they calculated ratios between prices and quantities, forming ratios composed of like units and comparing the two prices and the two quantities. The best-buy simulation was a way to test an explanation for this observation. Twelve best-buy problems were presented to each informant, at home, in a session set aside for that purpose. Participants were asked to decide which was the better buy. Some problems involved actual bottles, jars, boxes and cans from the supermarket. Others were presented as cards with written prices and quantities of items to be compared. The problems are laid out in chapter 5, Table 11, where there is a much more extensive analysis of the simulation experiment.

In the best-buy simulation experiment it was possible to discuss the problem and its solution with the participant each time an answer was given, so that it was clear that the participant had solved the problem, and not merely guessed the answer. In the supermarket we recorded information on the prices and quantities of each grocery item mentioned by a shopper, and which item was chosen, so there was evidence as to whether the shopper selected the better buy. But during problem-solving activity in the supermarket the shopper was struggling to buy groceries and provide a commentary on the process at the same time, while the observer was struggling to balance an unobtrusive approach against the desire to elicit complete information about solution procedures. Thus it was not always possible to gather evidence about problem-solving processes as precisely as in the best-buy simulation.[5] This experience, indeed, led us to develop the simulation experiment, in an attempt to check our observational findings.

All participants took part in the arithmetic session in which they worked on an 11-page set of 54 problems.[6] This was supposed to be a relaxed, certainly not a test-like occasion, at home, with a staff person from the AMP who had gotten to know the participants during initial interview sessions. However, we were not successful in removing the evaluative sting from the occasion. Participants did not believe our claim that this was "not a test in the usual sense." They reacted to the request that we be allowed to observe their math procedures with comments of "ok, teacher," by clearing the work space, and by talking about not cheating. They spoke with self-deprecation about not having studied math for a long time. Common requests were phrased as, "May I rewrite problems?" and "Should I . . . ?" This marked reaction itself constitutes data to be accounted for at a later point in the argument. Meanwhile, since participants were sure the exercise was a test, it will be referred to as such in the discussion which follows.

Their suspicions may have focused, quite appropriately, on the conventionally structured relations among the problems. The math test sampled a paradigmatic representation of arithmetic taken from school curricula, including integer, decimal and fraction problems as one dimension, and arithmetic operations (addition, subtraction, multiplication and division) as the other (Appendix table 2).[7] Additional problems, including negative-number arithmetic and a few that required knowledge of associative and commutative laws, were intended to explore arithmetic operations more broadly. In the same spirit, other problems contained both decimals and fractions. Since some lent themselves more easily to solution in one mode or the other, we thought that flexible use of solution strategies might indicate a general appreciation of their arithmetic properties.[8] The problems isomorphic with best-buy problems in grocery shopping asked for a comparison of two ratios expressed as fractions, for example, "circle the larger: 6/3 or 5/4." For there was reason to think that shoppers solving best-buy problems in the supermarket asked themselves which ratio was the larger. Another reason for posing the problems in this form had to do with precision. The request in the test setting to "circle the larger" was intended to leave the matter of calculating precision open, as it was in the market. The problems in the test situations each involved one easily reducible pair of terms and may have been easier to solve than the best-buy problems in the market and in the simulation experiment.

Some of the same arithmetic principles were addressed in the multiple-choice questions as in the math test. These included translations between numerals and written numbers, comparison of fractions to decide which was larger, conversion from fractions to decimals and vice

Table 4 *Relations among math scores*
N = 34

	Multiple choice	Math test	Number facts	Measure facts
Multiple choice	XXX	.86 (.001)	.34 (.03)	.34 (.03)
Math test		XXX	.33 (.03)	NS
Number facts			XXX	.44 (.005)
Measure facts				XXX

Note: Here and in the tables that follow, the decimals in parentheses are significance levels. Those not in parentheses are correlation coefficients.

versa, rounding and estimation, taking a simple average and questions about metrics. Only the summary score on the multiple-choice test has been used in the analysis which follows.

It seemed possible that specific number and measurement facts would be resources for transfer and that people would be more inclined to calculate in everyday settings if they commanded a ready fund of arithmetic facts. Therefore participants were asked to respond to the (orally) presented problems (e.g. 6×9? 18/3?) with an immediate answer, or to indicate that they would need more time to calculate. The same format was used to present questions about the equivalence of different units of length, weight and volume. The accuracy and timing of their responses were used as indices of their knowledge of specific arithmetic and measurement facts. Appendix table 3 lists these problems.

All of these data have been explored extensively using regression analysis as well as less robust nonparametric measures of association. Since these analyses tell the same story, I have given the simplest account wherever possible. The statistics reported here are presented in sets. Interpretive emphasis is placed on patterns of relations among variables.

From transfer of learning to situational specificity

Scores on the general and specific measures of school-like math are strongly correlated with each other (Table 4).[9] Further, years of

Table 5 *Arithmetic performance and schooling*
N = 34

	Age	Time since school	Years of school
Multiple choice	.52 (.001)	.56 (.001)	.44 (.005)
Math test	.45 (.004)	.53 (.001)	.47 (.003)
Ratio problems	.24 (.037)	.30 (.011)	.21 (.064)

Table 6 *Mean scores on math tasks*
N = 34

Math task	Mean score (in %)
Multiple choice	82
Math test	59
Ratio problems	57
Number facts	85
Measurement facts	66
	Average 70
Best-buy simulation experiment	93
Grocery shopping	98
	Average 95

schooling is a good predictor of performance on the arithmetic tests, as are age and years since schooling was completed, though in the opposite direction (e.g. the more time passed, the lower the score, Table 5). But if the context is broadened to include performance in the supermarket and in the simulation experiment, the initial findings must be reconsidered in the face of several different kinds of contravening evidence. There is a large disparity in success between the arithmetic test performance (average 59%) and those in supermarket and best-buy experiment (98% and 93% respectively, Table 6). Further, the extremely low variance in success rates in the supermarket and simulation experiment suggest that

Table 7 *Intercorrelations of math performances*

N = 34

	Multiple choice	Math test	Number facts	Measure facts	Best-buy problems	Super-market problems
Multiple choice	xxx	.86 (.001)	.34 (.03)	.34 (.03)	n.s.	n.s.
Math test		xxx	.33 (.03)	n.s.	n.s.	n.s.
Number facts			xxx	.44 (.005)	n.s.	n.s.
Measurement facts				xxx	n.s.	.39 (.03)
Best-buy problems					xxx	n.s.
Supermarket problems						xxx

those highly variable test scores are not closely associated with supermarket math "performance."[10] Table 7 shows not a single significant correlation between frequency of calculation in supermarket, and scores on math test, multiple choice test or number facts. There is a significant correlation between weight and volume facts (but not length) and frequency of calculation in the supermarket. But its place is unique in this set of nonsignificant correlations. Finally, the supermarket and best-buy exercises show an entirely different pattern of relations with schooling and age than test performance. Table 8 shows that success and frequency of calculation in supermarket and simulation experiment bear no statistical relationship with schooling, years since schooling was completed, or age.

The direction of the difference in problem-solving success between these settings contravenes the logic of learning transfer. Math is the central ongoing activity in the test situation and should command resources of attention and memory greater than those available in the supermarket where math competes for attention with a number of other concerns. School algorithms should be more powerful and accurate than quick, informal procedures (that's why they are taught in school).

Table 8 *Age and performance*

N = 34

	Age	Time since school	Years of school
Multiple choice	.52 (.001)	.56 (.001)	.44 (.005)
Math test	.45 (.004)	.53 (.001)	.47 (.003)
Ratio problems	.24 (.037)	.30 (.011)	.21 (.064)
Number facts	.24 (.082)	.12 (.251)	.20 (.123)
Measurement facts	.13 (.224)	.21 (.115)	.33 (.027)
Best buy problems	.08 (.279)	.16 (.124)	.00 (.494)
Supermarket problems	.02 (.494)	.04 (.384)	.01 (.461)

Finally, 98% accuracy in the supermarket is practically error-free arithmetic, and belies the image of the hapless jpf failing cognitive challenges in an everyday world.[11]

In best-buy problems in the supermarket, problem-solving processes often involved "left to right" calculation (decomposition of a number into hundreds, tens and ones starting with the largest and working through to the smallest), recomposition, rounding, ratio comparison, transformation of both problems and solutions in the course of problem solving, use of the environment as a calculating device, and other techniques not found in test situations. There were too few errors to describe in general terms, but there was one typical feature of arithmetic practice in the supermarket that would count as error in experimental terms: problems were occasionally abandoned in the middle of a calculation. A shopper would stop part way through the process and use some means other than math to resolve a quantitative dilemma, (e.g. postponing a purchase or "taking the big one because it won't spoil anyway." Arithmetic procedures used in the simulation experiment provided one further useful observation, that people found it much easier to operate with ratios that were evenly divisible into smaller units, especially when one was a multiple of the other, or both were divisible

Table 9 *Mean scores by number type and operation*

N = 34

Type of Arithmetic	Mean score (in %)
Integers	84
Decimals	67
Fractions	48
Addition	68
Subtraction	65
Multiplication	55
Division	55

by the same unit. Easily manipulable ratios are important in carrying out best-buy calculations. Putting these observations together helps to account for a third. People appear likely to abandon problems at times when particular numbers are unmalleable – difficult to relate to each other without editing them in ways that seriously distort their interrelations. This difficulty with arithmetic in the supermarket is understood, and exacerbated, by supermarket packaging and pricing policies which often arrange weight, volume and price in prime-number units. One further characteristic of math in the supermarket deserves comment. As will be clearer in chapter 7, problem solving in the supermarket is a process of transformation; something must first be transformed into a problem by the problem solver. Then the problem, solutions, number and their relations are transformed until a resolution is reached. Given that people are accurate at solving problems in this manner, it appears that they must be good at keeping straight about what those relations are.

There is clear discontinuity between this description and a parallel description of procedures and errors on the math test. In the test situation, essentially all problem-solving activity was dependent on pencil and paper and Arabic place-holding algorithms. Problem solvers worked from right to left, using borrowing and carrying routines for addition, subtraction and multiplication problems. In long division problems jpfs estimated quotients and checked them through multiplication and subtraction. There were differences in error rates among standard types of problems and operations on the math test (Table 9). Fraction problems were more difficult to solve than integers or decimals,

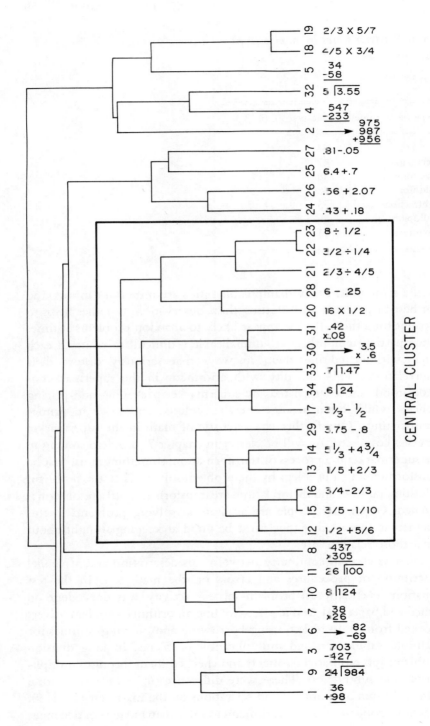

Figure 1 Alpair clustering of math problems

19	$2/3 \times 5/7$	
18	$4/5 \times 3/4$	
5	34 -58	
32	$5\overline{)3.55}$	
4	547 -233	
2	$\rightarrow$	975 987 $+956$
27	$.81-.05$	
25	$6.4+.7$	
26	$.56+2.07$	
24	$.43+.18$	
23	$8 \div 1/2$	
22	$3/2 \div 1/4$	
21	$2/3 \div 4/5$	
28	$6-.25$	
20	$16 \times 1/2$	
31	$.42$ $\times.08$	
30	$\rightarrow$	3.5 $\times .6$
33	$.7\overline{)1.47}$	
34	$.6\overline{)24}$	
17	$2\,1/3 - 1/2$	
29	$3.75-.8$	
14	$5\,1/3 + 4\,3/4$	
13	$1/5 + 2/3$	
16	$3/4 - 2/3$	
15	$3/5 - 1/10$	
12	$1/2 + 5/6$	
8	437 $\times 305$	
11	$26\overline{)100}$	
10	$8\overline{)124}$	
7	38 $\times 26$	
6	$\rightarrow$	82 -69
3	703 -427	
9	$24\overline{)984}$	
1	36 $+98$	

CENTRAL CLUSTER

multiplication and division more difficult than addition and subtraction. However, an exhaustive analysis of errors (Faust unpublished data), reveals a different pattern of clustering of problems (based on the Alpair clustering program, D'Andrade 1974) when they are sorted in terms of test-takers' performances – one central cluster and two peripheral ones (Figure 1). The central cluster contains the problems most similar because most often solved incorrectly. This cluster contains several fraction problems but not the fraction multiplication problems ($\frac{2}{3} \times \frac{5}{7}$; $\frac{4}{5} \times \frac{3}{4}$). Further, it includes a number of decimal problems and no integer problems. But the principle behind the errors seemed a puzzle since this set of problems clearly does not map onto the math categories that were used to generate the test. A further observation brought insight with it.[12] All – and only – the problems at the periphery of the diagram, could be solved directly as they were represented to the problem solver. (This group includes just those decimal addition and subtraction problems in which decimal point placement and alignment of numbers require no manipulation before or after solving them.) Those in the central cluster must be transformed and re-represented before they are solveable. Thus, the fraction–addition and fraction–subtraction problems must be expressed in terms of a common denominator; division of fractions requires inversion and multiplication, decimal points must be moved before the decimal problems are amenable to solution. The two decimal multiplication problems ($.42 \times .08$; $3.5 \times .6$) in the central cluster are only an apparent exception, for while arithmetic operations may be performed directly on these problems as represented, the decimal point must be assigned its proper location after the calculation, a transformation of the numerical solution.

An examination of problem-solving protocols for seven of the participants confirms these findings. Six of the seven missed the first three division of fraction problems, multiplying immediately instead of inverting the divisor first. All but one then worked out the algorithm and solved other problems correctly. A person who missed all of the problems had part of the rule available, "invert and multiply" but inverted the dividend instead of the divisor. Decimal point placement caused most of the difficulties in decimal problems (Faust unpublished data). Thus partial understanding of transformational rules seems to be at the heart of erroneous procedures on the test.

In sum, the only constant division in problem-solving success among the problems in the test lies between problems that are directly solvable and those that must be transformed before solving. It is the latter that engender errors. There is confirming evidence from other studies of adult math problem solving. Scribner (Scribner and Fahrmeier 1983) demonstrates that decimal point placement rules are a source of difficulty for the adults in her study. Larkin (1978) reports difficulties with the fraction inversion rule among adults. The rules for transforming problems in school lessons, learned as formulae, mainly by rote, seem very different from the ubiquitous and successful transformation of problems in the supermarket. The latter do not appear to involve formulaic rules at all. As the argument proceeds we shall consider more carefully the nature of transformational procedures in the supermarket and their differences from algorithmic procedures taught in school.

There are discontinuities in performances, errors and procedures between the supermarket on the one hand and test activities on the other, though the arithmetic problems are formally similar and the persons solving them are the same. It is not unreasonable to speculate that variation in arithmetic procedures is somehow related to the situations in which they take place. Two reasons seem especially noteworthy for taking this possibility seriously. The jpfs were unexpectedly accurate in arithmetic in the supermarket, to such a degree that it suggests there may be qualitative differences in the arithmetic procedures from those assembled in a testing situation (chapters 5, 6 and 7). Secondly, the jpfs who carried out calculations in the market successfully were experienced at shopping for groceries. That they struggled to produce half-forgotten algorithms for fraction and decimal transformations during the math test raises the possibility that they did not have comparably immediate and lively experience with school-taught arithmetic procedures. That is, it suggests that they may not have integrated school-taught algorithms as the "method of choice" into a number of situations of their adult lives. This too provides impetus for exploring the situational specificity of math activity.

Several critical points about transfer research have emerged in the course of the analysis. A narrow focus on transfer from one problem to another is not equivalent to, nor representative of, the experience of bringing knowledge to bear in diverse situations in the lived-in world. The two-problem approach creates too small a range of variation, under too simple circumstances to illuminate relations among people's everyday activities and the situations in which they occur. Thus even if conventional research were able to produce strong evidence of transfer, the validity of extrapolation from the experimental to any other situation would be doubtful. Secondly, learning transfer research assumes that success, or at least remediation for future success, depends on the conscious, attentive application of correct knowledge. Yet even the skeletal findings presented here call this assumption into question. Math activity was more salient and the object of more concentrated effort in the test situations than in the supermarket, while math was more accurate in the supermarket where it played a minor role in the ongoing activity of buying groceries. Relations between conscious explicit formulations of strategy and successful realizations in practice are clearly in need of further exploration. And finally, the learning transfer genre assumes that cognitive incapacity of one sort or another accounts for "failure to transfer." But the contrast between the success of supermarket shoppers and their performance on school-like tasks implies that there may not be just better and worse performances or more and less successful realizations of some basic arithmetic competence. Rather, there appear to be qualitatively different practices of arithmetic in different settings. It is worth considering the possibility that relations among persons, their activities, and contexts, are implicated in success – and failure – rather than merely cognitive strategies. If so, explanations of continuity and variation in math activities in terms of learning transfer will not suffice.

Convergent findings

Other studies confirm both the discontinuity of math performances between settings, and the pattern of differential accuracy of calculation found by comparing test with supermarket data.[13] All three studies – Scribner's analysis of working arithmetic in a dairy, Carraher, Carraher and Schliemann's in an open-air produce market in Recife, Brazil and an eloquent account of similar findings made by junior high school teacher James Herndon (1971) – compare everyday and school-related math, and involve experiments or tests that try to simulate everyday activities.

The juxtaposition of these studies with AMP research leads to both a new point and a new question. First, it is possible to document in detail a series of ways in which jpfs actively give meaning to, and fashion, processes of problem solving in the midst of ongoing activities in relevant settings. Each of the studies asks whether people know and use one form of arithmetic or two, or more. None casts a broad enough net across situations to document the possibility of an indeterminate number of arithmetics, nor in what terms they might be formulated.

But together the studies raise the question, and we shall come back to it at the end of the discussion.

The first is the Industrial Literacy Project. Focused on relations between school and everyday thinking skills, it pursued these questions through ethnographic field observation and simulation experiments. Scribner *et al.* (1982) located this investigation of arithmetic practice among workers in a commercial dairy in Baltimore, Maryland. Among other issues, she addresses educators' concerns about the adequacy of math preparation in school, arguing against the implied view that school is the only place to learn, and suggesting an agnostic stance on whether testing is a crucial source of predictions about future math performance at work (1982: 3).

> We presented individuals with simplified versions of work tasks under standardized and controlled conditions. Since many of these tasks involved quantitative problem-solving (e.g. counting, computations with decimals, and the like) we could regard performance on them as indicative of practical arithmetic skills. Most tasks were amenable to detailed process analysis, and for several we were able to extract from these analyses the higher order strategies or rules regulating modes of problem solution. During the course of the research, we also conducted observational studies of workers performing these tasks on the job.   *(1982: 5)*

The work tasks observed and simulated included making up delivery truck orders of dairy products for restaurants and other large customers, counting stock, and pricing delivery tickets. Formal arithmetic tasks included a test of math-fact knowledge, a computational test, a mental-math test and a set of negative-number problems.

Order forms are a ubiquitous part of most jobs in the dairy: for clerks, for those (called preloaders) who assemble orders to go out on delivery trucks, for truck drivers who deliver orders and for bookkeepers who keep track of sales and receipts. Scribner distinguished between jobs, some of which required work with numbers on order forms, others which involved the objects to which the orders referred. Some jobs had more restricted educational requirements for employment than others. Employees in different types of jobs differed in average amounts of schooling. Thus, she was able to explore variation in arithmetic practices across everyday situations and formal tests, among people with different amounts of schooling and work experience.

Like the AMP, the Industrial Literacy Project began with intensive observational work in everyday settings. From these observations (e.g. of preloaders assembling orders in the icebox warehouse) hypotheses were developed about everyday math procedures, for example, how preloaders did the arithmetic involved in figuring out when to assemble whole or partial cases, and when to take a few cartons out of a case or add them in, in order to efficiently gather together the products specified in an order. Dairy preloaders, bookkeepers and a group of junior high school students took part in simulated case loading experiments. Since standardized test data were available from the school records of the students, it was possible to infer from their performance roughly the grade-equivalent of the problems. Comparisons were made of both the performances of the various experimental groups and the procedures employed for arriving at problem solutions.

A second study was carried out by cognitive psychologists investigating arithmetic practices among children selling produce in a market in Brazil (Carraher *et al.* 1982; 1983; Carraher and Schliemann 1982). They worked with four boys and a girl, from impoverished families, between 9 and 15 years of age, third to eighth grade in school. The researchers approached the vendors in the marketplace as customers, putting the children through their arithmetic paces in the course of buying bananas, oranges and other produce.

M. is a coconut vendor, 12 years old, in the third grade. The interviewer is referred to as 'customer.'

Customer: How much is one coconut?
M: 35.
Customer: I'd like ten. How much is that?
M: (Pause.) Three will be 105; with three more, that will be 210. (Pause) I need four more. That is . . . (pause) 315 . . . I think it is 350.

The problem can be mathematically represented in several ways. 35×10 is a good representation of the *question* posed by the interviewer. The subject's answer is better represented by $105 + 105 + 105 + 35$, which implies that 35×10 was solved by the subject as $(3 \times 35) + 105 + 105 + 35$ . . . M. proved to be competent in finding out how much 35×10 is, even though he used a routine not taught in 3rd grade, since in Brazil 3rd graders learn to multiply any number by ten simply by placing a zero to the right of that number.   *(Carraher, Carraher and Schliemann 1983: 8–9)*

The conversation with each child was taped. The transcripts were analyzed as a basis for ascertaining what problems should appear on individually constructed paper and pencil arithmetic tests. Each test included all and only the problems the child attempted to solve in the market. The formal test was given about one week after the informal encounter in the market.

Herndon, a teacher who has written eloquently about American schooling, described (1971) his experiences teaching a junior high class whose students had failed in mainstream classrooms. He discovered that one of them had a well-paid, regular job scoring for a bowling league. The work demanded fast, accurate, complicated arithmetic. Further, all of his students engaged in relatively extensive arithmetic activities while shopping or in after-school jobs. He tried to build a bridge between their practice of arithmetic outside the classroom and school arithmetic lessons by creating "bowling score problems," "shopping problems," and "paper route problems." The attempt was a failure, the league scorer unable to solve even a simple bowling problem in the school setting. Herndon provides a vivid picture of the discontinuity, beginning with the task in the bowling alley:

> . . . eight bowling scores at once. Adding quickly, not making any mistakes (for no one was going to put up with errors), following the rather complicated process of scoring in the game of bowling. Get a spare, score ten plus whatever you get on the next ball, score a strike, then ten plus whatever you get on the next two balls; imagine the man gets three strikes in a row and two spares and you are the scorer, plus you are dealing with seven other guys all striking or sparing or neither one.
>
> I figured I had this particular dumb kid now. Back in eighth period I lectured him on how smart he was to be a league scorer in bowling. I pried admissions from the other boys, about how they had paper routes and made change. I made the girls confess that when they went to buy stuff they didn't have any difficulty deciding if those shoes cost $10.95 or whether it meant $109.50 or whether it meant $1.09 or how much change they'd get back from a twenty. Naturally I then handed out bowling-score problems, and naturally everyone could choose which ones they wanted to solve, and naturally the result was that all the dumb kids immediately rushed me yelling, "Is this right? I don't know how to do it! What's the answer? This ain't right, is it?" and "What's my grade?" The girls who bought shoes for $10.95 with a $20 bill came up with $400.15 for change and wanted to know if that was right? The brilliant league scorer couldn't decide whether two strikes and a third frame of eight amounted to eighteen or twenty-eight or whether it was one hundred eight and a half.
> (Herndon 1971: 94–95)

People's bowling scores, sales of coconuts, dairy orders and best buys in the supermarket were correct remarkably often; the performance of AMP participants in the market and simulation experiment has already been noted. Scribner comments that the dairy preloaders made virtually no errors in a simulation of their customary task, nor did dairy truck drivers make errors on simulated pricing of delivery tickets (Scribner and Fahrmeier 1982: 10, 18). In the market in Recife, the vendors generated correct arithmetic results 99% of the time.

All of these studies show consistent discontinuities between individuals' performances in work situations and in school-like testing ones. Herndon reports quite spectacular differences between math in the bowling alley and in a test simulating bowling score "problems." The shoppers' average score was in the high 50s on the math test. The market sellers in Recife averaged 74% on the pencil and paper test which had identical math problems to those each had solved in the market. The dairy loaders who did not make mistakes in the warehouse scored on average 64% on a formal arithmetic test.

Scribner's data, like AMP findings, contravene the view that arithmetic skill should decrease out of school and over time:

> Math fact scores were significantly and *positively* related to age, years in plant and years on current job and to no other background factors. Further, years in plant is negatively correlated with level of schooling.   *(1982: 30–31)*

She goes on to point out that:

> Among dairy workers, level of schooling had little effect on either theoretical (test) or practical (task) arithmetic problem-solving. The influence of amount of prior schooling was evident only on the written computations test.   *(1982: 33)*

There is evidence that workers made calculations which were arithmetically more advanced than they had the opportunity to learn in school.

> Although this blue-collar group's average educational level was 9th grade, some of the men had not completed elementary school. However, on the average, their knowledge of math facts and ability to do mental and written math with whole numbers and negative numbers were on a par with students who were above the 9th grade level in math achievement.   *(Scribner and Fahrmeier 1982: 17)*

They were also more flexible in choosing strategies for solving problems:

> workers demonstrate marked superiority over students in their use of flexible strategies . . .   *(1982: 26)*

These studies produced evidence that shoppers, dairyworkers and vendors invent units for calculation. The dairy loaders, for instance, receive orders from the bookkeepers in units of cases plus individual cartons of dairy products. The preloaders transform these into combination of full and partial cases of the products. This is not as easy as it sounds for some products have 16 cartons to a case, some 32 and some 48 creating in effect different number bases for different products. As they talk about, and work on, assembling an order in terms of cases and partial cases, the preloaders reduce the size of the numbers they need to remember. But more important, the units they use reflect the organization of their work. They don't carry cartons about separately or load them individually onto trucks; they work with cases, some full and others partially filled. In the Brazilian market prices change rapidly. In general, market sellers keep the prices in round units and change the quantities of produce at a given price. So price units remain relatively stable and easy to calculate. This makes it possible to negotiate with customers in a way that makes the most of old knowledge and past calculations. And the Weight Watchers invented units of measurement with great frequency (see chapter 6).

Conclusions

The results of the learning transfer experiments of chapter 2 ranged from negative to positive-with-limitations. As a whole perhaps "equivocal" and "unstable" describe them best. But when we investigate learning transfer directly across *situations*, the results are consistently negative, whether analyzing performance levels, procedures or errors. The Brazilian research group titles one paper "Life 10, School 0" (Carraher *et al.* 1982). Scribner recommends caution about the predictive value of school testing for success in the workplace and demonstrates greater problem-solving success with more complex arithmetic in the dairy than school grade level would predict. AMP findings concur. And Herndon uses the term "dumb class" with great irony, going on to a social, not psychological, analysis of the phenomenon so labeled.

These studies also show a consistency of findings concerning the active character of arithmetic practice. Grocery shoppers continually transformed and sometimes abandoned problems in the supermarket. Jpfs actively insisted that school math procedures be used on certain occasions, and invented quantitative units and flexible strategies. All of the studies demonstrated discontinuities in problem-solving processes between situations, and the uncoupling of math performances from schooling except during tests. The math observed appears to have a generative relation with ongoing activities and at the same time to be shaped by them. The studies converge in their methods as well; observational research was the basis for the development of experiments which simulated everyday activity. The experiments provided but one locus in comparison of activity across settings, rather than constituting a unique setting for the putatively value-neutral, transparent study of the instantiation of ideal forms of thought. Together these shifts in method made it possible to avoid the dilemma of prefabricated tasks and interpretations, by taking advantage of an observationally-derived understanding of practice *in situ*.

The studies analyzed here suggest some general dimensions by which activity might be constituted in situationally specific ways. First, if situations, occasions and activities are interrelated, these relations must shape arithmetic in practice. For instance, decimal/fraction conversions and ratio comparisons are surprisingly frequent in the everyday activities of AMP participants. It seems likely that they arise because the transport of materials, engaged in activity in one setting to another setting in which they are incorporated in different activity sometimes requires comparison and conversion. In shopping, food items are quantified in one set of terms, in cooking, others. Lumber is sold in board feet while furniture is designed and built in linear feet and inches. Orders in the dairy are presented in numbers of cartons, converted into cases by preloaders, and so on.

A second general dimension of difference in the constitution of activity across settings concerns relations between problem solver and problems. Are we to conceptualize them in objective or subjective terms, or both or neither? A contrast between the dairy project and the AMP is useful in considering the question. According to Scribner's analysis problems exist in the environment, concretely, and can be objectively assigned to school or work categories in a binary classification of kinds of arithmetic (theoretic or practical). In AMP observations in the supermarket some problems also appeared to be "out there" in the store. But whether the shopper "sees" the problem or not is the shopper's option. And if a problem must be recognized in order to exist, it is not possible to locate problems exclusively either in settings or in cognitive processing – both are involved.[14] AMP data further contain evidence that problems are sometimes externally given as commands, sometimes exist in the setting as invitations to calculate, and at still others can be negotiated with the setting and people in it or generated by the problem solver.

The variety of ways of constituting arithmetic problems is impressive. But perhaps more central to differences in arithmetic practices is that people also experience themselves, subjectively, as both subjects and objects in the world. In the supermarket the world is experienced as concrete, "out there." Individuals experience themselves as in control of their activities, interacting with the setting, generating problems in relation with the setting and controlling problem-solving processes. (In such circumstances it is possible to exercise alternatives to the solving of a particular problem, abandoning arithmetic for some other kind of solution. The outcome is not failure, but a different option.) In contrast, school and experiments create contexts in which children and "subjects" experience themselves as objects, with no control over problems or choice about problem-solving processes. Herndon's description of his students' response to "bowling" problems supports this claim.

Even though the basis for generalization is limited, it is important to emphasize that these contrastive cases do not establish a static contrast between school and all "other" situations, or between two kinds of arithmetic. The research in the dairy provides crucial evidence for this point. For in the dairy workers are, at one level, treated as instruments of labor. Orders to be filled appear, and workers are not free to generate creative lists of purchases for the customers. But though they do not control problems, they have a job to do, one in which they experience themselves as subjects acting in the world (or in the icebox at least). In this circumscribed field of action they have partial control over problem-solving processes, though less than in the supermarket. It would be difficult to argue for a dichotomous division of circumstances (and hence for "two maths"), given that configurations of relations of control and experience in the world are extremely diverse.[15]

A third general dimension of variation across situations concerns the salience of any given activity when it unfolds in different settings. Previously I argued that normative experiments face a dilemma, for they must characterize on *a priori* grounds the structure of "correct" knowledge for the experiment, making it difficult to seriously ac-knowledge, much less analyze, the variety of levels of structural relations generated by subjects. The dilemma is exacerbated by another conven-tion of experimentation: in practice, the target experiment activity is assigned a roughly constant (and high) level of salience in and across experiments (as well as in those other entangled setting, tests and classroom lessons). In contrast, the degree to which ongoing activity is organized in terms of mathematical concerns *varies* in the supermarket and other everyday situations. On some occasions it is the main ongoing activity, while perhaps more often it is not. Observed *in situ*, it is possible to examine the effects of differential salience on the ways or levels at which activity is organized, and thus on the varied character of arithmetic procedures in different situations. The next question is how to encompass such variation in an analysis (see chapter 5).

The last two dimensions – the complex possibilities for the consti-tution of subject/object relations between problems and problem solvers and the varied salience of math in different situations – suggest grounds for conceiving of math in practice as more varied than a small number of genres of knowledge, or binary divisions of practice. The three dimensions have each suggested middle-level analytic questions that might be posed in analyses of the activity of persons-acting, in setting. Other such questions, their more specific implications, and higher order assumptions and units of analysis are still to come.

The critique of learning transfer research developed in this chapter and the previous one challenges the credibility of the theoretical framework that gives centrality to learning transfer. There remains the perplexing question of why learning transfer theory and its functionalist underpinnings have endured for so long. An important part of the answer surely lies in its key role in the organization of schooling as a form of education and in justifications of relations between schooling and the distribution of its alumni into occupations. These have defended it from critical analysis in academic contexts, as elsewhere (e.g. Simon 1980: 81). The findings of transfer research, volatile and ambiguous, taken as a whole and over many years, suggest that were the ban on critical analysis lifted, the inadequacies of "learning transfer" could be seen to have theoretical roots. It is time to consider historical and theoretical antecedents to the widely distributed views – folk, pedagogical and academic – that compose a taken-for-granted world of problem solving, learning transfer, expert knowledge and everyday cognition. The next chapter offers an explanation for why these views have persisted and considers why a principled and satisfying alternative to a purely cognitive explanation of the cross-situational continuity of knowledge-in-use may not be possible within this perspective.

Appendix

Adult Math Project arithmetic exercises

Appendix table 1 *Math problems in supermarket*

Product	Ratios (larger package vs. smaller package)	
	I	II
refried beans	$ .57 20½ oz.	$ .49 17 oz.
yoghurt	.35 8 oz.	.47 6 oz.
yoghurt	.35 8 oz.	.43 6 oz.
canned chilis	.79 7 oz.	.49 4 oz.
rice	2.16 28 oz.	1.21 14 oz.
soy sauce	1.47 20 oz.	.59 16 oz.
shampoo	1.09 32 oz	.79 16 oz.
syrup	2.26 36 oz.	1.63 24 oz.
brown sugar	1.16 32 oz.	.59 16 oz.
crackers	1.24 16 oz.	1.32 1 lb.
canned fruit mix	.82 30 oz.	.69 29 oz.
flour tortillas	.67 20 oz.	.63 12 oz.
round steak	4.50 2 lbs. +	3.20 1 lb. +
canned tomatoes	.53 18 oz.	.33 16 oz.
stewed tomatoes	.42 16 oz.	.49 11 oz.
tuna	1.89 12½ oz.	1.39 9¼ oz.
tuna	2.32 13 oz.	1.89 12½ oz.
BBQ sauce	1.17 23 oz.	.89 18 oz.
cereal	1.35 16 oz.	.98 13 oz.
sugar	4.30 10 lbs.	2.16 5 lbs.
celery	.79 2 lbs.	.23 1 lb.
liquid detergent	2.72 64 oz.	1.63 32 oz.
crackers	1.23 16 oz.	1.03 12 oz.
crackers	1.23 16 oz.	.90 8 oz.
noodles	1.98 64 oz.	1.12 12 oz.
noodles	1.79 3 lbs.	.59 12 oz.
noodles	.69 2 lbs.	.59 1 lb.
Q-tips	1.29 300	1.17 170

Product	Ratios (larger package vs. smaller package)	
Q–tips	1.29 300	.79 54
milk	1.86 gallon	.95 ½ gal.
mustard	.75 24 oz.	.79 16 oz.
cereal	1.26 (−.10) 16 oz.	.97 (−.10) 12 oz.
ammonia	.49 1 quart	.39 32 oz.
applesauce	1.03 33 oz.	.81 24 oz.
paper towels	.93 100 ft.	.62 85 ft.
facial tissue	1.09 280 sheets	.53 200 sheets
facial tissue	.53 960 × 820	.75 825 × 945
cheddar cheese	5.29 32 oz.	1.59 9 oz.
paper towels	.93 11 × 14	.59 11 × 10
sugar	3.75 10 lbs.	1.88 5 lbs.
sliced ham	.97 5 oz.	1.09 4 oz.
peanut butter	2.21 40 oz.	2.45 36 oz.
peanut butter	2.21 40 oz.	1.05 18 oz.
paper towels	.82 119 sheets	.79 104 sheets
spaghetti mix	.69 double	.27 pkg.
honey	3.39 3 lbs.	1.80 24 oz.
honey	3.00 2 lbs.	1.64 24 oz.
bath tissue	.75 4 × 500 sheets	.45 1000 sheets
soft drinks	3.35 12 pack	1.69 6 pack
frozen fish	1.72 12 oz.	3.13 8 oz.
tomato sauce	.39 15 oz.	.18 8 oz.
cheese	5.09 2 lbs.	2.65 1 lb.
crackers	.77 16 oz.	.60 8 oz.
American cheese	1.99 16 oz.	1.55 12 oz.
refried beans	.57 20½ oz.	.33 17 oz.
butter	1.75 1 lb.	.50 ¼ lb.

Appendix table 2 *Math problems*

Add: (1) 36   (2)   975   Subtract: (3)   703   (4)   547   (5)   34   (6)   82
          $\underline{+98}$ 987 $\underline{-476}$ $\underline{-233}$ $\underline{-58}$ $\underline{-69}$
                  $\underline{+956}$

Multiply: (7)   38   (8)   437   Divide: (9) $24\overline{)984}$ (10) $8\overline{)124}$ (11) $26\overline{)100}$
          $\underline{\times 26}$ $\underline{\times 305}$

Add: (12) $\frac{1}{2}+\frac{5}{6}=$ (13) $\frac{1}{5}+\frac{2}{3}=$ (14) $5\frac{1}{3}+4\frac{3}{4}=$
Subtract: (15) $\frac{3}{5}-\frac{1}{10}=$ (16) $\frac{1}{2}-\frac{2}{3}=$ (17) $3\frac{1}{3}-\frac{1}{2}=$
Multiply: (18) $\frac{4}{5}\times\frac{3}{4}=$ (19) $\frac{2}{3}\times\frac{5}{7}=$ (20) $16\times\frac{1}{2}=$
Divide: (21) $\frac{2}{3}\div\frac{4}{5}=$ (22) $\frac{3}{2}\div\frac{1}{4}=$ (23) $8\div\frac{1}{2}=$
Add: (24) $.43+.18=$ (25) $6.4+.7=$ (26) $.56+2.07=$
Subtract: $.81-.05=$ (28) $6-.25=$ (29) $3.75-.8=$
Multiply: (30)   3.5   (31)   .42   Divide: (32) $5\overline{)3.55}$ (33) $.7\overline{)1.47}$ (34) $.6\overline{)24}$
          $\underline{\times .6}$ $\underline{\times .08}$

Add: (35) $\frac{6}{4}+.8=$ (36) $.63+\frac{4}{5}=$ Subtract: (37) $1.79-\frac{1}{2}=$ (38) $\frac{1}{2}-.2=$
Multiply: (39) $.24\times\frac{1}{4}=$ (4) $\frac{2}{5}\times .75=$ (41) $.59\times\frac{1}{2}=$
(42) $10-25=$ (43) $-48+37=$ (44) $-5+24=$ (45) -795 (46)   46
                                                            253      $\underline{-75}$
                                                          -309
                                                          $\underline{+166}$

(47) $3\times6+3\times4=$ (48) $2\times7\times8\times5=$ (49) $-3\times 4\times -5\times -6=$
(50) $4\times2\times -7=$
Circle the larger fraction:
(51) $\frac{6}{3}$ or $\frac{5}{4}$ (52) $\frac{20}{35}$ or $\frac{12}{18}$ (53) $\frac{8}{10}$ or $\frac{66}{60}$ (54) $\frac{8}{13}$ or $\frac{4}{7}$

Appendix table 3 *Math and measurement fact problems*

Addition	Subtraction	Multiplication	Division
$2+3=$	$8-4=$	$5 \times 7=$	$3\overline{)18}$
$57+114=$	$62-40=$	$10 \times 11=$	$5\overline{)20}$
$4+5=$	$31-11=$	$7 \times 3=$	$6\overline{)12}$
$7+9=$	$17-9=$	$6 \times 9=$	$9\overline{)72}$
$46+16=$	$10-6=$	$12 \times 8=$	$2\overline{)100}$
$300+120=$	$65-9=$	$9 \times 7=$	$3\overline{)24}$
$11+8=$	$80-20=$	$4 \times 10=$	$8\overline{)80}$
$24+12=$	$5-3=$	$3 \times 5=$	$7\overline{)84}$
$8+6=$	$19-5=$	$7 \times 8=$	$3\overline{)9}$
$12+9=$	$20-6=$	$9 \times 9=$	$11\overline{)22}$
$6+7=$	$350-50=$	$7 \times 12=$	$2\overline{)8}$
$10+5=$	$9-6=$	$6 \times 8=$	$3\overline{)12}$
$38+12=$	$15-10=$	$11 \times 8=$	$9\overline{)54}$
$9+3=$	$28-6=$	$5 \times 9=$	$6\overline{)36}$
$40+60=$		$8 \times 8=$	$5\overline{)60}$
$4+7=$		$12 \times 3=$	$8\overline{)56}$
		$4 \times 6=$	$4\overline{)24}$
		$9 \times 8=$	$10\overline{)60}$
		$3 \times 11=$	$4\overline{)36}$
		$10 \times 8=$	$11\overline{)110}$
		$8 \times 4=$	$3\overline{)6}$
		$2 \times 3=$	

Measurement facts:
How many:

inches in a foot?	millimeters in an inch?	feet in a yard?
yards in a rod?	feet in a mile?	miles in a league?
rods in a furlong?	inches in a yard?	teaspoons in a tablespoon?
tablespoons in a quarter cup?	ounces in a pound?	quarts in a gallon?
cups in a quart?	cups in a gallon?	gills in a pint?
ounces in a quart?	pints in a quart?	quarts in a peck?
pecks in a bushel?	tablespoons in a stick of butter?	

How much does a stick of butter weigh?

4

PSYCHOLOGY AND ANTHROPOLOGY II

The question is, "Why does the mind with its durable cognitive tools remain the only imaginable source of continuity across situations for most cognitive researchers – while we isolate the culturally and socially constituted activities and settings of everyday life and their economic and political structures and cyclical routines from the study of thinking, and so ignore them?" It is not this form of the question, however, that has exercised the minds of cognitivists. Rather, (negative) reactions to the study of cognition-in-context follow from strong beliefs and long-standing practices that create a taken-for-granted divide between cognitive processes and the settings and activities of which they are a part. I believe that the particulars of this position must be confronted. Cognitivists might well rejoin, "why take up the study of everyday thought in context?" For the very term "everyday," when applied to thought, has been imbued with pejorative connotations. Its analytic meaning typically has been derived by comparison to the ostensibly superior canons of scientific thought. Moreover, the study of activity *in situ* has been damned as a rejection of theory and a move towards descriptive particularism. Even granting intrinsic value to the study of "what people really do," it has been made to appear that doing so requires a lamentable sacrifice of methodological rigor – assumed to be impossible to achieve outside the experimental context – in order to gain relevance to the concerns of everyday cognition. I think this caricatured view of the study of socially situated cognition must be rejected, along with the problematic which claims that these issues are central ones.

In order to proceed we need to consider how everyday thought has been conceptualized and investigated in the past, thereby acquiring its specifically negative and residual character, while at the same time its elucidation remains among the ultimate goals of psychological research.[1] For the monological determinism of cognitivist theories has a history, one that still shapes discussions of the problem of continuity. Further, the accepted division of labor between the disciplines of psychology and anthropology is reflected in and acts upon their defining concepts, cognition and culture, which are also central to theorizing about continuity in activity across situations. It may be argued that all of this, and learning transfer too, has persisted in part because of recalcitrant dilemmas within a positivist conception of science generally, more directly shaped by a specific configuration of relations between culture and cognition.

The history: the myth of scientific and everyday modes of thought

The pejorative meaning of "everyday thought" has grown out of evolutionary thinking and its contemporary philosophy of science. Change away from nineteenth-century stereotypes of the savage mind has been more apparent than real, for in recent years the characteristics associated with everyday thought have been merely transposed from the arena of cross cultural to intracultural social categories and relations without changing their basic content. It is not difficult to demonstrate that "everyday thinking" is treated residually, by contrast with other "modes of thought," rather than as a phenomenon in its own right. For example, Bartlett (1958: 164) has suggested that:

> By everyday thinking I mean those activities by which most people, *when they are not making any particular attempt to be logical or scientific*, try to fill up gaps in information available to them . . .   (emphasis added)

He was echoing a very general view, with long-standing roots. Thus, late nineteenth-century social evolutionists, concentrating on the nature of reason and logic, were more concerned with the comparative analysis of rationality than with a unified theory of mind, or its "everyday" manifestations. Levy-Bruhl, to take a celebrated instance, defined as his problem the affirmation of the non-rationality of primitive thought – in contrast to the image of a western *homo logicus* – and argued bitterly against the universalist rationalism essayed by British anthropologists in explaining the existence of "primitive" beliefs (1910: 6–10). Levy-Bruhl and his contemporaries did not conceive the exercise to be one of theorizing about the nature of the mind – its characteristics were taken for granted as a set of basic assumptions whose analysis was clearly not the goal of the investigation.[2]

As far as the mentality peculiar to our society is concerned, since it is only to serve me as a state for comparison, I shall regard it as sufficiently well defined in the works of philosophers, logicians and psychologists, both ancient and modern, without conjecturing what sociological analysis of the future may modify in the results obtained by them up to the present.   *(Levy-Bruhl 1910: 19)*

The enterprise was given form by late nineteenth-century students of relations between culture and cognition in a comparative framework in which categories of thinking operations and taxonomies of modes of thought were elaborated in the service of evolutionary schemes (not coincidentally related to categories of child development, social class, and gender as well). The dichotomy between mind and body underlying Western epistemologies provided the framework for a similarly dichotomized sub-classification of rational and scientific modes of thought in opposition to primitive, non-rational or irrational ones. Subsumed within this set of categories, "everyday" thought was also defined in contrast with "scientific" thought. This particular dichotomy found its way into the work of Tylor, Levy-Bruhl and Boas (among others) as a minor implication of the classificatory opposition between primitive and scientific modes of thought.[3] But it has recently become more central, and explicit, in the investigation of thinking (Neisser 1976; Goody 1977; Cole, Hood and McDermott 1978; Bronfenbrenner 1979). It appears that "everyday thinking" has taken on, or taken over, the characteristics attributed to primitive thought, by virtue of its identical relationship with the characteristics ascribed to scientific thought. Goody illustrates (from the work of Levi-Strauss) what he calls the "Grand Dichotomy" between modes of thought assigned to separate stages of culture (1977: 146ff.).

Domestic Cultures	Wild Cultures
'hot'	'cold'
modern	neolithic
science of the abstract	science of the concrete
scientific thought	mythical thought
scientific knowledge	magical thought
engineer(ing)	bricoleur(age)
abstract thought	intuition/imagination/perception
using concepts	using signs
history	atemporality; myths and rites

He sums up:

In the simplest terms, /this/ is a contrast between the domination of abstract science together with history, as against the more concrete forms of knowledge . . . of 'primitive' peoples.   *(1977: 148)*

This and other schemes of types of thought have, as their negative pole, imagined descriptions of primitive thought: emotional, concrete, alogical, closed, magical. Above all, it is that which is not objective, utilitarian and rational. The question is, however, where these conceptions of "civilized thought" have come from. Barnes, an historian of science, argues that their historical and artifactual basis lies in an antiquated empiricist philosophy of science. He speaks of their role in anthropology, but the analysis is equally apt for psychology.

> Attempts to understand or explain preliterate systems of belief have frequently led anthropologists to compare them with ideal 'rational' models of thought or belief; in practice such comparison has been used to separate beliefs into those which are 'rationally' intelligible and hence natural and not in need of explanation, and those which deviate from this ideal and are consequently puzzling and in need of explanation. It is clear that the form of many anthropological theories has been partially determined by the ideal of rationality adopted and in practice this ideal has usually been presented as that which is normative in the modern natural science, that is to say modern anthropological theory has been profoundly influenced by its conception of ideal scientific practice. This conception has, however, been derived less from familiarity with the natural sciences than from familiarity with the philosophy of science and the abstract discussions of 'scientific method' to be found therein.   *(Barnes 1973: 182)*

I have argued that cognitive experimental research relies on *a priori* normative models as source and inspiration for the development of experimental tasks and the interpretation of activity in experiments. Barnes indicates the historical basis of this practice. Issues of rationality – directly, and in discussions of higher and lower levels of explanation and generalization, hierarchical versus low level multiple classification structures and procedures, and concrete versus abstract "thinking" – are dimensions frequently built into experimental tasks, as they were also preoccupations of Levy-Bruhl's. These categorical distinctions were and are emblems of "rationality": that is, operationalization of cognitive processes in the laboratory consists of building tasks to reflect norms of "scientific thought," rather than scientific (or any other) practice. This helps to account for the hypothetical nature of psychologists' generalizations from subjects' performances in laboratories to activity in everyday settings (see Bartlett 1923: 284; Lave in preparation), for it is the relations of those performances to an idealized "rational science" that count, not their relations with everyday practice. Further, to organize cognitive experimentation in terms of an *idealization* of one so-called "form of thought," both makes it impossible, by definition, for subjects to respond adequately, and rejects the value of their responses (and by extrapolation "everyday thought") on *a priori* grounds.[4] In this respect conventional cognitive studies are of a piece with a colonialist anthropology.

There has been, then, only an apparent shift within psychology and anthropology away from simplistic taxonomies of modes of thought. Negative, residual terms, such as the law of participation and mystical identity, have fallen out of use. But the change has gone no further than an increased number of taxonomic categories, and these of an unsurprising kind. Thus, Bartlett (1958), less ethnocentric than most but unable to transcend the dualism, contrasted closed (puzzle solving) thinking to open-ended ("adventurous") thinking, and expanded the second term to include everyday, natural scientific, mathematical, artistic, and (speculatively) religious and legal thinking as well. And, in a different time and theoretical orientation:

> At a commonsense level, most of us believe that there are differences in cognitive style among lawyers, physicists, economists, accountants, and historians. Yet there has been almost no careful work on the nature of those differences.
>
> *(Simon 1976: 260)*[5]

It appears that the expanded taxonomies merely mark a shift in the sociological arena from contrasts between "civilized" and "primitive" cultures to differences between occupations – and between social classes. Basil Bernstein argues, in effect, for a substantive parallel between cultural distinctions concerning modes of thought and differences between social classes within industrial European society.[6] It is a complex argument in which socialization provides the link between class and cognition:

> Without a shadow of a doubt, the most formative influence upon the procedures of socialization, from a sociological viewpoint, is social class . . . The class system has deeply marked the distribution of knowledge within society.   *(1972: 163)*

These assumed (admittedly, ideal-typical) differences between social classes are characterized by Bernstein (1972: 162–164) in familiar dichotomous terms.

Upper class	*Lower classes*
orders of meaning	
universalistic	particularistic
explicit principles	implicit principles
freed from context	tied to context
the metalanguage of public	tied to local
forms of thought	relationships and to a
	local social structure

Upperclass	*Lower class*
	Speech codes
elaborated	restricted
reflexive	not reflexive
change possible	no access to self-generated change
articulated symbols	condensed symbols
	(Modes of thought)
rationality	metaphor

C. R. Hallpike, who has argued that "primitives" are retarded at a preoperational level of cognitive development, echoes Bernstein's distinction between public and local social structures and their relations to forms of thought, implying class distinctions as well:

> Rather than contrasting primitive man with the European scientist and logician, it would be more to the point to contrast him with the garage mechanic, the plumber, and the housewife in her kitchen.   *(1979: 33)*

Goody, on the other hand, in criticizing the set of dichotomous categories given above, does not erase the great divide, but domesticates it, by locating it within a single subject:

> The notion of a shift of emphasis from magic and myth to science and history has been the commonplace of anthropological discourse since its very beginning . . . Another current of opinion has concentrated upon analysing the technical achievements of simpler societies and calling attention to the mythical or magical elements of our own . . . The very existence of these two trends . . . points to the inadequacy of the notion of two different modes of thought, approaches to knowledge, or forms of science, since *both* are present not only in the same societies but in the same individuals.   *(1977: 148, emphasis added)*

It is difficult to avoid the conclusion that even today the domestication of the savage mind and the savagery of the domestic mind are viewed as fundamentally the same thing.

Indeed, the principles of "rationality" used to characterize "civilized" or "scientific" modes of thought have not much shifted since plucked casually from the common-sensical ambience by Levy-Bruhl and his contemporaries. Nor has there been marked change away from the assumed inadequacy of "primitive" thought: "because the milieu of primitive societies is cognitively less demanding than our own, the cognitive development of its members will be correspondingly retarded" (Hallpike 1979: 31–32). Cultural and cognitive deficit explanations of school and experimental performances are based squarely within this tradition. More subtly perhaps, there is evidence that for many psychologists, everyday thinking has been viewed as simplified, less demanding, than that required in experiments (e.g. Slovic, Fischoff and Lichtenstein 1976. Cf. Cole, Hood and McDermott 1978: 22ff.). It may well be that life outside the laboratory is also assumed to be simpler because it is conducted by members of the lower classes and "housewives."

The characterization of everyday thought as "simpler" than that demanded in cognitive experiments or "science," may be questioned on several grounds. It stands in direct contradiction to a widely held view among scientists that their special goals are precisely those of reductive simplicity. Claims for the simplicity of either everyday life or the scientists' view are inadequate, however. For relations between science and the world it purports to investigate are mutually entailed in one another. Science studies just that portion of the complex everyday world that we think we *can* know. This in turn is typically defined in terms of the ideology of empiricism which itself elevates rationality to an ideological construct.

Secondly, there are compelling arguments that positive science in Western thought is – like all deep, pervasive, complex systems of belief – tautologically constructed. Polanyi speaks to this issue in comparative cross-cultural terms:

> the stability of the naturalistic system [of 'science'] which we currently accept . . . rests on the same logical structure [as Azande beliefs about poison oracles]. Any contradiction between a particular scientific notion and the facts of experience will be explained by other scientific notions; there is a ready reserve of possible scientific hypotheses available to explain any conceivable event. Secured by its circularity and defended further by its epicyclical reserves, science may deny, or at least cast aside as of no scientific interest, whole ranges of experience.
>
> *(Polanyi 1958; excerpted in Marwick 1970: 337)*

Though Polanyi waivered in his constructivist claims (1958), there are increasingly well-supported constructivist arguments based on empirical studies of the practice of science that deserve serious attention from cognitive theorists of all persuasions. They weave a picture of the unexceptional character of science as everyday practice (e.g. Latour and Woolgar 1979; Knorr-Cetina and Mulkay 1983; Lynch 1982; Traweek in press).

And third, "rationality" implies an antithetical concept of "irrationality." But the very opposition between "rational" and "irrational" thought runs into epistemological difficulties. For it always raises the question, how do we *explain* "irrationality"? In other words, wherein lies the rationality of irrationality? A classic answer lies in the notion that "irrational" thought and (ritual) practice are to be explained by their

functions. Thus, Parsons (1957) suggests that Malinowski's functionalism was a response to the dilemma created by his assumptions that the
"savage" was both a rational empiricist *and* a serious believer in the
efficacy of ritual.

> There is a sense then in which Malinowki's central problem was to make both types of
> behavior humanly understandable to the modern European through a theory of
> function of some sort. Above all an adequate theory had to account for the fact that
> both types of behavior characterized the same people under different circumstances.
>
> *(1957: 54–55)*

But to defend the existence of ritual on functional grounds as
Malinowski did, is to defend the privileged truth of nineteenth-century
canons of rationality. Instead, it is worth taking seriously Sahlins'
argument (1976) that rationality is the great rationalization of Western
culture, the principle by which we close and tautologize our own system
of thought. Within its bounds is, by definition, whatever "makes sense"
to us. The rest, the residual category – including "primitive," and more
recently "everyday," thought – lie outside. Indeed, it is because this is so
that our own epistemology and theory must become the subject of self-
reflection. To ignore this – especially in the name of "getting on with the
empirical task of science" – is to condemn ourselves, our operations and
our findings to a procrustean binary logic that mires both psychology
and the artifices it creates in an inescapable tautology.

Dual divisions

Cognitive studies in psychology and anthropology are mired in other
divisions, differences which they defend in ways that are exceptionally
difficult to overcome. For example, both disciplines have overlooked
their common theoretical views, preferring instead to emphasize their
self-styled differences on grounds that psychology has the distinction of
being theoretically oriented while anthropology is descriptive. They
also emphasize their methodological differences. It will be argued, as we
review this state of affairs in more detail, that the effect has been to sustain
the conceptualizations of culture and cognition that were encoded in
their formal division into disciplines at the turn of the century.

From a conventional cognitive psychology, in which continuity of
activity across settings is assumed to be a function of knowledge stored in
memory and general cognitive processing, any move toward a theory of
cognition-as-socially-situated must appear as a descent into atheoretical
particularism. Treating cognition and culture as isolatable units of

analysis leads to such fears: for cognitive "universals" and the specificity of culturally organized contexts imply one another, as we shall see. At another level, the characterization of psychology as a nomothetic discipline and anthropology as ideographic reflects the same division precisely.

The issue of context offers an illustration of the dilemmas that such attributions create. Thus, a contextually grounded theory of cognition requires a *theory* of situations. Social anthropology is an obvious place to look. But given that relations between psychology and anthropology have been couched in nomothetic/ideographic terms, cultural (social) context is consigned to an agenda of descriptive particulars, challenging the very possibility of a general theory of situationally specific activity. How this state of affairs has helped to sustain belief in learning transfer, and created barriers to the development of a theory of cognition in context requires further discussion.

The association of anthropology and psychology with mutually exclusive categories of descriptive specificity and theoretical generaliz- ation has a long tradition. It has been raised in remarkably similar terms in debates since the social evolutionists of 1900, then by Boas and, in their turn, the critics of Boas (e.g. White 1949), and continues in critiques of contemporary context-specific approaches to cognition (e.g. Cole 1981).

> Boas' success in criticizing existing theory without being able to replace it won him many detractors who complained that he had introduced "historical particularism" into anthropology, opening the floodgates to local descriptions and trivia-mongering in the place of real theory.   *(Cole 1981: 20)*

He cites Jahoda's parallel critique of the work of LCHC:

> [this approach] appears to require extremely exhaustive, and in practice almost endless explorations of quite specific pieces of behavior, with no guarantee of a decisive outcome. This might not be necessary if there were workable "theory of situations" at our disposal, but as Cole admits, there is none. What is lacking in [the context specific] approach are global theoretical constructs . . . of the kind Piaget provides, and which save the researcher from becoming submerged in a mass of unmanageable material.   *(Cole, 1981: 20–21)*

Studies of situated cognitive practice are distinguished from cognitive stage theories in ideographic/nomothetic terms in the same fashion as Boas' work and evolutionary anthropology and the two disciplines. Thus, Campbell (1961: 338) contrasts them:

> The great difference in task must be recognized between [anthropology] the descriptive, humanistic task of one who seeks to record all aspects of a specific cultural

instance and the [psychologist's] task of the abstractive and generalizing "scientist" who wants to test the concomitant variation of two isolated factors across instance in general.

He goes on to argue that both anthropology and psychology revolted against "the theoretical excesses of a previous generation" (1961: 339) to avoid the biases which theory introduces into the objectivity of fieldwork, and stresses the shared positivist epistemology of American anthropology and psychology. But nonetheless he concludes that there should be a mutually respectful, though definite, division of labor. Cole describes the existing division between the fields in a similar fashion (without, however, subscribing to it):

> In a certain sense, psychology and anthropology represent a division of labor with respect to explaining human nature; anthropology provides a description of the content of human experience while psychology describes the processes that interpret experience. At least with respect to their accounts of individuals, anthropology and psychology have historically played out the content-process distinctions in the construction of disciplines.
> *(1981: 9–10)*

From the perspective of psychologists, then, many of whom begin with a belief in the universality of cognitive processes, all that culture *can be* is content – an assembly of particular knowledge, and/or context – an assemblage of situational particularities. Anthropology, as the discipline which studies culture, is the descriptive study of those particularities. Indeed, from this perspective, the notion of the theoretical study of culture is at best regarded suspiciously, at worst denied entirely. But it is precisely these divisions of labor and caricatures of disciplines that have led to the absence of meaningful discourse at a theoretical level between disciplines. It is also such assumptions – particularly the universality of cognitive processes – that mistake theory and theoretical discourse *sui generis* for a metaphysic concerning the nature of cognition and culture. That this metaphysic has a hegemonic hold on the study of cognition is intimately related to the role of positivism as the central ideological tenet of the symbolism and epistemology of Western science, an issue to which we shall shortly return.

Closely related to the issues discussed so far, and the arenas in which they are played out, is a methodological divide that conventionally separates psychology and anthropology, rigor versus relevance. Campbell provides but one of a series of papers in which anthropologists and psychologists have focused explicitly on relations between their disciplines (e.g. Boas 1910; Rivers 1926; Bartlett 1937; Köhler 1937; Nadel 1937; Campbell 1961; Edgerton 1974; LCHC 1978, 1979; and Price-

Williams 1980). He sees psychology as an abstractive, scientific testing approach to the study of human activity, as opposed to the descriptive recording, participant observation methods of the anthropologist. The opposition here is ambiguous. One interpretation is that the two terms stand in a trade-off relationship with one another – one may give up a certain amount of, say, experimental control, for a certain amount of assurance that the observer's and subject's perceptions of the situation are ˌcongruent. Thus, to learn about peoples' activities in the settings of their everyday lives would require suspension of laboratory control over some of the circumstances in which activity takes place.

A different interpretation better describes current research practice: that the two methods, laboratory experimentation and participant observation, in fact form another simplistic opposition, this one concerning the appropriate means of seeking truth. For, on the whole, discourse about relations between anthropology and psychology has been chauvinistic on both sides, and not productive of synthesis or even communication. Edgerton (1974: 63–64) suggests an explanation for this heated opposition:

> I believe that most cross-cultural psychologists are committed to experimental procedures as their ultimate means of verification . . . Because the conflict is at the level of a basic belief about how truth is best ascertained, it is often exacerbated by unspoken assumptions . . . Anthropologists have always believed that human phenomena can best be understood by procedures that are primarily sensitive to context, be it situational, social, or cultural. Our methods are primarily unobtrusive, nonreactive ones; we observe, we participate, we learn, hopefully we understand. We rarely experiment, and then only under special conditions. This is our unspoken paradigm and it is directly at odds with the discovery of truth by experimentation which, at least as many anthropologists see it, ignores context and creates reactions.

That is, he argues that the issues are epistemological ones concerning the nature of procedures by which we may arrive at "truth." He emphasizes the fundamental nature of opposition between the underlying assumptions glossed here as "rigor" and "relevance" and warns that, "it may take a revolution in Kuhn's terms" to bring about a reconciliation of the two paradigms.

It is remarkable that papers about relations between anthropology and psychology do not call for *theoretical* rapprochment: the level of argument is in fact almost uniformly methodological. This reflects the fact that the two fields are dominated by a positivistic view of social science in which theory is believed to grow out of empirical observation: it is consistent with this shared epistemology that they should identify methods used to collect data as the starting point for a dialogue about rapprochment and view their differences as methodological ones. But this diagnosis insures that the two fields will continue to have irreconcilable disagreements, for as usually couched, one method pitted against another, the debate is, I think, unresolvable.[7]

A common epistemology

So far I have described a series of dichotomously polarized issues that have sustained limitations on debate between paradigms and disciplines over a considerable period of time. I have yet to discuss the sources of the coherence with which the issues reinforce one another. They take their shape, the great divides are formed, in terms of a positivist epistemology which specifies a series of assumptions on which they are based: rationality exists as the ideal canon of thought; experimentation can be thought of as the embodiment of this ideal in scientific practice; science is the value-free collection of factual knowledge about the world; factual knowledge about the world is the basis for the formation of scientific theory, not the other way around; science is the opposite of history, the one nomothetic the other ideographic; cognitive processes are general and fundamental, psychology, correspondingly, a nomothetic discipline; society and culture shape the particularities of cognition and give it content, thus, sociocultural context is specific, its study ideographic; general laws of human behavior, therefore, must be dissected away from the historical and social obfuscations which give them particularity. These propositions entail one another in complex ways. To challenge any one of them draws the rest into question as well. A quest for better understanding of everyday cognition in context that questions conventional relations between the socially organized world, culture and cognition – and hence the whole field of assumptions – is unavoidably, therefore, a fundamental epistemological question.

To understand better the relations between culture and cognition implied in the shared epistemology of positivistic cognitive studies (whether in anthropology or psychology), it may be useful to review central features of the conception of social order and the relations of individuals to that order. Normative functionalism, from Durkheim and Wundt to Parsons and cognitive studies today, posits a functioning social order in equilibrium, and individuals molded and shaped through socialization into performers of normatively governed social roles and practices. Society is conceived of as external to the individual, having a separate (and for experimental purposes separable) existence from the individuals who pass through it.[8] It locates relations between culture and cognition within the mind of the experiencing individual, in memory and in accumulation of past socializing experiences. Change in the character of society and of mind is conceived of as an evolutionary matter requiring sweeping time spans. Thus, when the investigation is confined to a human lifespan or more narrowly, childhood, or even more narrowly, current cognitive practices, society and culture are assumed for all intents and purposes, to be constant. The evolutionary view of mind, encompassed by and following from the theory of social order, has already been characterized in some detail: two modes of thought, one civilized, professional and rationally scientific; and the other (a residual mode), primitive, metaphorical, expressive, non-rational and characteristic of novices. Culture, in this scheme, is equated with accumulated factual knowledge, increasing in individuals and societies alike with the evolutionary move toward individualism and all that goes with it. Durkheim laid out the position generally current at the turn of the century (1915; Durkheim and Mauss 1963). Its contemporary guise requires elucidation.[9]

Cognitive scientists discuss expertise in a particular knowledge "domain" e.g. chess, as on the order of 50,000 chunks of knowledge (Simon 1980: 83–84; Norman 1980; originally formulated in Simon and Barenfeld 1969). Anthropologists with an interest in cognitive science have incorporated this quantitative formulation into longstanding views of culture as accumulated knowledge (Roberts 1964; D'Andrade 1981; Romney, Weller and Batchelder 1986). D'Andrade extrapolates from 50,000 chunks of knowledge in an area of professional expertise (note the emphasis on professions/occupations here as elsewhere in discussions of modes of thought), to the person who might have several hundred thousand to several million chunks of information, to the information pool – the culture – of a society (a hundred to 10,000 times what a person knows.)[10]

An attempt to decode cognitivists' assumptions about cognition and culture, is presented in Figure 2 (based primarily on analysis of the text of Simon 1980). From the figure it appears that culture, that is, knowledge, is context-free, value-free, body-free and factual. It consists of hierarchically organized discrete chunks. Culture and the (professional) mind are seamlessly related, both composed of knowledge. Knowledge is arranged in the mind in condition/action pairs, that is, as means/ends relations – the forms of instrumental rationality. The social world is

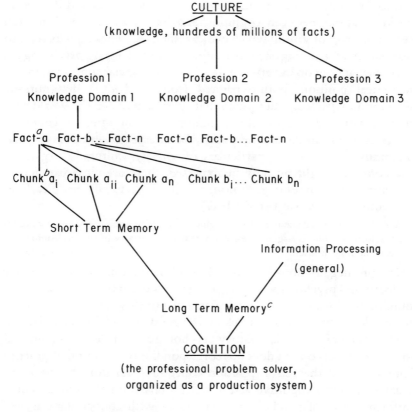

Fact: a constellation of chunks

Chunks: perceptual configurations, visual, auditory

Long Term Memory: a well-indexed encyclopedia, entries are chunks; production systems

Figure 2 Culture in cognitive theory

acknowledged only in the form of professional occupations, translated immediately into knowledge domains. Correspondingly, cognition is not that of a whole person, but only of the person conceived of in a professional role, and only of course, as a rational problem solver.

We must look elsewhere for the – absent – social context of cognitive activity.[11] It is conceived of in terms that have not changed in a surprisingly long time, surprising because even the revolution of information processing psychology away from behaviorism did not lead to a reformulation of relations between the person and the object world; relations between cognition and its "environments" are still treated in terms of stimuli which evoke responses. Neisser (1976; see also Norman 1980) has suggested that information processing psychology is merely what goes on in between. It follows that social context is, in this theoretical position, both separated from, and in a deterministic relationship with, cognition, such that (were activity in the world ever the object of study) apparent variation in the deployment of cognitive processes would in the end necessarily be interpreted in terms of what "naturally" varies — the particulars of socially, culturally organized situations. As might by now be expected, there are close parallels in contemporary sources (e.g. Simon) to pronouncements made early in the century (e.g. Chamberlain 1917):

> A man, viewed as a behaving system, is quite simple. The apparent complexity of his behavior over time is largely a reflection of the complexity of the environment in which he finds himself.   *(Simon 1969: 25)*

The privileged "non-context" of experimentation has been a major device within psychology for relegating issues about the interrelations of thinking and social context, and in particular the hegemonic character of the world-around, to the status of the residual and implicit. But to conduct the practice of laboratory psychology "as if" experiments had no sociocultural context does not correspondingly exempt that practice from a general theoretical position concerning relations between the social world and cognitive activity.[12] Emphasis on the fundamental, uniform nature of psychological processes, with concomitant assignment of variability to a particular configuration of the social world, is a position, one which asserts the hegemony of the latter.

If problems with conceptions of cognition in relation with the social world stem from their artificial separation, relations of culture and cognition suffer opposite difficulties. Culture and knowledge are equated with each other, the former addressed only as a feature of memory. It is consistent with this position that learning-transfer proponents characterize memory metaphorically as a warehouse or attic, the repository of a lifetime's accumulation of (the culture's accumulation of) knowledge (cf. Kvale 1977). Memory takes on the character of a place where cultural acquisitions are stored, and where development toward increasingly integrated and "rational" general knowledge is to be expected. Simon's (1980) equation of expert knowledge with a well-indexed, easily accessible, encyclopedia provides an excellent example. The same metaphor has currency in developmental psychology.

Giddens cites Bruner (1974) as an example in which development is conceived of (inappropriately) as a set of "stored competencies" (1979: 129).

The main difficulty with this view is that the nexus of cognition/culture relations is never constructed in the present, but always assumed to have an existence because of events which took place in the past.[13] "Warehouse" and "toolkit" metaphors for the location of culture in memory make it possible to abnegate the investigation of relations between cognition and culture by, in effect, defining culture as "what people have acquired, and carry around in their heads," rather than as an immediate relation between individuals and the sociocultural order within which they live their lives.[14] In practice this has meant that cognitive researchers have been able to proclaim the important role of culture in cognition without looking beyond the standard unit of analysis: the "cognitive processes" of a particular individual in response to a laboratory task. But this approach provides no basis for accounting for relations, especially generative relations, between people-in-action and the social world around them.

The view that culture is the evolutionary accumulation of knowledge along with increasingly complex technology and social forms, and mind and culture but two aspects of the same phenomenon, has prevailed in cognitive theory through most of the last century (Kvale 1977; LCHC 1981). A crucial problem has emerged from this sustained equation of culture and cognition. If culture and cognition are treated as aspects of a single phenomenon, they must both in the end be allocated to the same nexus in the social world. There are two immediate possibilities. The first, heavily represented among cognitive psychologists, collapses culture and cognition into representations in the mind (cf. Minick 1985). The concept of "culture" is simply transformed into that of "knowledge," and culture dispensed with altogether.[15] The second, heavily represented in anthropology, locates culture and cognition together by transforming them into a superorganic system of meaning, "an information pool." In this case cultural structures such as language become reified constructs, but cognition, as an individual generative process, drops out of the equation. Neither appears to offer a satisfactory solution.

Further, having merged culture into the concept "knowledge," the functionalist position treats the *term* "culture" as if it referred to some large, bounded untheorizable, particular social entity, a society.[16] One unfortunate consequence of these confusions of analytic categories is to reduce any unit of analysis which insists on the integral nature of individual cognition and its context, to a component, a literal subunit of the society (culture), leaving no basis for disentangling the sociocultural order from the individual's experience of it. Further conceptual elaboration of these categories seems unlikely so long as the culture–knowledge–society terms are used in the conflated fashion just described.

There is one further problem concerning the treatment of culture in cognitive research, in this case as part of much broader Western cultural practices. Sahlins argues that it is characteristic of this social formation, perhaps uniquely, to transform in ideological terms that which is culturally commonplace and "normal" into the natural, to biologize it.

> When we render the conventional as the useful /or rational/, it also becomes for us "natural," in the double sense of inherent in nature and normal in culture.
>
> *(1976: 72–73)*

"Cognitive processes," viewed in this light, become obvious candidates for reexamination as culturally constituted phenomena. Cognitive theory might then be analyzed as a mode by which the cultural is so "naturalized."

Conclusions

The chapter began by asking why there has been such a long history to the interpretation of continuity in activity in terms of learning transfer. The most general answer lies in the durability of a positivist epistemology of science and division of disciplines. If cognitive transfer has persisted as an apparently satisfactory account of the social reproduction of knowledge-in-use since the turn of the century it has done so as one small aspect of a much larger nexus of theory and practice. Thus, recent proposals for cross-disciplinary collaboration, and for more contextually sensitive theory and method, must almost certainly founder on all the grounds elaborated here.

Questions have been raised about the context-free characterization of cognition, the methodology which goes with it, the conception of culture as factual information, and the adequacy of a normative view of the exemplary person as a rational, professional scientist and problem solver. It seems clear that to move away from the conceptions of persons, culture, the social world, and the everyday that have been called into question, they must be treated as objects of analysis rather than as unexamined explanatory devices. The problem is not merely one of method, nor for that matter can we treat method as separable from the problematic of which it is an integral part.

It is also possible to begin to move in positive directions. From this point I shall take the situated character of activity (including cognition) as given, and begin to explore its dimensions. This process will help make plain prerequisites for a more consistent conceptualization of culture and cognition and their constitution and relations in a social world. Some information has been already been assembled about everyday arithmetic: various studies suggest that it is qualitatively different in different situations, peculiarly accurate, and actively constructed in series of transformations of relations of quantity. We can return to analysis of arithmetic practice in the supermarket, trying not to replicate the assumptions or practices of functionalist theory, while attempting to develop both empirical evidence and theoretical motivation for a theory of practice.

II
Practice in theory

5

INSIDE THE SUPERMARKET (OUTDOORS) AND FROM THE VERANDA

This chapter returns once more to the analysis of arithmetic practice, and will draw on the empirical project in more positive terms, looking for ways to theorize about the unfamiliar forms of everyday activity. We could begin with the most common questions people have asked about the Adult Math Project: How much math is there in everyday activity? What does or does not transfer from school? One can respond to these queries, but in spite of the intrinsic interest of the distribution of frequencies of problems or problem-solving procedures in the lived-in world, these are not the most useful questions for an inquiry into relations among math activities across settings.[1] We shall ask instead how activities come together and shape each other on different occasions, and what are the processes which generate qualitative differences among arithmetic activities. And we shall ask *what* structuring resources are brought to bear in a given situation to give quantitative relations their form and meaning. To begin, a distinction must be made between math-in-practice and math conceived as a system of propositions and relations (a "knowledge domain"). The term "knowledge domain" connotes a body of knowledge structured *as such*, a bounded "conceptual space." In practice, this abstraction has enabled and legitimized the analysis of processes of problem solving as if they were poorly realized or simplified versions of a putative knowledge structure. But this taken-for-granted claim must be examined more closely, for it is likely that the shape and efficacy of everyday arithmetic depends upon its generation out of the articulation of structuring resources across occasions and situations; knowledge of formal codifications of math may (or may not) play a part. I shall try to show that activities-in-setting provide fields for action that structure each other. In practice, such resources are to be found not only in the memory of the person-acting but in activity, in relation with the setting, taking shape at the intersection of multiple realities, produced in conflict and creating value.

In order to illustrate some of the conceptual underpinnings of a theory of practice – the notion of multiple ongoing activities, the concept of structuring resources, their proportional articulation, and ways in which they shape processes that generate and resolve arithmetic dilemmas – this chapter compares two experimental studies of proportional reasoning. They have similar research goals and involve the same math problems, but the experiments are generated in very differently articulated structuring resources and have quite different outcomes. The comparative analysis also offers an opportunity to develop methodological implications of AMP research. The concept of structuring resources will be introduced first, in a series of examples at several analytic levels, as they vary in proportional articulation between major social arenas over time and between experiments.

Structuring resources

Suppose you are asked to solve a math problem like 75×114. A school taught scenario is one possibility: Get out paper and pencil, use a place holding algorithm, write 114, below it $\times 75$, draw a line beneath, multiply from right to left, 5×4, carry 2, 5×1 is 5 plus 2 is 7, 5×1 is 5, move to the left, 7×4, carry 2, 7×1 plus 2, 7×1, writing down the answers all along. Then add down the answer columns. Or, use a calculator, punch in 7, then 5, the multiply button, then 1, 1, 4, the total button, and read the answer on the display. Or, ask a friend, "how much is 75 times 114?" "Well, let's see . . . 75 hundred is 7 thousand 5 hundred and 750 is 8,250. Remember that. Okay. And 4×70 is 280 and 4×5 is 20. So that's 300. What have you got?" "8,250." "So its 8550." The product may very well be the same in each case, but the process has been given structure – ordered, divided into units and relations, in action – differently in each case.

However, it is probably never the case that only one thing is going on at a time. People routinely shop for groceries and do math at the same time. I can read and knit. Sometimes the process of knitting gives shape to the reading. I might read while knitting a row, but wait to turn the page until the row is finished, or stop reading in order to pick up a dropped stitch. At other times I read to the end of the page before starting a new row, knitting faster if the plot thickens, slightly tighter when it gets tense. Knitting projects look more promising if they don't require constant attention, hard-cover books appeal partly because their pages stay open better. Knitting is a structuring resource for the process of reading and reading provides structuring resources that give shape and punctuation to the process of knitting. They shape each other, but not necessarily equally. Usually one is the ongoing activity, the other is given shape more than it shapes the first.

A different example involves math and grocery shopping in unequal proportions. If given a "going to the store" problem to do in a math class most people would treat the story as having no substantive significance – it is there to disguise mathematical relations. The same people generating math dilemmas in the supermarket are likely to organize quantitative relations to fit the issues and concerns of buying food (as we shall see). Neither math nor shopping would be organized in the same fashion across the two situations. The proportional contribution of each to the process of activity as a whole varies from one occasion to the other, there is no fixed procedure for math or shopping, nor do they have symmetrical organizing effects on one another.

A much broader example of the articulation of structuring resources involves relations between the structuring of school math curricula and everyday math practices at different times in the history of public schooling. Arithmetic instruction was introduced into British elementary schools about 1750, brought into the school from the marketplace (Cohen 1982). The curriculum consisted of what Cohen calls "denominate math," systems of weights, measures and their equivalents, for different branches of commerce – the latter provided the structuring resources for the school curriculum. It organized teachers' and children's day-to-day activities. Perhaps they first learned fish sellers' weights and measures, then grain sellers', then carpenters', then cloth merchants'. Whatever the order, major units of learning would have been given order by commercial occupations. Perhaps within a single system of measurement units were learned first, then price/unit equivalents for each one, and so on. Again, the concerns and activities of the marketplace provided the structuring resources for school activity.

By about 1820 the math curriculum in the US looked somewhat less like a survey of the quantitative practices of the craft/mercantile world and began to take on an institutionalized structure of its own (math lessons on addition, then subtraction, then multiplication, then the rule of three). The curriculum was no longer ordered specifically in mercantile terms (though it was still controversial because of its commercial connections. Cohen 1982). Sometime since then, certainly by the end of the nineteenth century, there was a reversal of the impact of everyday math on school math curricula, such that what had become the relatively independent teaching of math as a structure in school settings, began to be justified as a universalistic and rational prescription for structuring arithmetic practice in other aspects of everyday life (including commerce). This claim is a familiar one, reflected in the belief that math practices outside school should be replaced by those taught in school. There is a common assumption that part of what makes school math a superior substitute for everyday varieties is its algorithmic character (it is assumed to have no other qualities as such, except its infallibility). There is a widespread preoccupation with the responsibility of schools in the preparation of children for life after school. And further, there is an assumption that without such preparation school alumni might be unable to do math.

There has been a long and gradual shift, then, in the proportional contributions of school-generated and non-school math structuring resources to normative visions of everyday practice. The shift has led to the structuring of math lessons as specific, algorithmic prescriptions for a universally applicable set of procedures to be employed outside school. The ideology of schooling claims légitimate hegemony of school arithmetic over the math practices of alumni in the settings of their after-school lives.

The formal scholastic structure of mathematical knowledge, treated as an end in itself, as mathematical expertise, has also been taken to be the proper template for fashioning experimental studies of logico-mathematical cognition. As I argued earlier, such expertise is the yardstick of choice against which to measure and evaluate subjects' performances. Results and conclusions are then extrapolated from experimental settings to the unexamined activities and settings of the lives of jpfs. Like school curricula, experiments have been designed on the basis of assumptions that one form of practice should organize all occasions of practice.

However, when doubts are raised about the ecological validity of experiments, as they have been by Bronfenbrenner, Neisser, Cole *et al.* and others, they pose, whether intentionally or not, questions about the articulation of structuring resources in experiments and other settings. Calls for ecologically valid research open up a broad field of relations between normatively derived models of good thinking and everyday activities and transform this field into an object of analysis. Questions follow: is it valid to extrapolate from experimental findings to activity outside the laboratory? If it is not automatically appropriate, what are alternative sources for the characterization of everyday activity and how are they to be reconciled with laboratory-shaped characterizations of cognitive processes and the problem-solving capabilities of jpfs? Further, who is to decide what cognitive phenomena are significant objects of study, and how? Are guidelines to be found in normative models of cognition, in an investigation of the activities of peoples' lives, in some combination, or in other sources altogether?

So long as it is assumed that math takes one universal form, transported to all settings and carried out in a uniform way, the answers to these questions may be assumed to be simple, and can be simply assumed. There would be no question about the validity of extrapolating laboratory findings to other settings. But if math practice takes form in situationally specific ways (the very term "ecological validity" introduces this possibility), it implies that the formal mathematical properties of potential problems are not sufficient to determine what problems will emerge in practice. Other factors in the situation shape problems: ongoing activities, the structure of the setting, and their relations. If so, then experiments, grocery shopping, and cooking situations are ones within which (at least) two things are going on at once. Among them they should generate multiple realizations of math in practice.

To construct ecologically valid experiments requires a stipulation of how realizations of math other than a normative – scholastic one will figure in the investigation. Is the activity to be investigated the application of school math or grocery shopping (math) or some other form? Is the conclusion to this question consonant with the experimenter's beliefs about what is (or should be) going on "out there?" If not, what articulation and weighting of activities is to prevail in interpreting experimental results? There are no ready-made answers to these questions. In practice, research that has tried to address questions of ecological validity has included varied, generally conflicting strategies for connecting experiments with situated activity outside the laboratory without rethinking their theoretical underpinnings, construction, or interpretation. Sometimes the results seem almost absurd. In one of the experiments discussed below, researchers interpret grocery shoppers' responses to their grocery shopping math problems, e.g. "I always buy the large sizes; I don't like to shop often" as a "primitive /reasoning/ strategy" (Capon and Kuhn 1982: 452), because the response is not a mathematical solution. Such a conclusion could only be justified from a position in which the structuring of math in a scholastic frame of reference is invoked in the interpretation of math in other settings. A subject's description of her general shopping strategy is read only negatively – as a failure to use "real" mathematics. This, in turn, is taken as evidence of cognitive incapacity.

Comparison of the two proportional reasoning experiments may help to make the argument clearer. In one of these studies Capon and Kuhn investigated adult levels of cognitive development, focusing on unit price calculations for supermarket products.[2] The other is the best-buy simulation experiment of the AMP, sketched in chapter 3. I shall first present the rationales, tasks and interpretive schemes of the experiments. Their results, discussed next, tell a clear story and establish two points: problem-solving success rates are quite different in the two experiments, and the experimenters' analyses of subjects' strategies is based on quite different principles of interpretation. Analysis in terms of structuring resources follows the description of the experiments.

Just outside, and inside, the supermarket: divergent views

Capon and Kuhn (1979; also Kramer 1981) set up a cardtable outside a supermarket, stopped customers who were about to do their shopping, and asked them to calculate which of two bottles of garlic powder, then two bottles of deodorant, was the better buy. They interviewed "50 female shoppers" in a low-middle income area in Southern California. In a second study (1982) they expanded the sample to include 100 women shopping at a supermarket in a middle-income area of Cambridge, Massachusetts using essentially the same procedures (Table 10). They reported that only 32% of the subjects in the first experiment were able to use proportional reasoning to solve a 2:3 ratio problem and only 20% for a more difficult ratio. Only 44% of the 150 subjects succeeded in solving both problems. This stands in contrast to a much higher rate of success in selecting the best buy in the AMP simulation experiment.

Capon and Kuhn began with a concern that, "not all subjects in an adult population perform at the highest stage in Piaget's development sequence, the stage of formal operations" (1979: 450). They intended to investigate formal reasoning in a naturally occurring setting out of concern that previous research – almost exclusively formal testing – did not address the question of variability in everyday functioning. They

Table 10 *Best-buy problems (Capon and Kuhn experiment)*

Unit price problems	Best buy	Unit price	Unit price difference	Target ratio
A. *Garlic powder*				
Bottle 1 $ .41 1.25 oz.	2	32.8 ¢/oz.		$P_2P_1{}^a$ (disguised
			.3 ¢/oz.	2:1)
Bottle 2 $ .77 2.37 oz.		32.49 ¢/oz.		
B. *Deodorant*				
Bottle 1 $1.36 8 oz.	1	17 ¢/oz.		Q_1Q_2 2:3
			.6 ¢/oz.	
Bottle 2 $2.11 12 oz.		17.58 ¢/oz.		

^{a} P = price, Q = quantity. Subscripts distinguish grocery items.

emphasized that no other study "has attempted to assess formal reasoning in any of the actual naturalistic settings in which it might be expected to occur" (1979: 450).

> The subject was supplied with pencil and paper. The interviewer said, "Suppose this were a product you used a lot of. When you went to the store to buy some, you found you had a choice between these two sizes. How could you tell which one is the better buy?" If the subject responded in the vein that, "You would have to figure it out," the interviewer asked the subject to go ahead and do that. If the subject said that either "the bigger one" or "the one on sale" was a better buy, she was asked, "How could you check to make sure the (sale/bigger) one is actually the better buy."
>
> *(1979: 450)*

The AMP simulation experiment took place in participants' living rooms. The exercise included bargain problems, best-buy problems and unit-price problems. This choice reflected terms and type of problems that had appeared in earlier conversations with the shoppers. Where different combinations of prices and quantities formed easily decomposable ratios, we thought there might be corresponding differences in procedures for solving the problems. For bargains, people might simply recognize that one was larger and cost less than the other. Our best-buy problems would lead to the comparison of the two prices or two quantities first (then the remaining pair). When price-quantity relations were the easiest to decompose we expected shoppers to carry out unit-price calculations. And we wondered whether precise ratios

Table 11 *Best-buy simulation problems*

	Problems	Best buy	Unit price	Unit price difference	Target ratio
I. Bargains and simple comparisons					
A. Potato chips					
Bag A	$1.09	7½ oz.	C	14.5 ¢/oz.	A − B = .9 ¢/oz.	C = Bargain
Bag B	$1.09	8 oz.		13.6 ¢/oz.	A − C = 4.5 ¢/oz.	
Bag C	$ .83	8 oz.		10.0 ¢/oz.	B − C = 3.6 ¢/oz.	
B. Barbecue sauce						A = Bargain
Bottle A	79¢	18 oz.	A	4.4 ¢/oz.		
					1.4 ¢/oz.	
Bottle B	81¢	14 oz.		5.8 ¢/oz.		
II. Best buy problems					
C. Peanuts						$2/1\ P_1/P_2$
Can A	90¢	10 oz.	A	9.0 ¢/oz.		
					2.3 ¢/oz.	
Can B	45¢	4 oz.		11.3 ¢/oz.		
D. Pepper						$2/1\ Q_1/Q_2$
Box A	59¢	2 oz.	A	29.5 ¢/oz.		
					7.5 ¢/oz.	
Box B	37¢	1 oz.		37.0 ¢/oz.		
E. Jam						$3/2\ Q_1/Q_2$
Jar A	$1.50	18 oz.	A	8.3 ¢/oz.		
					.5 ¢/oz.	
Jar B	$1.05	12 oz.		8.8 ¢/oz.		
F. Raisin bran						$4/3\ Q_1/Q_2$
Box A	$1.58	20 oz.	B	7.9 ¢/oz.		
					.4 ¢/oz.	
Box B	$1.13	15 oz.		7.5 ¢/oz.		
G. Mustard						$5/2\ P_1/P_2$
Jar A	75¢	16 oz.	A	4.7 ¢/oz.		
					.3 ¢/oz.	
Jar B	30¢	6 oz.		5.0 ¢/oz.		
H. Hot sauce						$2/1\ P_1/P_2$
Bottle A	74¢	7 oz.	A	10.6 ¢/oz.		
					1.7 ¢/oz.	
Bottle B	37¢	3 oz.		12.3 ¢/oz.		

Table 11 *cont*

	Problems		Best buy	Unit price	Unit price difference	Target ratio
I. Corn						$2/1\ Q_1/Q_2$
Can A	39¢	17 oz.	A	2.3 ¢/oz.		
					.6 ¢/oz.	
Can B	25¢	$8\frac{3}{4}$ oz.		2.9 ¢/oz.		
J. Maraschino cherries						$3/2\ P_1/P_2$
Bottle A	$1.49	13 oz.	B	11.5 ¢/oz.		
					.5 ¢/oz.	
Bottle B	$ .99	9 oz.		11.0 ¢/oz.		
III. Unit price problems						
K. Sunflower seeds						$1/10\ Q_2/P_2$
Package A	30¢	3 oz.	A	10.0 ¢/oz.		
					1 ¢/oz.	
Package B	44¢	4 oz.		11.0 ¢/oz.		
L. Olives						$1/6\ Q_2/P_2$
Can A	21¢	3 oz.	B	7.0 ¢/oz.		
					1 ¢/oz.	
Can B	30¢	5 oz.		6.0 ¢/oz.		

Note: in the last column P=price; Q=quantity. The ratios given are those around which the problem was designed. Subscripts refer to the first and second items being compared. Thus P_1/Q_1 would indicate the ratio between the price of the first item and the quantity of the first item.

would be treated differently from disguised ratios which would require transformation to obtain simpler ratios before solving. (The problems are given in Table 11.)

Instructions for the best-buy experiment were roughly similar to Capon and Kuhn's but with some characteristic differences as well. The person was first asked several questions. "When you go shopping, do you ever find yourself comparing two items in order to find out which one gives you the most for your money?" (Everyone answered "yes" to this question.) "About how often (e.g. on the order of once a shop, once a week etc.)?" "How do you figure out which is the better buy?" (e.g. mental arithmetic, paper and pencil, a calculator, other). "Have you ever run into a situation where you couldn't figure this out using _____ (fill in the method)? If so, what do you do?" After getting the above information the participant was told:

> Now I have some problems of this type for you to do. Each problem will have two or three items, either the actual items or written on notecards,[3] and I want you to tell me which one gives you the most for your money. Assume that the quality of each item is the same and that you have no other preference except for getting the most for your money. Please talk through the problem while you are figuring it out, so that I can follow the steps you are going through in making your decision.

If people said they could not decide, or that a problem was too difficult, they were asked: "what information would you need to answer this question? Tell me exactly what needs to be done to help you decide and I will use this calculator to get any intermediate steps done." After each problem there was discussion to clarify any parts of the procedure which were not clear from the person's description.

We were initially concerned about how much uniformity to impose (or resist imposing) on the shoppers' problem-solving methods. We decided that the initial attempt should be done without calculational aids. If two rounds of calculation were required, however, we wanted to make sure that they would be able to use the method they preferred in the supermarket on the second round. But when shoppers told us how they solved problems in the store, and we observed what they actually did while shopping, it became clear that our concern was misplaced. In response to the question, "what would you do if you couldn't figure out a best-buy problem on the first try?" two shoppers suggested they could use a calculator; two others suggested using pencil and paper; two said they would just take the larger item; three thought they would recalculate in their heads; 13 said they would redo the calculation and if that didn't work, abandon the problem. One suggested reading store (unit price) labels. These were, of course, hypothetical responses to a hypothetical question. We also knew what the same people did while actually shopping. During our trips to the market a calculator was used only once, on a single item, and no one used paper and pencil. There were a number of instances of multiple rounds of calculation, suggesting that besides abandoning problems, people often did them over (without invoking additional calculational aids). So, when shoppers made second attempts to solve a problem in the simulation experiment, we did not offer them any new supports, though the experimenter occasionally carried out a specific numerical calculation on request.

Capon and Kuhn were also concerned with minimizing the impact of simple numerical calculation difficulties on the outcome of the experiment. They therefore did not count an arithmetic error as a mistake if the strategy used was logically complete.

For the comparative analysis AMP best buy simulation data were coded as similarly as possible to Capon and Kuhn's categories.

Capon and Kuhn   Adult Math Project

Subject's response   Subject's response

(1) is extraneous, task-extrinsic e.g. a   (1) (not a category in AMP analysis)
     shopper reports she would buy
     "the small one; I'd never use the
     big one up." (1982: 450)

(2) is extraneous, task-intrinsic e.g.   (2) is to choose the larger item
     "reasoning oriented to the task
     objective, and an inference was
     based on one or two additional
     cues in the task situation" (1982:
     450) e.g. buy the one on sale, or
     the larger.

(3) uses weight and price information   (3) is incomplete
     but fails to draw inference.

(4) subtraction: used subtraction   (4) a difference strategy: produces a
     operations and made an inference   judgement of whether the
     "With the bigger one you get 32   marginal difference in quantity is
     more grams for 36 more cents."   worth the marginal difference in
     (1982: 451)   price.

(5) weight ratio diagnosis, including   (5) best-buy calculations, comparing
     various conceptually correct   two quantities or prices first; the
     calculations.   result to the remaining ratio.
                                                       There were several variants.

(6) direct ratio. "These strategies   (6) unit price calculation, of which
     involved the calculation of direct   there were several variants.
     ratios, either price per unit weight
     or weight per unit price prior to
     the inference, and are highly
     generalizable." (1982: 451)

(7) (not a category in their analysis.)   (7) inspection: "bargain" problems
                                                       were solved primarily through
                                                       recognition that one was both
                                                       cheaper in price and a larger
                                                       quantity.

AMP analytic categories were intended simply to reflect differences in price and quantity relations among the problems, while Capon and Kuhn intended their six response categories to fall along a rough scale of progressively more advanced cognitive strategies.

> The strategies described in these categories reflect a range from primitive strategies based on factors extraneous to the data to logically correct, completely generalizable strategies. *(1982: 450)*

Table 12 *AMP best-buy simulation solution rates*

Number correct	Number of people
less than 9	0
9	1
10	5
11	6
12	12

Note: maximum possible = 12
   N = 24

Problem:	A	B	C	D	E	F	G	H	I	J	K	L
15 Solution errors:	0	0	0	0	2	4	4	0	0	4	0	1
3 Transcript errors:	(1)						(1)		(1)			

Note: 12 problems, N = 24

I have summed them up as follows:

Level (1) the strategy is irrelevant, or if relevant uses a non-arithmetic rule of thumb (responses they coded as one or two).
Level (2) the strategy is incipiently inferential (response types three and four).
Level (3) the strategy is properly inferential, but specific (response type five).
Level (4) the strategy is universal, fully formal operational (response type six).

By their analysis the first two levels were conceptually incorrect. The third was correct but not "highly generalizable" (1982: 451).

In the AMP simulation, everyone solved at least 9 of the 12 problems correctly (average 11.2). Table 12 gives the distribution of scores. In the combined data from the two Capon and Kuhn experiments slightly over half (53%) were conceptually correct. However, subjects who employed adequate strategies occasionally drew erroneous conclusions about which was the better buy, even following correct calculations. In the end only 44% of the subjects succeeded in giving completely adequate solutions (see Table 13). There is clearly a substantial difference in solution rates; the 93% AMP solution rate is approximately double the average 44% figure for correct solutions using Capon and Kuhn's category five and six strategies.

Solution rates for different types of problems in the AMP experiment are compared in Table 14. Unit price problems (those for which the highest level of reasoning would be required in Capon and Kuhn's terms) were solved as often as bargain problems. Both were solved

Table 13 *Solution and error rates in the Capon and Kuhn experiments*

1979	(N = 50)	1982 (N = 100)	combined (N = 150)
For both problems Categories 1–4 (conceptually *incorrect*)	55%	43%	47%
Categories 5–6 (conceptually *correct*)	45%	58%	53%
	100%	100%	100%

Deodorant problem only (Comparable information on garlic problem not provided in the C & K papers):

Categories 5–6 correct	40%	60%	50%
Categories 5–6 correct (after subtracting inferential errors)	32%	55%	44%

Table 14 *Average solution rates, AMP best-buy simulation problems*
N = 24

	Bargain[a] (A,B) problems	Best-buy (C–J) problems	Unit-price (K,L) problems	Overall (A–L)
Average correct	94%	91%	98%	93%

Average correct, by increasingly difficult ratios	
2:1 precise ratios (C,D)	97%
2:1 disguised ratios (H,I)	92%
All easier ratios (C,D,H,I,K)	99%
2:3 ratios (E,J)	88%
More difficult ratios (F,G)	81%

[a] Letters refer to problems, see Table 11

Table 15 *Number of strategies used by shoppers (AMP)*

Number of strategies	Number of shoppers
1	0
2	0
3	12
4	12

slightly more successfully than the "best-buy" problems, the subset most closely equivalent to the Capon and Kuhn problems. As might be expected if the ability to simplify ratios affects success, problems with more malleable ratios had higher average solution rates than problems involving a 2:3 ratio as in the deodorant problem. Fewer people solved problems with 4:3 and 5:2 ratios correctly, though still a large majority of the shoppers (81%). There was only a 5% difference in success rates between the disguised and undisguised ratios.

The 15 errors in the AMP experiment fall into two types. Either the shopper did not succeed in solving the problem (nine cases) or insisted that the two items were equally good buys (six cases).[4] The four problems with the most difficult ratios accounted for 14 of the 15 errors. In addition there were 15 attempts to solve a problem in which the experimenter carried out a calculation for the problem solver, of which 14 were successful. Four people received two such assists, seven one assist and 13 none, suggesting that this procedure contributed relatively little to individual or collective performances. Three other responses were not analyzed due to an undecipherable tape recording.

Capon and Kuhn treated problem-solving strategies as fixed attributes of individuals. They compared the strategies each person used on the two problems and found that 74% responded with just one, 14% used strategies that differed by one step in the scale of strategies, and 12% by two steps (1979). This relatively consistent use of a single strategy indicated to Capon and Kuhn that their results had tapped stable differences of mental development. In the AMP simulation experiment each participant used at least three strategies and half of them used four (Table 15). Seven of the shoppers used the same strategy on more than half the problems. Table 16 shows, however, that the strategies they preferred were not the simple or erroneous ones. The data also

Table 16 *Majority use of a strategy (AMP)*

Strategy	Number of users	Number times used if used on more than half of the problems
Unable to complete	0	0
Size	0	0
Difference	0	0
Ratio	1	7
Unit price	4	7
	1	8
	1	9

Table 17 *Strategies across problems in Capon and Kuhn's experiments*
N = 150

Strategy	Very disguised 2: 1 ratio Garlic	2: 3 ratio Deodorant	Difference
Irrelevant	9 (6%)	14 (9%)	(3%)
Size or on sale	24 (16%)	24 (16%)	(—)
Incomplete	24 (16%)	24 (16%)	(—)
Difference calc.	7 (5%)	14 (9%)	(4%)
Ratio comparison	44 (29%)	31 (21%)	(8%)
Unit price	42 (28%)	49 (33%)	(5%)

demonstrate that each person who did something "primitive" *also* used ratio and unit price strategies as well.

The pattern of strategy frequencies for the problems in Capon and Kuhn's experiments (Table 17) supports their claim that the strategies their subjects used were substantially the same across problems (1979: 451). But AMP data challenge the conclusion that this finding reflects stable personal attributes. In the AMP simulation experiment, participants matched strategies to types of problems (Table 18). That is, bargain problems were overwhelmingly solved by inspection, and problems in which a unit price ratio was easier to transform than the other arithmetic relations were solved by unit-price calculations. The best-buy problems

Table 18 *Strategies across problem types (AMP)*

N=24

Strategy	Bargains	Best buy	Unit price
Inspection	23 (96%)	0(–)	0 (–)
Ratio comparison	0 (–)	90 (47%)	3 (6%)
Unit price	2 (4%)	75 (39%)	45 (94%)

Table 19 *Strategies for ratios of varying difficulty (AMP)*

N=24

Strategy	A 2:1 Ratios	B 2:3 Ratios	C 4:3 and 5:2 Ratios
Ratio	77%	23%	10%
Unit Price	21%	54%	60%
Other Strategies	2%	23%	29%

Strategy	Difference: A – B	Difference: B – C
Ratio	54%	13%
Unit Price	33%	6%
Other Strategies	21%	6%

were solved more often with a best-buy strategy than a unit-price strategy, though both were used. The latter provides a clue as to why the Capon and Kuhn problems were approached rather similarly. If the problems and strategies (for best-buy problems only) are regrouped by ratio difficulty, it becomes clear that a best-buy strategy was most often used on problems with 2: 1 ratios, and unit price comparisons when they were more difficult. In general, the distribution of strategies for difficult ratios, that is 2: 3, 4: 3 and 5: 2 ratio problems were very much alike (Table 19). It appears that the garlic and deodorant problems presented comparably difficult ratios. Table 19 further discourages a developmental interpretation. As problems became more complex, developmental limitations should have been intensified. Yet there was an increase in unit price calculations as ratio difficulty increased.

In sum, as constructed, Capon and Kuhn's experiment offered two possible explanations for constancy of activity across problems; they attributed the constancy to developmental characteristics of the individual but could equally have argued that using similar strategies on both problems was an active, flexible response to problems that closely resembled one another. Since they did not perform an experiment that would distinguish between the two hypotheses, their claim that similar activity reflected stable attributes of the individual is difficult to justify. We did perform that experiment, varying the difficulty of ratios within and across problems. Our results support the alternative explanation.

The "easy ratio" method of the jpfs is not a prescriptive algorithm for uniform activity across occasions. Arguably, it would be easier to keep straight about the meaning of various ratio comparisons were just one method automatically applied to all problems. Nonetheless jpfs do not simplify their lives in this fashion; in fact, the ratios they compose out of prices and quantities have different meanings and implications for grocery shopping decisions. Characteristically, it is not the changing meanings of quantitative relations that appear difficult for the shoppers so much as the numerical recalcitrance of the quantities involved.

The conclusions to these experiments differ in expectable ways. Capon and Kuhn caution that "the present data do not contradict the notion that performance is enhanced when the problem context is concrete and familiar." They seem to have in mind a simpler everyday world. They conclude that formal operational reasoning is "far from universal," a formal operational strategy not available to "many of the subjects," and "there does in fact exist significant variability in level of logical reasoning among an adult population." They suggest that increasing unit pricing in stores won't help if many people do not have the ability to use them. The remedy lies in substantial consumer education (1979: 451). Capon and Kuhn thus reiterate themes common in the learning transfer research of chapter 2: it is easier to solve problems in everyday situations than in the laboratory, subjects' difficulties are cognitive, the cure is to make appropriate strategies consciously available to them.[5] In contrast, the AMP simulation experiment recommends against ranking proportional reasoning strategies in (or out of) the supermarket. It supports the view that shoppers are generally efficacious in solving best-buy problems, they use a variety of strategies, flexibly in relation to (among other things) the arithmetic properties of particular price and quantity ratios.

Two articulations of structuring resources

Math activity in these experiments appears to derive from differently articulated structuring resources in at least three respects. One is the proportional role assigned to theoretical models on the one hand and observation *in situ* on the other in the construction of experimental tasks. A second will emerge in a comparison of the dilemmas of subjects as they search ambiguous experimental scenarios for clues to the intended meaning of the task. And the third arises in problems of interpreting experimental results. This will take us back to the question of context. In each case we shall ask in what proportions structure and meaning in activity are derived from a normative mathematical knowledge structure and from the structuring of everyday activity.

Capon and Kuhn began with a Piagetian model of formal operational approaches to ratio comparison. There is no evidence that the lived-in world directly influenced their choice of research topic, in fact it appears the other way around: given a determination to study proportional reasoning, they asked themselves, "where would you find ratio comparisons in a mundane situation?" Unit price comparisons in the supermarket had this form, and met the ideals of formal operational arithmetic and good consumer behavior at the same time. Thus, the theoretical importance of mathematical operations structured the search for a relevant everyday activity. It did not lead Capon and Kuhn to observational research inside a supermarket, nor did the location of their experiment outside a market lead them to investigate how grocery shopping activity might have shaped arithmetic.

The AMP approach, described previously, may be quickly summed up. It began with an ethnographic question, "what sort of math occurs in grocery shopping?" It led to observation in the supermarket and the singling out of best-buy problems because they looked rather like "real math" (a point at which normative conceptions of mathematical knowledge shaped the construction of this experiment). It appeared that people approached such problems by seeking out easily simplified ratios. A simulation experiment was designed to explore this hypothesis about problem-solving procedures in the market.

Both mathematical activity and grocery shopping activity were implicated in the construction of the experiments. But each experiment gave the structuring of these activities characteristic weight at a sufficiently fundamental level to have a consistent impact on a variety of aspects of the process of experimentation. Thus, Capon and Kuhn's experiment, with the exception of its location, the garlic powder and the deodorant, and perhaps the impact of shoppers' responses on the description of coding categories, drew almost exclusively on a putative mathematical knowledge domain and a theoretical model of cognitive development as structuring resources for its construction and interpretation. The AMP drew on an ethnographic account of grocery-shopping practice, but with a counterweight in the choice of school-like math episodes from among the multitude of goings-on that might have been singled out for further investigation. As a result, Capon and Kuhn took the view that they were observing proportional reasoning (or not). The same activity from an AMP perspective, was interpreted as either everyday grocery shopping arithmetic practice or some school-like experimental contrivance.

The second issue concerning structuring resources follows from the first. Both the AMP and Capon and Kuhn studies were committed to investigating cognition in "natural" settings. They assigned subjects the same experimental task (to solve best-buy problems as if they were in the supermarket). But the "as if" signals a problem. Subjects find themselves in one situation, an experiment, while there are signs that they are expected to act as if they were in a different situation, e.g. grocery shopping. At the same time conventional experimental practice bars experimenters from explaining their intentions to subjects who are thereby left to guess them. In the experiments discussed here subjects seemed to draw similar conclusions about the predominant structuring resources shaping a particular experiment, but differed sharply between experiments, reflecting differences in their structure quite accurately.

It is worth considering why there was such definite variation in subjects' interpretation of the situation between experiments. Participants in the best-buy simulation seemed to conclude that they were to proceed more or less as they would in the store while participants in Capon and Kuhn's experiments – given pencil and paper and invited to show their work – appeared to view the exercise as a test. There is suggestive evidence in favor of this surmise. The difference in problem-solving success rates between the two simulation experiments was similar to that between performances in everyday math activities and school-like tests in the dairy, market vendor, and AMP studies. Further, in these studies there was a relation between schooling and performance on school-like tests but not between schooling and performance in everyday settings. Capon and Kuhn (1982) demonstrated a relation between schooling and the strategy level employed by their subjects. Taken as a whole the evidence suggests that their subjects interpreted the experiment in terms of a test-like scenario.

The third issue in which the proportional articulation of structuring resources is paramount is contained in two small clues to striking differences in the general conclusions of the experiments. The first clue is a discrepancy of judgment: Capon and Kuhn and the AMP made conflicting evaluations of the difficulty of 2: 3 ratios. Capon and Kuhn continually referred to a 2: 3 ratio as "simple" (1979: 450, 451; 1982: 450), while the same ratio in the AMP study was characterized as "difficult." This raises questions as to the frame of reference within which such judgments are made. Capon and Kuhn do not make explicit the context within which 2: 3 is a simple ratio. It appears that they think the ratio is "simple mathematics," that is, simple with reference to the knowledge domain of mathematics. The AMP judgment was made with reference to arithmetic in practice in the supermarket and simulation experiment: shoppers found it hard to figure a precise 2: 3 ratio in the course of grocery shopping when unamenable relations among numbers made it difficult to transform them. This small discrepancy takes on more serious dimensions in relation to conclusions about the general mathematical well-being of the subjects. Where the ratios were conceived of as simple, and failure to calculate was taken as evidence of serious mental incapacity, experimenters concluded that shoppers were inadequately prepared for real life. Described as difficult, in AMP research, they contributed to a considerably more sanguine view of the capabilities of jpfs.

The second clue is to be found in the observation that Capon and Kuhn ascribed a higher level of mathematical sophistication to unit-price strategies than to best-buy strategies. This reflects a confusion over both the mathematical and grocery shopping properties of these strategies. Figure 3 may help to clarify what is at issue. Capon and Kuhn claim that the unit-price strategy is superior to a best-buy strategy because only the former is "universal." The distinction between more and less universal cannot be a mathematical one, however, for a proportional comparison of a ratio of two prices to two quantities is mathematically equivalent to the comparison of two price/quantity ratios. Capon and Kuhn explain that it refers to the fact that the shopper is free to compare the unit price of one item to that of any other item in the supermarket, while the direct comparison of two quantities (and prices) limits the result to those particular items. But we observed in the supermarket that price comparison arithmetic is used almost exclusively

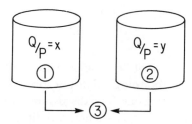

Which has lower unit price ?

"Best Buy" Calculation

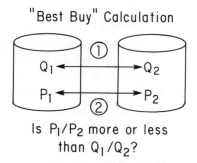

Is P_1/P_2 more or less
than Q_1/Q_2?

Figure 3 Unit price and best-buy calculations

at points in decision processes where only two or rarely three candidates remain for a single grocery item (Murtaugh 1985a).[6] The ability to make universal comparisons is irrelevant in the supermarket. To assert the value of "freedom" to compare grocery items as a property of the supermarket context betrays a lack of first-hand observation in the market and suggests that the context for this claim was a "conceptual space," a math-for-itself world where "general is always better."

We have discussed the forming or shaping of activity at a level of value and judgment brought into play when experimenters *act* – when they make up tasks, interpret performances, and thus in each case, doing several things at one time, assign greater value to some than others. Subjects also have to judge how they are supposed to, and/or want to, respond. In the course of the simulation experiments the actors together created conditions in which action with and about mathematics-as-an-end-in-itself took its shape partly from grocery shopping in some circumstances, while the reverse was true in others. Differently structured activity followed from their asymmetric impact on one another.

Validity and method

Other issues that have fallen within the rubric of "ecological validity," are central to a theory of practice. Three methodological implications of the comparative exercise deserve further comment. The discussion will focus on differing views of the meaning of experimental validity, a comparison of strategies used in the simulation experiments with those observed in the supermarket, and the role of explanation and description in the research.

The AMP assumed that "validity" referred to complex (not uniform) relations between activity in an experimental setting and elsewhere in the lived-in world. Capon and Kuhn took internal cognitive states as the critical comparative reference point. This assumption became clear when they discussed the possibility that their experiment might not have tapped higher level strategies that could have been available to some subjects.

> Even though subjects classified into Categories 1 and 2 did not make reference to either the price or quantity data, it is possible that proportional reasoning was within their competence. However, as the interview itself and motivational incentives [$1; a chance to participate in a $50 drawing] were designed specifically to minimize the performance/competence gap, we regard this explanation of Category 1 and 2 performance as extremely unlikely.   *(1982 fn. 4: 451)*

A theory of experimental validity is embedded in this analysis. Strongly motivated performance is taken to be the most accurate or representative indicator of the upper limits of competence. Authenticity is to be gained by insuring that subjects are highly motivated to perform. This strictly internal concept of validity in practice preempted a focus on relations between activity in the experiment and the lived-in world. Commitment to one led to silence on the other, illustrating in yet another way the conflict inherent in turning a functionalist cognitive theory into a situated theory of practice.

Questions concerning ecological validity have so far been posed while comparing experiments. We have yet to compare strategies in the experiments to strategies in the supermarket. It was possible to code these strategies in much the same terms as in the experiment (Murtaugh 1985a). Neither of the experiments matched the distribution of problem-solving strategies in the supermarket (Table 20), though this observation must be treated with caution; for the frequencies of problem-solving strategies were affected as we varied the numerical

Table 20 *Strategies for solving best-buy problems in two simulation experiments and in the supermarket*

Strategies	Capon and Kuhn	Best-buy simulation (best-buy problems only)	Supermarket
Difference	14%	9%	22%
Best-buy ratio	18%	47%	35%
Unit price	27%	39%	5%

properties of prices and quantities systematically in the simulation experiment. Two simple observations seem warranted, nonetheless: there was a larger proportion (22%) of the unorthodox-looking "difference calculations" (coded as strategy four) and a notably smaller proportion of unit price calculations (5%) in the market than in the experiments.

In subtraction or difference calculations, the shopper took the difference between prices, then the difference between quantities and made a marginal utility judgment. Such calculations take the form, "I will get two ounces more for six cents. Is it worth it?" There is a question about quantitative relations to be resolved, but not a problem for which there is a numerical solution. More important, the answer depends on considerations other than those contained in the arithmetic relations alone. Capon and Kuhn treated this strategy as only incipiently inferential, and dismissed it as inadequate. But additional examples from the supermarket suggest that this form is simply structured less in terms of math as an end in itself and more in relation to other aspects of ongoing activity. Examples may illustrate better how difference calculations involve arithmetic relations directly relevant to, indeed generated out of, the activity of grocery shopping.

Example 1: A shopper considered two rolls of paper towels, one costing 82 cents, the other 79 cents. The shopper noted the number of sheets in each roll, 119 versus 104, and proceeded to reformulate the problem, saying, "That would be three cents more and you get 11 more, 15 more sheets." She concluded that the larger roll was "probably a better . . . buy." The shopper's decision is, precisely, whether to spend an additional three cents for 15 sheets. That is, she must judge whether the marginal value of the additional quantity is worth the marginal cost, a different and more relevant question than whether the larger or smaller size has the lower unit price.

(Murtaugh 1985b: 36–37)

Example 2: A shopper compared two boxes of sugar, one priced at $2.16 for 5 pounds, the other $4.30 for 10 pounds. She explains, "The 5 pounds would be four dollars and 32 cents, versus four dollars and 30 cents. I guess I'm going to have to buy the 10-pound bag just to save a few pennies." In this case, a unit price calculation would have revealed that the larger size costs 0.2 cent less per pound than the smaller size. Instead, this shopper compares prices for ten pounds of sugar, the quantity she has already decided to purchase, store and use. The answer returned by this calculation ("a few pennies") is easily interpreted as the amount of money actually saved by selecting one alternative over the other.   *(Murtaugh 1985: 35)*

The marginal value assessments appear to be instances of activity-shaped, heterogeneously related relationships, generated in grocery shopping activity. In these examples the elements (prices and quantities) and relations (ratios and comparison of ratios) of a unit-price calculation have more salient relations elsewhere than with each other. Prices are compared with alternative uses for marginal sums of grocery money and quantities and units of quantity are compared with concerns about managing food. Inventory is one such issue – how much sugar may be bought at one time without waste or spoilage. Another issue is storage capacity as the shopper considers the sizes of five and ten pound packages relative to shelf height and space available in her kitchen. This process of transformation of quantitative relations may be described as "dissolving" problems (in both senses of the term), making them disappear into solution within ongoing activity rather than "being solved." Such transformations pose a challenge to scholastic assumptions concerning the bounded character of math problem solving as an end in itself.

Satisficing and marginal value "calculations" are common, and cognitive psychologists have explained them primarily as a result of the information processing limitations of the mind. But this interpretation depends on the view that the arithmetic relations and elements of, say, two grocery items, are the only relations involved in their comparison. This, of course, fits the conventional model in which an encapsulated arithmetic problem-solving structure (the steps in the calculation) *replaces* ongoing activity-structure (e.g. putting together tonight's dinner) in the supermarket. On the contrary, it appears that in practice, relations among arithmetic elements and other kinds of concerns in the world are often equal to, or more important than, the arithmetic relations among those same elements, and relations of quantity are merged (or submerged) into ongoing activity. "Processing limitations" would offer an absurdly impoverished account of the structuring of these relations.

To say that processes of marginal value assessment and satisficing produce arithmetic relations that dissolve in ongoing activity, is another way to express the idea that grocery shopping activity creates fields for action within which arithmetic activity is enabled, though not determined. Further, shoppers' concerns about meals, family food preferences, inventory and nutrition plainly motivate arithmetic activity more strongly than the reverse, since arithmetic in the supermarket often serves these other-than arithmetic intentions and purposes. This proposition also helps to explain the comparatively low frequency of unit-price calculations observed in the market.

> The behavior of shoppers in the supermarket indicates that price per ounce is not a particularly useful piece of information. Shoppers apparently feel that it is not worth the effort to calculate the price per single ounce, when a single ounce is neither purchased nor consumed. In contrast, the procedures that shoppers do employ reflect concerns for both price and quantity . . . Shoppers do not perform calculations as ends in themselves; rather, they transform quantitative information in ways that will highlight relationships among items that are relevant to their concerns.
>
> *(Murtaugh 1985b: 192)*

The third methodological issue follows from this discussion. It is important to note that we have been engaged in interrogating observational research in the supermarket for an explanation of findings generated in an experiment. In the light of discussions of the traditional nomothetic/ideographic division between experimental and ethnographic methods (chapter 4) this deserves further comment. In research on adult math practices, we have employed experimental methods as a means of augmenting understanding of everyday scenes. This view has influenced our interpretation of experimental findings: simulation experiments make it possible to confirm tentative descriptions of activity derived from observation in the supermarket. But for an explanation, for light on why problem solving takes a particular form, it is necessary to go back to ongoing activity in the supermarket itself.

Even such a reversal of description and explanation maintains a separation of function, however, and this does not describe the research process closely enough. AMP research might be described as an iterative implementation of Bartlett's suggestion that observation should precede experimentation. We began in the supermarket, constructed experiments on the basis of this inquiry, and have gone back to the ethnographic material in search of an explanation for our findings. As the focus has shifted from ethnographic to experimental forms, to observation *in situ* again, description and analysis have been part of the project as a whole in all its phases, rather than uniquely divided between methods (or disciplines).

Iterative, multimethod research does seem to follow from and reflect a theory of practice. It begins with an assumption that all empirical methods generate situations structured partly in the desire to inquire, and that in some respects, therefore, what is learned is an artifact of the process of inquiry. Thus, the structure of the AMP simulation experiment bore certain relations and resemblances to everyday activity-in-setting, but limited ones. Because of their exotic, hybrid structure, both Scribner and the AMP "bracketed" simulation experiments with formal tests on the one hand and observations in everyday settings on the other, and referred interpretations of the results of simulation experiments to activities of the same people in test and everyday settings. Simulation experiments are useful primarily in a comparative context, as descriptive devices for exploring activities whose meaning must be sought through observation in their customary contexts.

Consigned to a single method, it is not possible to assess the artefactual contribution of method to findings. Such is not the case when a multiple method approach is employed. In research in which methods and situations are varied, there is the possibility of validating one's understanding through iterative investigation of situationally specific differences. When any socially organized experiment is treated as asocial, experimenters will remain silent about its organization and the expectations and interactions of the participants. The argument here is that differences in activity among settings, including the – no longer privileged – experimental setting, can be grist for an analysis that does not depend for validity on the view that people act in narrowly consistent ways in all settings.

Conclusions

This chapter has presented a series of examples of multiple activities and their mutual shaping in ongoing activity. The central idea is that "the same" activity in different situations derives structuring from, and provides structuring resources for, other activities. This view specifically opposes assumptions either that activities and settings are isolated and unrelated, or that some forms of knowledge are universally insertable into any situation. Different situations, and indeed different occasions subjectively experienced as "the same," are instead viewed here as *transformations* of structuring resources given a realized form through their mutually constitutive articulation, weighted in different proportions from place to place and time to time.

The articulation of structuring resources is not likely to vary in an evenhanded way, as if all possible articulations were equally probable. Thus, it seems obvious that math is almost always more structured by, than structuring of, grocery shopping in the supermarket. But it is still an important question as to how the relatively stable proportional articulations of structuring resources that give practice in the lived-in world its apparently routine and expectable qualities, is constituted. And this question surely implicates the constitutive system of social order in the broadest sense.

We may note very briefly that scholastic institutions reflect and are in part realizations of a common constitutive order. In comparing school curricula and experimental ideologies earlier in the chapter I argued that the proportional emphasis on mathematico–scholastic structuring in these two institutionalized arenas was harmonious, perhaps identical. School and academic psychology clearly affect each other directly but they also share a common history and a common social context as well. An analysis of the specifically cultural and historical character of this web of interrelations is implicit in the several examples chosen to illustrate the idea of structuring resources and their proportional articulation. A theory of practice does take learning, thinking and knowledge to be historically/culturally specific, socially constituted, and politically tempered, and argues that they structure the social world writ large as well as being structured by it.

Finally, it should not be too surprising that alumni of schooling – all of us – share the beliefs that shape the social institutions. School alumni respond accordingly as subjects in experimental situations (as chapter 7 will demonstrate further). It follows that taken-for-granted "natural" values about proper math structuring that permeate cognitive theory, schooling and folk ideology are better descriptions *of each other* than of the practice of arithmetic in everyday settings. But we need not stop there. The next two chapters take up further conceptual developments needed for a more direct examination of everyday practice.

6

OUT OF TREES OF KNOWLEDGE INTO FIELDS FOR ACTIVITY

The previous chapter explored the articulation of activities (math and grocery shopping) whose interrelations shaped their structure differently in two experimental situations. But activity is not the only source of structuring resources. People's social relationships give structure to their activities. People experience "problems" subjectively in the form of dilemmas and, so motivated, "problem-solving" activity often leads to more or less enduring resolutions rather than precise solutions. "Math" and standard crystallized forms of quantity such as those to be considered here – the system of currency and systems of measurement as well as algorithmic arithmetic – carry meaning and values *as such*, and these too are subjectively experienced. All of these sources of structuring resources for activity, being more than the quantitative relations to which they give shape, help to account for the characteristic fate of formal knowledge structures in practice: they are transformed from standardized forms into situationally specific realizations in practice, and when they are addressed as formal systems, more often than not it is to incorporate (only) their symbolic significance into ongoing activity.

We will begin to consider the meaning of "real" math, and with it the meaning of money and measurement, in contemporary American parlance in the following discussion. Next, distinctions made here between dilemmas and problems, and problem resolutions and solutions, need explanation. Two sources of data provide evidence for this analysis: measurement practices of the Weight Watchers and money management interviews with the shoppers. In the Weight Watchers study, the dieters were motivated by quantitative dilemmas and their measurement practices in the kitchen reflected different resolutions to these dilemmas. Open-ended interviews with the grocery shoppers made it

124

clear that the means by which they managed money reflected and were shaped by their activities and relations with each other and the dilemmas these engendered. Both the knowledge that "real math" is culturally highly valued *and* its transformations contribute to the structuring of math practice. One puzzle to be addressed is how these conflicting understandings are fit together. We will see that they grow out of, and in turn create, dilemmas which motivate the shaping of math in practice.

The socially organized meaning of "math"

It would have been helpful to be able to report participants' views about the meaning and implications of formal mathematics. What follows does draw on their beliefs as these have been inferred from their uses of arithmetic in the supermarket and reactions to the testing situation. But in large part I am able to present only an impressionistic summary of diffuse conversations and observations of a more casual variety.

It appears that, in this culture at this time, mathematics is a reified object as a career, academic discipline and body of knowledge. It is a subject in school and an object, "real math," in folk belief. It has been given form by, and in turn has given form and substance to, a host of meanings, values, and symbolic properties which people share. Knowledge of math is taken to be a measure of sheer mental brilliance; it provides the kind of truth with which there is no possible argument, and is thus a technology of authority and the symbolic medium for asserting the authority of technology. It indicates exactitude, rationality and "cold" logic which stand in mutually exclusive relations with intuition, feeling, and expression. In short, its meanings *as such* are different from its instrumental and literal contents and meanings.

"Real math" in social practice is also "incorrigible," in the terminology of phenomenological sociology. That is, part of the cultural meaning and value of mathematics comes from the strong supposition of its immutable reality ($7+5=12$; a meter is a meter any time, any place). The Pythagorean Theorem is beamed into outer space because its "universal" properties recommend it as a form likely to be recognized by extraterrestrials. Arguments have been advanced, however, that these apparent eternal verities are socially constructed, "artful social accomplishments." Pollner (1974: 43 quoting Gaskings) begins with a definition:

> An incorrigible proposition is one which you would never admit to be false *whatever* happens: it therefore does not tell you *what* happens . . . The truth of an incorrigible proposition . . . is compatible with any and every conceivable state of affairs. (For example: whatever is your experience on counting, it is still true that $7+5=12$)

He pursues the implications of this view for relations between knowledge and practice.

> If such a proposition tells you nothing about the world, what, then, is the point of it – what does it do? I think that in a sense it is true to say that it prescribes what you are to *say* – it tells you *how to describe* certain happenings. Thus the proposition "$7+5=12$" does not tell you that on counting $7+5$ you will not get 11 (This, as we have seen, is false, for you sometimes do get 11.) But it does *lay it down*, so to speak, that if on counting $7+5$ you do get 11, you are to describe what has happened in some such way as this: *Either* "I have made a mistake in my counting" or "Someone has played a practical joke" . . .   *(1974: 44)*

Pollner goes on to argue that these explanations are more than a linguistic implication of the discrepancy between experience and incorrigible beliefs. (I have paraphrased his argument slightly.)

> The incorrigibility . . . is a continual accomplishment: [it] is assured in no other way than through the artfulness of . . . practices for orienting to it as such which includes the use [of mathematical propositions] as the incorrigible mandate for and constraint upon the search for accounts which reconcile the discrepancy between [formal propositions] and subsequently observed events.   *(1974: 44)*

If, as he argues, "incorrigibility" is constructed, then cognitive theory in particular, and schooling pervasively, have sustained and been sustained by assumptions about relations between knowledge and practice that are too simple. Familiar relations between normative models and practice reflect these assumptions. Beliefs in one universal, unimpeachably true form of mathematics, applicable in canonical forms that themselves have no specific characteristics, meaning, or value, are direct expressions of the common cultural reifications of math. It seems difficult, if not impossible, to avoid such views if incorrigibility is assumed to be a natural property of mathematics rather than a social accomplishment. But if "mathematics" is the product of social work and symbolic fashioning, surely math in practice is more and other than it is claimed to be by practitioners and teachers. Further, we have seen that quantitative relations are not confined within mathematical boundaries. The analysis of difference calculations in the previous chapter provided an empirical basis for arguing the nondeterminant structure of math in practice – that quantitative relations can have closer, more salient, relations to other kinds of relations than to each other. Under these circumstances, the symbolic significance of "real math" is a structuring resource that helps to shape activity.

Aspects of everyday activity in the classroom contribute to, as well as reflect, the symbolic properties and meanings of algorithmic arithmetic. The properties of "formal" systems of money, measurement (and math) have been institutionalized in "problem-solving tasks" in school and in research on cognition. In school, money and measurement are addressed, perhaps exclusively, in arithmetic classes. Classroom arithmetic lessons provide a powerful locus for teaching rational, utilitarian interpretations of arithmetic, money and the standardized dimensions of material goods. In this context the transformation of relations of quantity is reduced to problem-solving procedures, that is, to means/ends relations. Children are taught the units and equivalents among units of currency and also about their relationship with the decimal notation system. This approach incorporates implicit messages that money, *like* arithmetic, is an objective system of units and relations with which to calculate. And since math and money, according to common belief, are objective and universal, when accurately applied they should produce correct, rational means for action. (If in doubt about whether alternative interpretations are possible, contrast this characterization of money with its role as a fetishized object in Marxist theory.)[1] In short, standard systematizations of quantitative relations are transmitted to children in school, specifically characterized as instrumental means to reach goals defined elsewhere, taught as if they had no symbolic value or connotations of their own. But these *are* some of the central meanings and values ascribed to systems of quantity and their prescribed uses in this society. And we should expect to find them enacted, drawn upon as structuring resources, in everyday math practice.

Measured change

It may well be the algorithmic, scientific, objective connotations of math that attract new disciples to Weight Watchers, although, as we shall see, exact measurement and its meanings are variously transformed in practice. The Weight Watchers study explored the activities of nine new members of the dieting program as they incorporated new measurement practices into meal preparation over a period of weeks (de la Rocha 1986).[2] All of the participants demonstrated the usual level of success at formal arithmetic, averaging 60–70% on the general math test. The math involved in preparing meals according to the Weight Watchers program was not as difficult as the math at which they were successful on the test. Yet the dieters differed sharply in their uses of arithmetic in the kitchen. Thus "competence" (that is, as measured by test performance) was by no means a major structuring force in fashioning the frequency and accuracy of calculation in the kitchen, and we must look elsewhere for an explanation of the differences between the dieters' calculational activities. There is a second salient pattern, this one across time. The more expert the Weight Watchers, the less they calculated. There was a clear trend for all of the cooks to make fewer calculations as they became more familiar with the program, while maintaining a constant level of accuracy in food portion control, and continuing to lose weight (de la Rocha 1986). An explanation for both of these patterns lies in the dilemmas which motivate dieting activity and lead to different resolutions for different people and at different times.

The dieters invented accurate portion control while reducing their engagement in weighing and measuring by establishing equivalences between formal measurement stipulations of the diet program and their own activity while they cooked meals in their kitchens. Measurement tools and directions for weighing and measuring foods were pervasive in the dieting procedures laid out in the Weight Watchers manual. Early in their experience with the program, while the dieters were unfamiliar with the complex rules, they did take advantage of the properties of a food scale and measuring devices, though not necessarily in standard fashion. But by the end of five weeks the dieters were measuring much less often with measuring scales, cups, and spoons. As they incorporated measurement activity into cooking and serving meals, standard representations of quantity were set aside in favor of more direct dealings with the real thing. Thus, a process that had several stages on day one:

> Look up allowed serving size of a glass of milk. Get out measuring cup, milk carton, and drinking glass. Pour milk in measuring cup. Pour milk from measuring cup into glass. Wash measuring cup and later the glass

Became:

> Get out glass and milk carton. Pour milk into glass up to just below the circle of blue flowers. (Wash the glass.)

Dieters took advantage of the sociocultural structuring of the settings of dieting activity, among them, store packaging and conventional units of food like "a slice of bread" in addition to the idiosyncrasies of household containers. This made it possible to find equivalents for, and thus eliminate, measuring activities. They invented units (a "big" spoonful; four swallows = four ounces). Foods were treated differently depending on whether they were solid, liquid or somewhere in between. These characteristics affected the ease with which dieters invented units and equivalents for measurement purposes. Thus, out of 134 invented measuring *devices*, 97% were used to measure liquids. But of 72 invented *units* of measure 63% were applied to solid foods and only 21% to liquids. The structuring of settings and their furnishings, including food, offered resources for establishing quantitative relations in activity, increasingly over time (de la Rocha 1986: 235). In sum, the articulation of formal measurement prescriptions in the Weight Watchers program with measurement activity in meal preparation gradually shifted from partial structuring in formal terms to very little, and to gradually increased structuring by cooking activity and dieters' strategies for losing weight.

The latter speak to issues of motivation and the values that shape practice. The dilemmas of dieting cooks involved conflicting motiv-ations concerning weight, its relations with beauty on the one hand and solace on the other. The first dictates "don't eat" while the second suggests "have another cookie." A diet is a notably temporary resolution to the dilemma. Dieting itself presents further dilemmas. The Weight Watchers program advocates "scientific portion control" and their approach is to regulate weight by precisely controlling the amounts of each food eaten. As the milk example suggests, however, precise measurement takes time, organization, and work, in settings where the cook is often under pressure to produce meals efficiently for a hungry family.

The dieters as a group responded by measuring almost exactly half the items they ate (de la Rocha 1986: 223). But their approaches to dieting divided them into two separate camps. From interviews about their history as dieters, they appeared to have relatively long term, consistent resolutions to dieting dilemmas (de la Rocha 1986, chapter 4). Some espoused the view that meticulous control of food portions was the way to control weight. Others expressed their approach as "so long as you feel hungry you must be losing weight." Each of them did indeed conduct her diet in accord with one philosophy or the other. School biographies and math test scores had no predictive value for measure-ment practices in the kitchen, but the long-term dieting styles clearly shaped measurement activity differently. Methodical dieters used formal measurement techniques on 61% of the food items they recorded in their food diaries, while the "go hungry" dieters measured only 26% of the time. Thus dieting dilemmas seem to have motivated activity in characteristic ways, accounting better than differential knowledge of arithmetic (or of the dieting system) for differences in quantitative activity in the kitchen.[3]

In short, the Weight Watchers study suggests a series of conclusions that confirm those of the analysis of best-buy calculations and raises questions to be pursued in the money management study. Math, for dieting cooks, was not an end in itself, nor was it a salient structuring resource for the activities of which quantitative relations were a part. It did not take form through the interpolation of school math or the formal measurement prescriptions of the diet into these activities. Nor were the dieters' practices a matter of default in the face of ignorance of the structure of relevant school arithmetic. Math, while cooking meals and dieting, seemed to be structured in relation with dilemmas that motivated dieting and cooking activities. Dieters transformed resolutions to long-term dilemmas into short-term strategies that shaped the flow of cooking activity. This description of the management of quantitative relations in dieting reflects two general shifts in analytic approach: to a different conception of trouble, of activity-stopping snags within ongoing activity rather than prefabricated "problems," and to a focus on the person-acting (in activity, in setting) as the unit to be analyzed, rather than the "problem solving attempt."

The measurement practices of the Weight Watchers did not appear to be determined by the structure of math or of cooking yet they were not independent of either one. Their proportional articulation shifted over time towards the structuring of quantitative relations into ongoing cooking activity. Evidence and argument here support a claim that opportunities, such as routine meal preparation, which enable the realization of measuring activity, don't determine its structure, and may not share it. Structure results from and unfolds in the articulation of activities, social relations, and their settings. There is a term, "fields for action" in the phenomenological sociological literature and in the work of Bourdieu that captures this view rather well. The nested, enabling, and other characteristics of fields for action will be developed more fully as we proceed. These complexities suggest we might inquire into alternative characterizations of prerequisites for action in contrast with notions of scripts, trees or other map-like guides or prescriptions for understanding for conventional studies of cognition treat the structuring of action as something that precedes it. The view is consistent with an emphasis on thought distanced from experience as the canonical form of human experience to be investigated, but it is not compatible with the everyday math practices just described, nor with a theory of practice.

Money management in practice

Money management practices offer a clear example of the ubiquitous transformation of standardized, "universal" forms of knowledge into situationally specific forms and categories of quantification. This section explores some of these transformations (and incidentally their cultural specificity, which may become clearer in contrast with the uses of special purpose monies in other cultures). It appears that multiple activities and social relations converge on, or are condensed in, the structure of money management and measurement practices. In particular I shall try to show that social relations – dieters' relations with their families, and especially relations among family members concerning the management of money – shape and are expressed in the ways in which canonical systems of knowledge are transformed in everyday activity. The categories and relations of money management practices also provide a rich field within which to address the warning (chapter 1) that a theory of practice may easily become a thinly disguised form of utilitarian individualism. Relations between rationality as a global value, the situation-specific dilemmas that motivate math in practice, and the specific character of values as experienced and acted upon, are central to this discussion.

Anthropologists have described the special purpose monies of "primitive" cultures, where beads may be exchanged for pigs or iron bars for women, but not the reverse, making translations between systems of exchange impossible (Bohannon 1955; Polanyi, Arensburg and Pearson 1957). In contrast, Western cultures have a universal monetary system and medium of exchange that in principle provides a universal standard. The strength of the distinction is called into doubt, however, as soon as a close look is extended to the ways in which jpfs manage family finances.

Money passes through families interviewed in the AMP in a cyclical flow which can be described in phases. It is brought into the family as income, held temporarily by various compartmentalized means ("stashes"), and finally used to meet expenditures. The flow of money occurs in varied media of exchange, including cash, checks, and credit cards (both general- and special-purpose). Incoming funds shaped into stashes and by media for transactions, are used to create, in practice, special purpose monies. It will be argued here that they are used to create categories that may not be treated as equivalent, and that these prohibitions have the same moral character as those surrounding special purpose monies in other societies. Participants in the AMP gave the impression that a universal standard of value and medium of exchange was *not* an advantage, and that effort went into creating paths and flows of money which both produced and reflected the specific character of different value-expressing everyday activities (see also Douglas 1967).

There are many examples of the creation and use of special purpose monies by the people we interviewed. For example one elderly couple (C, the wife; E, the husband) maintained a joint account and two separate sets of checking and savings accounts, one for bills and daily expenses, the other for larger expenses, gifts and taxes. The wife was responsible for paying the bills from one account, the husband for tax related expenditures. C explained:

> I have a checking account I pay my bills out of. And then we keep a small checking account out of that other money. But we don't write checks on it unless, like, for example, Little E – little E – six foot six – needs something or godsons need something, it comes out of that money . . . [*Later*]: Now taxes, anything on that, that's E's. Anything big, like when we ran into this thing like the surgery. That just, of course wouldn't fit my figures at all. All that came out of his money. Eighteen thousand dollars . . .

Besides contrasting in ownership, this couple's stashes differed in the quantity of funds routinely stored, in the categories of activity and/or persons for whom they were used, and in the size (and perhaps metaphorically the importance) of the expenditures made from each account. Relative size was a pivotal descriptor in C's account of her family's customary stashes. From her statement it appears that the husband and wife, their accounts, and the expenditures paid from the accounts, contrasted as big to small. So economical was the description that at moments it is difficult to tell which – persons, accounts, or payments – are so designated.

Other examples of compartmentalized distinctions between banked stashes of money included Christmas club accounts and accounts created in order to hold funds for unusual expenditures in the yearly cycle (property and other taxes, vacations, or the schedule of home and car insurance payments). Were the universal character of the reified system of currency the major organizing principle for stashes, one might expect each family to have a general pool of family funds (like a general mathematics), used for all possible purposes, rather than particular funds corresponding to particular aspects of the lived-in world. But instead, categories of funds reflected and also supported the social relations and categories of activities into which people organized their lives.

The set of stashes for a given family was not independent of the institutionalized properties of money within the banking system. Banks charge for check writing, especially for small accounts, and people rationed the number of checks they wrote. One method was to designate a limited set of uses for such an account, as C and E had done. Stashes were also dependent on the quantitative characteristics of their contents – the defining features of C and E's stashes partly reflected an organization of their activities into categories for which roughly similar sized payments were expected. Those correspondences had a condensed character, reflecting multiple relations, as in C's description of her family's stashes.[4]

AMP participants used a number of exchange media in varying relations with stashes. These provided many possibilities for differentiation among stash/expenditure combinations. Most regular monthly bills were paid by check. But the meaning of the transactions was affected by the identity of the check writer and the account on which checks were drawn. Cash had customary uses defined sometimes by size ("under $10 I pay cash"), sometimes by category of expenditure ("I always pay for gas with cash"). Participants had a variety of cash stashes, generally one in the billfold of each adult, children's allowances and piggy banks, a "petty cash" fund in a teapot-equivalent, a dish of change for parking meters or laundry. Stashes of cash, like checking accounts, were designated for special uses (e.g. "quarters are for laundry, not for video games," or vice versa). Their use was circumscribed by special restrictions on ease of access and by their various purposes, and the contents of only certain stashes could be transformed or moved to other stashes, and then only in specified ways. They were also given form by stipulating conditions under which they could or must be replaced, and by arrangements for replenishing them consistent with their customary rate of use. The expenditure of cash was modified to fit flow rates and replenishment routines. So, to use cash or not for a particular expenditure was a multifactor decision involving knowledge of the state of the stash *vis à vis* typical cycles of cash in- and out-flow as well as the everyday meanings associated with different stashes.

In sum, the number and kinds of incommensurate stashes and media into which money was organized within each family were shaped by the physical characteristics of family members, their relations with each other and the meanings attached to these relations, their activities, the organization of banking, the physical characteristics of money, and amounts of money to be expended. *What* was reflected and supported was rich and complex. As important for the present argument is the point that *reflection* and *support* – of social categories, social and symbolic relations, activities and institutions – are pervasive relations between invented quantitative units and the lived-in world.

Dilemmas and resolutions

The formation of incommensurate stashes appears to grow out of contradictory values about how money should be managed. There is a belief in Western culture that within the family, money is to be used to express and create solidarity and collective well-being. This conflicts with values supporting the utilitarian character of exchange, and adversary relations between buyer and seller in the world at large. In turn, this presents families with dilemmas about how to negotiate the entry, internal circulation, and expenditure of money.

The problems begin with paychecks. A paycheck inextricably belongs to a family member. Yet once money is associated with the family, it must be transformed into collective property. In twenty-five interviews only one family reported routine direct transfers of cash from one spouse to the other. This was, however, viewed as too much like a payment, connoting utilitarian exchange of work for pay rather than mutual support by husband and wife in maintaining a household. Though the husband in the exceptional case described the transfer of funds as an even split of his salary, the wife was keenly aware of the contradictory interpretations which could be placed on the transaction.

There were several common strategies for transforming money from individual income into collective resource. AMP participants deposited money into a checking account on which both spouses wrote checks. Often the spouse drawing most heavily on the account was not the one who made the major deposits. When both spouses worked, both paychecks were often deposited into a single family account, erasing the association of specific sums with particular individuals. The individualistic connotations of paychecks were sometimes "laundered" away by allocating one to a specific category of expenses for the family, so that in effect it was redefined in terms of its uses rather than its source.

Thus, income from part-time employment was sometimes described as "earning the family vacation." A somewhat less important method was for both spouses to deposit cash, often in equal amounts regardless of income, into a stash marked for specific types of expenditures.

In Western cultural forms of money management, conflict between individual and collective values is expressed as the suppression of individual ownership in order to achieve collective values. But relations between individual and collective resources are not "natural" properties of the monetary system or of some universal division between domestic and public domains. It is perhaps easier to see this by contrast with African cultures described fairly shortly after Western money became common. In some cases the individualized character of forms of wealth had been a positive factor in reaching collective goals (Parkin 1980). Customary stashes took the form of individually known and named cattle. Individualization of these non-concealable resources was crucial in realizing collective commitments to furnish brideprice among a wide network of kinsmen. The introduction of Western currency had an adverse effect on this project, since it was not possible to track particular dollars over the years between a promise to contribute and an actual contribution, as it had been with a familiar herd of cattle. It may have been just the uniform characteristics of Western currency that destroyed accountability in that case, while providing an expressive medium for the transformation of income into collective resource in the present case.

Turning from the stashing of income to its expenditure, the problem of collectivization appeared to be relatively less difficult than that of individualization. Family members were part of a collective social unit and at the same time individuals with varied independent commitments outside the family. There was conflict between the collective definition of family resources and activities and the independence of family members. One way to illustrate this is to compare money management in one-marriage families with the organization of money in families where both spouses had been married previously.

Figures 4 and 5 illustrate quite different systems of money management created by two AMP families to provide a framework within which household decisions, calculations and plans could be defined and resolved, not necessarily in that order. Figure 4 shows the flow of money for a young couple without children. Husband and wife pooled their wage-based incomes in joint checking and savings accounts. Most expenses were treated as communal ones (even personal clothing), and paid from the joint checking account. In the other family (Figure 5) each

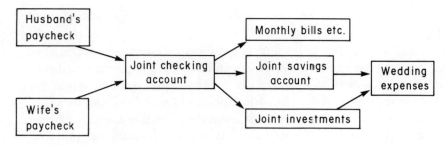

Figure 4 Money management: young family

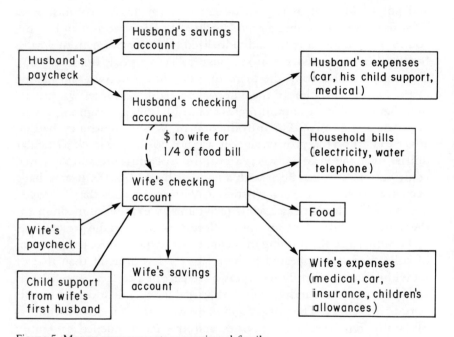

Figure 5 Money management: reconstituted family

spouse had been married previously. The wife's children lived in the household while the husband's children lived with his former wife. In contrast with the first family, this couple kept their finances separated. They had no joint accounts, and in paying for household bills each wrote a separate check for half of the total from her or his own checking account. The only direct transfer of money was the amount the husband gave the wife each month to cover one quarter of the food bill, the rest of which she paid from her account. Not all participants in the AMP who had remarried went to such lengths to keep separate finances, but they were more similar to the second family than the first. The relative lack of collective money management appeared to grow out of, and reflect, the complexity of financial arrangements about children, whose expenses involved former spouses as well as household members. At the same time, differences in financial arrangements between families reflected differences in their views of just how seamless a family should be.

Another dilemma associated with balancing individual and collective funds in the family had to do with the amounts, and in what media, spouses (and children) had monies for which they were not accountable to the family. Accountability started with the question of how much income was generated by the individual, and went on to questions about the kinds of stashes in which it was assembled and on what it was spent. For instance, C discussed what she and some other participants described as "mad money."

> Interviewer: Do you have a sense of how much cash you have on hand?
> C: Every bit. I'll tell you that's a joke especially around here . . . I keep about one hundred dollars in mad money in the back of my wallet and E'll say, "Honey could I have twenty dollars of your mad money?" See, I keep about one hundred dollars that don't count. That's mad money. But they all pay me back.
> Interviewer: What kinds of things do you buy out of mad money?
> C: Things you want to buy. I love to do ceramics. They're foolish because you know I have no place to put all the things that . . .
> Interviewer: Is that separate from the cash you might use if you're going out to lunch or something?
> C: Really you shouldn't spend it on lunches. Nobody else probably thinks the way I do about some things.
> Interviewer: Why do you say that?
> C: Well, everybody, all the women, all the ladies I know, they put their money in their purse, just dump it in their purse, and they just spend it the way they want to spend it. I don't do that. If I don't have it to spend, if I want to buy something that I feel isn't necessary, I always can take it out of my grocery money. If I didn't have any mad money, I just wouldn't buy it. I wouldn't even charge it. I wouldn't charge anything that I felt was foolish. Because I don't think that's a necessary evil.

"Mad money" generally came from collective funds, most often from household expense money. Women who did not have wage income obtained personal funds through a series of transformations: from spouse's income, to collective funds for collective expenditures, to surplus skillfully saved in running the household, and finally to individual pocket money. These funds reflected their history by deriving meaning from their contrast with the routinely practical uses of the original stash from which they came. By contrast, men often took personal funds directly out of their paychecks, though occasionally they turned over income to their wives and received spending money back – part of the laundering process to produce collective monies. (An example of this type is the "small account" C and E wrote checks on only if E or the godsons needed something.) Mad money might occasionally be used for family expenses, but the boundary between mad money and collective funds was maintained by the requirement that it be paid back, not simply absorbed into other uses.

Families in which spouses had significantly different incomes, where the wife worked part time and/or for very low pay, were similar to families in which the wife did not work for pay, with respect to the balance and management of personal and collective funds. However, families in which each spouse earned an income sufficient to support a household, tended to find the individuation of some funds for private use less difficult. The majority had three bank accounts – two individual ones and a collective account. Each person contributed substantially to the joint account, reserving a smaller portion in the others.

Contradictions as fundamental as collective/individual funds, and communal/individual accountability for their expenditure precluded a single, simple solution to the problem of allocating funds between their arrival and expenditure. Instead, there were conflicts to be resolved, entailing a series of arrangements that allowed the same funds to be treated sometimes as collective (though brought into the family individually), and occasionally as individual (even though taken from a common fund). Or the contradictions were resolved implicitly in the obvious symmetry of three bank accounts and three "persons" (the third being the collectivity). In all cases the proportional emphasis on conflicting values was at least partly realized in the relative amounts categorized in separate ways. Given the contradictory values which underlay these complex processes, "management" is an appropriate term for the transformation into practice of the properties of the universal standard provided by money (in theory). The process of transformation is complex. People must be able to track and control their funds while masking and reversing the meanings of money-in-flow.

Let us sum up what is situationally specific about the management of money. To begin with, in contradiction-resolving activity, stashes, media of payment and their combinations are used to transform legal tender into incommensurate categories and paths for funds coming and going through the family. They reflect family relations differently for different families. And the particular unitization of money in a given family shapes spheres of exchange so that they are commensurate with activities, social relations, values and occasions on which issues are resolved.

But further, this discussion of money management, like the Weight Watchers study, has framed the issue of problem solving in terms of contradiction-motivated dilemmas and their partial and shifting resolutions, and this too helps to account for the assembly of quantitative relations in situationally specific ways. What motivates problem-solving activity in everyday situations appears to be dilemmas that require resolution. It is necessary, in managing contradictory principles, to arrive at a resolution in specific terms and not necessarily in stable ones for a dilemma has no factual solution, no general, in principle, correct answer. It is a matter of conflicting values and viable alternatives, which are neither right nor wrong, and none of which is entirely satisfactory. Furthermore, the notion that resolutions to dilemmas are specific is not to be confused with notions that these are "concrete." It is surely an abstraction to say there is "no money in the house," in excuse to the plumber who is waiting to be paid, while standing next to a stash of grocery money in a kitchen drawer and mad money in one's purse on the counter. "Specific" in this context implies that stashes, transaction media or their combinations are integrally related to the ongoing activity of persons-acting-in-setting, of which they are a part. It follows that where a resolution is in order, people are almost certain to have more than one occasional resolution to a dilemma. There is a shift here in the conception of problem solving activity from a value free, context free technology of means, to a value laden, conflict driven, situationally-specific direct form of experience.

Money management practice, in theory

Money management and measurement as practice seem to grow out of multiple contradictions specific to the organization and meaning of social relations in activity in the lived-in world. Other reoccurring dilemmas may be discerned in the examples discussed here, that involve conflicts between the reified meanings of formal systems of quantity and the situation-specific characteristics of math in practice. Each is resolvable in varied, only moderately stable ways.

First, the stronger the incorporation of money management and measurement into ongoing activity, the more situationally specific – and effective – quantitative transformations are likely to be. But this stands in contradiction with the value and prestige placed on universalistic systems of quantification as reified strips of knowledge by the society at large. The supermarket math data illustrate this very well; the participants' situation-specific procedures are efficacious while the shoppers deny their value (sometimes even their existence).

Two other sets of conflicting principles are closely related. The more that arithmetic practice is an integral part of customary ongoing activity, the greater the contradiction with the common requirement that activities be easily communicated to others. And the more specifically tailored to private circumstances, the more difficult it is to argue that procedures have the legitimacy and weight of broadly shared conventions.[5] The discussion of mad money illustrates both. Mad money was a named stash, integral to C's money management practices. Its specific characteristics were understood by her family. But C addressed its lack both of general communicability and face legitimacy in the short discussion with the interviewer reported above, first by interrupting herself to translate her private category into a publically understandable form, "see, I keep about a hundred dollars that don't count. That's mad money." Then she asserts that her private system lacks broad legitimacy, "Nobody else probably thinks the way I do . . . Everybody . . . just . . . spends it the way they want to." The use of relations of quantity as a code for the meanings and symbolic properties of formal systems of quantification as such is quite common. The following chapter provides a more extensive example, concerning a shopper's use of arithmetic as a means of defending her commitment to rational shopping.[6]

Values attached to formal mathematics and the monetary system were discussed earlier. They reflect and instantiate an ideology of utilitarianism, objectivity and its keystone, rationality. One further contradiction in the use of math and money in practice comes from the conflict between this set of "rational–universal" values and the conflict-born specific values of ongoing activity and personal relations that shape the generation of quantitative relations in practice – values such as dinner on time, no flat tires, and occasional frivolity. The uses of money are evaluated and interpreted by AMP participants most saliently in specifically moral rather than general utilitarian terms, confirming that the categories of money management are part of a socially constituted moral order. Further, by various stratagems (paying back "borrowed" mad money, for example) people seek ritual means to prevent disordering or polluting them (Douglas 1966). Thus, "under $10 I pay cash" is potentially a utilitarian response to an objective problem, but it is also a ritualized response that preserves the meaning of "paying cash." C says, "if I didn't have any mad money, I just wouldn't buy it. I wouldn't even charge it." Mad money may not be spent on what she calls "necessary evils," for frivolity has strict moral limits.

If money is employed and evaluated so as to preserve moral categories and family relations as well as to express them, then they are neither (only) objective nor utilitarian. They do not meet criteria for rational action, and if not rational must fall under the rubric non- or irrational, in the conventional cognitivist view. But the empirical studies described here challenge the interpretation of compartmentalized, specific, efficacious processes for the transformation of quantity as evidence of the irrationality or even of the simplicity of quantitative aspects of everyday activity. Generative, system-maintaining, value-driven, multilevel activity seems a better analytic description of relations of quantity in practice. Prescriptions recommending calculation to achieve utility, rationality and objectivity are eclipsed in practice by more urgent values concerning the production and reproduction of ongoing activity and social relations. At the same time everyday actors place strong value on the rationality of practice. It is integral to the cultural fashioning of everyday life. But expressions of allegiance to canons of rationality do not themselves provide the fundamental principles enabling and shaping values-in-practice. Instead, expressions of utility and rationality are constructed through processes of action that are founded on other needs and values. Such processes are generated in the complex structure of lived situations, rather than in the underdevelopment of the human mind.

Conclusions

On the one hand, in the description of everyday practice it is difficult to detect problems to be solved or conventional scholastic problem-solving activity (e.g. encapsulated, procedure-driven interruptions that stop and restructure ongoing activity into arithmetic forms). On the other, it appears that fields for action – stashes, measuring devices, the process of choosing each grocery item – enable and are reproduced by ongoing activity, generatively and variously structured from among the obvious and often routinely available resources of persons' concerns, settings and activities. Though "problem solving" is a key concept in cognitive theory, the evidence assembled in this and previous chapters provides grounds for the conclusion that it does not have a correspondingly broad and fecund role to play in the analysis of everyday activity in its customary settings. How, then, are we to conceive of what might better be termed the transformation of quantitative relations? The response here is necessarily brief, but will be taken up again in the following chapter. The focus is on relations between fields for action and the process of problem management, illustrated by one further example from the Weight Watchers study.

At one point early in that study each dieter was asked to prepare a lunch of two open-faced sandwiches, one cheese and one peanut butter (for the extended analysis, see de la Rocha 1986, chapter 6). Each of the nine began by getting out a plate and laying two slices of bread on it. This had several effects simultaneously. It was a means of appropriating the problem, and at the same time created a field for action and a resolution shape to the problem. It is plausible to suppose that they had to recognize that something was problematic, represent it, implement a resolution, and evaluate the results. It is not impossible to point to aspects of the dieters' activity that fit each of these analytic categories of problem-solving action. But in general these occurred in no determinate sequence and in fact, nine different patterns were found. Further, as we shall see also in examples from the supermarket (chapter 7), one move often implemented several categories of action at once. Once enabled, sandwich making (and calculations about proper amounts of cheese and peanut butter) unfolded in an undetermined way, making use of many possible resources for structuring action, taking certain elements as incorrigible for immediate purposes, creating a specific articulation between the dieting and cooking worlds converging in and through activity in setting. Processes of problem management like these are dialectical in character, and we have borrowed Bartlett's (1958) term "gap-closing" to acknowledge their form.

The discussion has distinguished between conventional beliefs about the constitution of "problems" in contrast with conflict-generated dilemmas. Calculational episodes cannot be classified as constant members of either category. A continuation of the peanut butter sandwich exercise illustrates the point. Initially some of the dieters engaged with a calculational dilemma concerning how to follow the diet rules while making a peanut butter sandwich. But this generated a new dilemma: In making the sandwiches the dieters discovered that the formal solution called for an extraordinary amount of peanut butter. As the dieters realized this they exclaimed about it with vehemence, and scraped off the excess with alacrity (though knowing that the quantity on the bread was an accurate solution to the calculational problem). The calculation became simply the solution to a puzzle, while the peanut butter was a true dilemma. There were other snags involving math in the observational data on the Weight Watchers that evoked strong feelings, but more of them were limited in affect and action, "Let's see, I'll need twice as many tomatoes in the salad since David and Brian are coming to dinner." That is, math is sometimes a dilemma, but it is also the case that calculation is often unproblematic. It as often generates dilemmas as resolves them. This suggests that conventional assumptions about the importance attributed to "problem solving" in cognitive studies is both exaggerated and impoverished. At the same time it indicates the importance of considering whether and how quantitative relations are problematic if we wish to understand ongoing activity.

This and the previous chapter have discussed structuring resources and the transformation of the structuring of activity in relation with different activities. I have argued that at one and the same time the structuring of ongoing activity reflects and supports, produces, and helps to reproduce the routine character of everyday activity. What is the nature of these multiple and varied connections? The question becomes more insistent as the multiplicity of ties embodied in activity and the articulation of structuring resources takes a more central role in the argument. Certain plausible responses may be eliminated. Alternative structuring resources are not independent of each other, such that the implementation of one excludes others from consideration, without changing any of them in the process. On the contrary, I have emphasized the ways in which activities structure each other differently on different occasions. They proceed at the same time, given shape by their mutual articulation. Further, structuring resources for different activities are not causally dependent on one another. For example, knitting and reading, or grocery shopping and arithmetic calculation, each can go forward without the other, though organized differently when articulated differently with other activities. Relations between such activities appear to mutually constitute them. That is, the complex structure of ongoing activity (of which the transformation of quantitative relations is a part) is generated in their dialectical articulation.

The concept of dialectical relations requires elaboration, and must be extended to questions of relations between activity and its settings. This, in turn, presupposes a discussion of settings in their own right. For while much of the discussion has been about the multiple relations that give situationally-specific activity its shape as persons act, we have not yet addressed the question of why this specificity of activity is anchored within settings. To do so the setting, too, must be treated as an analytic object. The two questions will be considered together in the next chapter, in an analysis of the dialectical constitution of arithmetic practice in the supermarket.

7
THROUGH THE
SUPERMARKET

Before exploring arithmetic practice in the supermarket it may be useful to present a primer of dialectical percepts and examples to give more precise meaning to the proposition that practice is constituted in a dialectical relation between persons acting and the settings of their activity.[1] The task is a very general one, for I assume that social processes of all kinds are dialectical in character. This implies first that while the focus is clearly on the everyday activity of persons acting in setting, the properties ascribed to it must be consistent with the properties of a general dialectical theory of social order of which practice is a part. Secondly, conceived in dialectical terms, central aspects of activity include its self-generative and open character, whose structuring grows (dialectically) out of conflict. Dialectical theory describes self-generative processes in formal terms as thesis, antithesis and synthesis. These apply directly at the level of sociocultural order and its open working out over time. But "conflict" rather than "contradiction" seems a more appropriate term for the multiplicity of experienced disjunctions of social practice which motivate activity (see Giddens 1979, chapter 4).

Dialectical theory has the capacity to avoid certain theoretical entanglements that could well prevent the working out of a theory of practice. One of these is an idealism which leads to the conclusion that to understand cognition and the social world one need only study cognition. It also recommends against an environmental determinist interpretation of a material world coercing behavior from individuals whose activity is reduced to a material base. And it provides a principled alternative to the most obvious strategy for salvaging an encompassing theory from these extremes: an eclectic claim that both ideal and material aspects of the world are important in shaping activity, without specifying their nature or interrelations in consistent, unified terms. Characteristically the eclectic view emerges as only a program, one that stands in contradiction with the research practice of those who espouse the broad view. For example, Capon and Kuhn's formal commitment to ecological validity is disjunctive with the structuring of their experiments and explanations in intra-individual idealist terms. An antidote to this alternative, in dialectical spirit, involves opening up theoretical assumptions and their history to critical analytic scrutiny (an enterprise for which the book itself is intended as an example). And units of analysis, though traditionally elaborated separately, must be defined together and consistently, their relations being primary in the development of the terms. The tenet that the terms of dialectical relations are mutually constitutive underlines the importance of this point. The "primer" consists of a small number of specific questions that are central to a dialectical analysis coupled with short illustrations. (I shall leave to the next chapter further exploration of dialectical concepts and a discussion of a dialectical theory of social order consistent with a theory of practice.)

A primer for dialectical analysis

At the end of the previous chapter I argued that a dialectical relation is more than a declaration of reciprocal effects by two terms upon one another. Thus, to say that grocery displays in supermarkets influence shoppers' choices, while these affect how the store displays products, implies causal relations between the two, but not a dialectical relation. A dialectical relation exists when its component elements are created, are brought into being, only in conjunction with one another. For instance, the math problem and its resolution were mutually constitutive in the apple-buying episode (chapter 1). Constitutive relations between shelf displays and decision making in grocery shopping are pervasive in examples to be presented in this chapter: the intention to demonstrate good shopping procedures to a third party leads one shopper to search a shelf display of noodles visually and physically, in selective ways. The display was arranged so that differences in sizes and brands of products were salient aspects of the shopper's setting, calling attention to certain specific categorical possibilities which she might utilize in the demonstration. The shopper's activity was constituted in relation with these structuring resources. Conversely, neither the experience nor the context would be accessible in a particular realized form without the other, as an example of a shopper buying enchiladas will demonstrate.

The role of contradiction and conflict in analysis of activity, social practice and social order is crucial. Weight Watchers are caught in contradictions about the nature of womanhood in American society, and between the conflicting demands of family and diet. Contradictory principles govern the meanings of money within families, which motivate money management practices. In this chapter we shall encounter further dilemmas in the activity of grocery shopping. It is not the case, however, that setting and persons-acting somehow stand in contradiction. It is, rather, that arenas of activity such as supermarkets are products of the contradictions of political economy and sociocultural structuring, and persons-acting are caught in subjectively contrived versions of the same contradictions, out of which activity is (dialectically) fashioned.

An analysis in dialectical terms must account for various potential outcomes of activity in setting, its reproduction, or change, as well as the possibility of its transformation. The latter has received more attention in previous chapters, in discussions of the mutually transforming character of multiple activities, social relations and systems of meaning. The dairy loaders (Scribner 1984a; Scribner and Fahrmeier 1982) provide an additional example: they begin their careers using literal solutions to dairy-order arithmetic problems, but the context of stacked cases containing cartons of various sizes transforms the structure of categories for describing orders. The solution procedures are transformed as well, into "non-literal" solutions. This in turn changes the salient interrelations of full cases, partially filled cases, and different categories of dairy items in the cold storage locker, in the loaders' experienced version of them. Or in Weight Watchers, learning to prepare simple "clump" meals within the parameters of the program acts as a curriculum. But when mastered, the clump meals are boring. This is a precondition and motivation for transforming future meals (and the curriculum) into more interestingly complex culinary accomplishments.

In the analysis of structuring resources in knitting and reading, school math curricula, and simulation experiments I argued that activities were likely to structure each other in unequal proportions. This proposition is a specific example of a dialectical relation. Thus, the mutual constitution and transformation of the terms of a dialectic are rarely, if ever, symmetrically based on equal contributions to their articulation. A dialectical analysis then, needs to address the proportions of the relations of each in the constitution of the other. Indeed, proportional contributions to the articulation of ongoing activity must be empirically determined. For if activity is dialectically constituted, it is not possible to determine beforehand whether in a given instance it is being reproduced, transformed or changed. Given that the relations between the terms of contradictions are structural features of sociocultural order, reproduction is far more likely than either transformation or change. But delineating the possibilities and probable forms and their conditions of production is part of the analytic task.

Also basic to a dialectical approach is a view that unfolding activity is an open ended structure-in-process, and that reproduction of activities over time *is* a production. When people act it is a multi-level, multiple-purpose phenomenon, generating fields for action that support the generation of particular kinds of experience. Money stashes are such fields, as are "routine choices of grocery items" in the supermarket, as we shall see. Activity helps to reproduce the field for activity that encompasses it (further discussed in chapter 8). Action and the reproduction of activity-in-setting are two parts of the same process. This general implication of dialectical analysis, like the concept of articulated structuring resources, has been encountered earlier in more specific form. It was argued in particular that problem solving is never only that, partly because its routine production also entails producing conditions for its reproduction.

Activity such as arithmetic problem solving does not take place in a vacuum, but rather, in a dialectical relationship with its settings. So far, discussion of this concept has been confined to criticism of "context" in cognitive theory. But a more viable concept requires specification before we can proceed to the central task of the chapter, to give empirical instantiation to the proposition that "cognition" is constituted in dialectical relations among people acting, the contexts of their activity, and the activity itself.

Arenas and settings

It is exceptionally difficult to theorize about context, because the most relevant theoretical traditions do not take experience in the lived-in world as their analytic object. They tend to ignore the embodied, inescapably "located" nature of activity in time–space, perhaps because it is inconsistent with other assumptions. Thus, problems, and more broadly, knowledge domains, have been conceived of as the context of problem-solving activity in a functionalist, cognitivist, view. And, given the radical separation of individual and the social world (e.g. of cognition and context) implied by the conventions of cognitive studies, either a cognitive locus of "context" or an environmentally determinist one is possible within this tradition. It should not be surprising, then, to discover a well-developed behaviorist view in which the context of activity is equated with environment, which determines behavior. Barker, who has provided the most extensive analytic framework and amassed formidable data on "behavior settings," takes this position (1963a, 1963b, 1968).

> It is common observation that the *same* people and objects are transformed into different patterns as they pass from one variety of setting to another. This is exemplified by numerous pairs of behavior settings in Midwest and Yoredale with essentially the same people and objects as component parts but with quite different patterns . . . It is common observation, too, that *different* sets of people and objects exhibit the same pattern within the same variety of setting . . . obviously, whatever it is that impresses the characteristic array and flow of behavior settings upon their interior entities and events is largely independent of the persons who participate in them. *(1963b: 28)*

His analytic scheme (Barker 1968) for identifying behavior settings involves a number of components, including inhabitants, objects, space, time, behavior, leaders, and "behavior mechanisms" (e.g. thinking, eating, reading). Each contributes to the formation of settings, but to different degrees in different settings. This conception has two unique features. Behavior settings are never identified one at a time, in isolation from each other, but instead, by a process of distinguishing boundaries between contiguous settings (contiguity involves each and all of the components). Secondly, Barker started with exhaustive lists of possible behavior settings for a whole town. He experimented with an index of setting differentiation until the units derived by applying the index to a wide range of possible settings corresponded to his intuitive ideas of the contours of regular activities, rather than to subunits of activity, or to clusters of activities.[2] His work makes it difficult to ignore the possibility that there is in some respect an objective character to the organization of the arenas of activity. At the same time, the environmental determinist view has a crucial limitation. For by treating behavior as something caused by environmental configurations it excludes the *relation* between persons acting and settings as an object of investigation. But specification and analysis of this relation is a fundamental requirement for a dialectical analysis.

In contrast with a behavioral view, phenomenological analyses focus on dyadic interaction. Certainly this captures the quintessentially social character of human experience and its largely interpersonal character. But a phenomenological characterization of "context" as the environment of social interaction is akin to the cognitivist one, and rather like that in a popular game on the beaches of Southern California. Two players, each with a wooden paddle, try to hit a ball back and forth without letting it fall to the sand. The problem is that in the game, as elsewhere, it is difficult to avoid constituting activity directly in relation with the time-space locus in which it occurs. Even though partners in conversation and interaction are corporeal, embodied phenomena themselves and part of space–time *loci*, it is all too easy to conceive of the object of analysis – interaction – as in the air, out of context, or to conceive of "context" as entirely an artefact of interaction, ignoring the lessons of Barker's findings. Thus, in spite of affirmations of the *sui generis* character of social situations, phenomenological analysis of context has focused almost exclusively on its properties as interactionally constructed, its specificity, indeterminacy and superordinate character (e.g. Goffman 1964; Knorr-Cetina 1981a).

In sum, the functionalist position has limitations that a more socially interactive view of the world partially overcomes. It has difficulty accounting for the discontinuities it has constructed between individual and social order. As a theory of the person ratiocinating in isolation from the social world it has produced the psychology of rationality criticized throughout the book. The phenomenological position enjoys continuity between socially relating individuals and the society they interactively construct. But correspondingly, it is unable to account for macro-social, political–economic structures which, it appears, individuals can neither create nor negotiate directly but which somehow contribute to the public aspect of specific contexts. One has system without individual experience, the other experience without system.

A setting for activity cannot adequately be conceptualized as a weighted list of environmental components such as that of Barker, nor as an intersubjective construction, nor for that matter as a knowledge structure. And it certainly is not a direct realization of political economy, writ small. To avoid the one-dimensional character of each of these characterizations, a setting is conceived here as a *relation* between acting persons and the arenas in relation with which they act. (See Figure 6 for a diagrammatic representation of relations among arena, setting, person-acting and activity.) The supermarket, for instance, is in some respects a public and durable entity. It is a physically, economically, politically, and socially organized space-in-time. In this aspect it may be called an "arena" within which activity takes place. The supermarket as arena is the product of patterns of capital formation and political economy. It is not negotiable directly by the individual. It is outside of, yet encompasses the individual, providing a higher-order institutional framework within which setting is constituted. At the same time, for individual shoppers, the supermarket is a repeatedly experienced, personally ordered and edited version of the arena. In this aspect it may be termed a "setting" for activity. Some aisles in the supermarket do not exist for a given shopper as part of her setting, while other aisles are rich in detailed possibilities.

The relationship between these newly differentiated units of analysis, "arena" and "setting," is reflected in common uses of the term *context*. On the one hand, context connotes an identifiable, durable framework for activity, with properties that transcend the experience of individuals, exist prior to them, and are entirely beyond their control. On the other hand, context is experienced differently by different individuals. The apparently contradictory features of the term may be accounted for by recognizing that in ordinary usage context refers to relations between arena and setting rather than to a single entity. There is a distinction to be made here between the constraints imposed by the supermarket as arena and the constructable, malleable nature of the setting in relation with the activity of particular shoppers. Because a social order and the experience of it mutually entail one another, there are limits on both the obdurate and malleable aspects of every context.

A setting is generated out of a person's grocery-shopping activity and at the same time generates that activity. In short, activity is dialectically constituted in relation with the setting. For example, a shopper pauses for the first time in front of the generic products section of the market, noting both the peculiarly plain appearance of the products, divested of brand names and other information to which he is accustomed, and the relatively low prices of these products. This information provides potential new money-saving strategies. This in turn leads the shopper to attend to the generic products on subsequent shopping trips. The setting for these future trips, within the supermarket as arena, is thereby transformed; any change in the setting within the arena transforms the activity of grocery shopping. For instance, shoppers fairly often gave evidence of experiencing a delayed reaction when walking past a display. They would stop, turn back along the aisle, and pick up a previously forgotten item. Neither the setting nor the activity exists in realized form, except in relation with the other.

With these concepts in mind, the substantive analysis begins with the supermarket as arena and as setting. The ethnographic description is selective, designed to present those aspects of shopping most directly related to small-scale arithmetic problem solving. I shall argue that grocery shopping in the supermarket acts on price-arithmetic indirectly, by giving shape to the situation-specific generation of what it means for something to be problematic in the supermarket setting. This in turn shapes the character, meaning and fields for action of price arithmetic.

The supermarket as arena and setting

The arena of grocery shopping is the supermarket, an institution at the interface between consumers and suppliers of grocery commodities. Many of these commodities are characterized in consumer ideology as basic necessities, and the supermarket is the only avenue for routinely acquiring them. Typical supermarkets keep a constant stock of about 7,000 items. The arena is arranged so that grocery items remain stationary, in locations assigned by store management and suppliers, while shoppers move through the store, pushing a cart, searching for the 50 or so items they buy on a weekly basis. The arena may be conceived of as an icon of the ultimate grocery list; it is filled with partially ordered sequences of objects that may be obtained independently, laid out so that a physical progression through the entire store would bring the shopper past all 7,000 items.

A shopper's progress through the arena, however, never takes this form. The supermarket as "list" and the shopper's list are of such different orders of magnitude that the fashioning of a particular route through the market is inevitable. Part of what makes personal navigation of the arena feasible is the ordered arrangement of items in the market and the structured nature of shoppers' expectations about the process of shopping and what they will buy. The setting of grocery-shopping activity is one way of conceptualizing relations between these two kinds of structure. It may be thought of as one locus of articulation between persons-acting and the structured arena.

The resulting complementarity or synomorphy (Barker 1968) of the structure of peoples' experience and expectations as actors on the one hand, and the organization of arenas on the other, is part of what is meant by setting. Its articulatory nature is to be stressed; a setting is not simply a mental map in the mind of the shopper. Instead, it has simultaneously an independent, physical character and a potential for realization only in relation to shoppers' activity. These together constitute its essential character.

An example from the supermarket illustrates the mutual relations between setting and person-acting, such that together they generate activity in setting. A shopper and the observer were walking toward the frozen enchilada case. Until the shopper arrived in front of the enchilada display, it was as if she were at not just a physical but a cognitive distance from the enchiladas. In contrast, she and the enchiladas, in each other's presence, brought about an entirely different quality to the activity:

> Shopper: [speaking hesitantly, eyes searching the shelves to find the enchiladas]: Now these enchiladas, they're around 55 cents. They were the last time I bought them, but now every time I come . . . a higher price.
>
> Observer: Is there a particular kind of enchilada you like?
>
> Shopper: Well, they come in a, I don't know, I don't remember who puts them out. They move things around too. I don't know.
>
> Observer: What is the kind you're looking for?
>
> Shopper: Well, I don't know what brand it is. They're just enchiladas. They're put out by, I don't know. [Discovers the display of frozen Mexican dinners.] Here they are! [Speaking vigorously and firmly.] They were 65 the last time I bought them. Now they're 69. Isn't that awful?

Here, the shopper's demeanor before and after she located the enchiladas points to the relevant contrast. There was, on the one hand, her vague characterization of the product she intended to purchase before she located it and, on the other hand, her precise description and vigorous tone once it was in sight. This difference – between activity and setting in transition (before she found the enchiladas) and activity in setting (as she finds them) – is ubiquitous, illustrating what is meant by the integral and specific character of particular activities in particular settings.

Grocery-shopping activity is made up of relatively discrete segments like the enchilada purchase. The shopper stops in front of one display after another and goes through a process of deciding which item to transfer from shelf to cart. In most cases it is possible to face the display, locate an item, and take it from the shelf without moving away from an initial position. Within a particular shopping segment, size and brand are taken into account in that order in making decisions, while quantity and price are considered at the end of decision processes (Murtaugh, 1985a). The complexity of search processes varies across items: many selections are made without apparent consideration, as part of the routine of replenishing staple supplies. More often than not, however, shoppers can produce an account for why they routinely purchase a particular item rather than an available alternative.

Much of the decision making which occurs as shoppers place themselves in physical relation with one display after another is of a qualitative nature. Shoppers care about the taste, nutritional value, dietary implications, and aesthetics of particular groceries. Store management and commodity suppliers respond with large amounts of persuasive information about products, much of it printed on the item itself. Shoppers face overwhelming amounts of information, only a small part of which is relevant in the process of making their grocery choices, and then only when they establish a new choice or update an old result. In general, through time, the experienced shopper transforms an information-rich arena into an information-specific setting. These transformations of past experience, fashioned in relation with the supermarket setting, form the basis of what appear to be habitual procedures for collecting items purchased regularly.

Conventional assumptions treat calculation as a cognitive function and its context merely as a stage on which action occurs. But activity-in-setting, seamlessly stretched across persons-acting and setting often turns the latter into a calculating device. One shopper found an unusually high-priced package of cheese in a bin. The weights of the packages he had already inspected varied within only a small range. Weight, price per pound and price were printed on each package but not the steps in the calculation of price per pound. He suspected an error. To solve the problem, he searched through the bin for a package weighing the same amount and inferred from the discrepancy between their prices that his suspicions were correct. Had the calculation not been fashioned in relation with the setting, he would have had to divide weight into price, mentally, and compare the result with the price per pound printed on the label. Calculation of weight/price relations devolved on the structured relations between packages of cheese and the activity of the shopper who searched among them for an instructive comparison. Another shopper exploited the fact that packages of chicken thighs each contained six pieces. She compared package prices and chose a cheap one to ensure small size, explaining that she would select a moderate-priced package when she wanted larger serving portions. In this case also, weight/price relations were enacted with setting. The Weight Watchers' inventions for incorporating measurement into cooking activity provide a host of additional examples (de la Rocha 1986).

Shoppers describe themselves as engaged in a routine chore, making habitual purchases. The setting and the general intentions of the shopper ("doing weekly chores," "grocery shopping, again") come into juxtaposition repeatedly in such a way as to make it both customary and useful for the shopper to claim that shopping is "the same" from one occasion to the next. The similarity is a production and a claim by the shopper, and it is more than a matter of mechanical reproduction. For example, grocery lists almost always include nonspecific categories such as "treats" for children. The category is reproduced from week to week, but the specific treats vary, often in response to treat-like features of the setting (e.g. a candy sale, a new fruit in season).

Shoppers do not usually organize their activity to conform to the order of their grocery lists, which would involve greater physical effort than ordering it to conform to the market layout. One commented that, "I usually shop in the department that I happen to be in. I check my list to see if I have anything on the list, to save me from running all over the store." Saving physical effort is a useful rationale for using the structuring resources of the setting to organize the sequence of decisions about grocery items. But a more general – and generative – principle is at work. Personal grocery lists order items differently than these same items are organized in the supermarket arena. Within grocery shopping the segments of activity, like the items on the list, are relatively independent, and hence one segment is rarely a sequentially ordered condition for another. Almost by default, then, the structuring resources of the setting (e.g. the shoppers' versions of the layout of goods on the shelves and aisles) contribute proportionally more to the structuring of activity than the inventory of items to be purchased. This gives the appearance of a choice between mental and physical effort, when the choice is in fact between a more or a less compellingly structured component of the whole activity-in-setting. When the structure of shoppers' lists does involve interdependent items (e.g. buy cream only if the mushrooms look good), the resource for sequencing activity might well be the list instead of the market layout, or some mix of the two.

In sum, an activity-in-setting that is labeled by its practitioners as a routine chore is in fact a complex improvisation. Descriptions of the activity as "habitual" and "routine" lead shoppers to interpret their own activity as repetitive and highly similar across episodes, rather than to treat its nonmechanical, generative variability as a defining charac-teristic. These considerations must surely affect the manner in which shoppers come to see certain parts of activity-in-setting as smoothly repetitious and others as problematic.

Arithmetic activity in grocery shopping

Grocery-shopping activity in the supermarket setting generates fields for action within which shoppers will experience some events as problematic. Grocery-shopping dilemmas in turn are fields for action for arithmetic problem solution or resolution. In the dialectical relations between "routine" grocery shopping and the supermarket setting, repeated interactions produce a relatively smooth "fit" between activity and setting, streamlining each in relation to the other, and generating expectations that the activity will unfold unproblematically and effortlessly. In relation to this expectation "problems" take on meaning as conflicting possibilities for activity, or troubles with ongoing activity, that snag or interrupt the process of shopping. Where both expectations and practice over time lead to relatively unproblematic activity, snags and interruptions are recognized, indeed generated, so as to be limited in scope, in relation to the activity as a whole. (As part of a routine activity they must themselves, in some sense also be routine.) Shoppers generate snags in collaboration with the setting. Likewise, in this specific setting, the articulation between person-acting and setting is such that problem-solving processes are on the whole malleable in relation to the shopper's ongoing shopping activity. Persons-acting are free to transform, solve or resolve a problem, or abandon it in favor of other options. In the parlance of the AMP, they "own" their own problems. Generated in mid-action, while deciding what particular item to transfer from shelf to cart, problems are born of values in conflict (the big one? the cheapest?) and are themselves actions upon the world.

A second factor shaping fields for arithmetic activity in grocery shopping is the nature of choices to be made by the shopper. The supermarket is thought of by consumers as a locus of abundant choices, for which the stock of thousands of items constitutes the "evidence." But this view is contradicted by a different order of circumstances: the shopper cannot provide food for the family if she leaves the supermarket empty-handed due to attacks of indecision. That is, the shopper, faced with abundant alternatives, cannot avoid making choices. Conversely, because choices must be made, it is to the seller's advantage to proliferate decision criteria in the shopping setting – structuring resources for the process of arriving at a choice. The shopper's experience of choices as abundant helps to maintain the conflict between varied choices and the necessity of choosing. This conflict is not itself generally recognized, much less viewed as problematic, by shoppers, but in conjunction with the routine and dialectical character of shopping it contributes to the structuring of arithmetic activity.

These characteristics – the generative routine and the contradictory quality of routine choices – together with the dialectical form of activity-in-setting shape the rationalizing character of arithmetic calculation in the supermarket. The term *rationalization* has been proposed as a hallmark of everyday decision-making (e.g. Bartlett, 1958). It is used in common parlance to refer to after-the-fact justification of an action or opinion. The term contrasts sharply with folk characterizations of rational decision-making in which evidence should provide logical motivation *for*, and before, a conclusion. But activity-in-setting, in dialectical terms, is complex enough that a description of the activity as "marshaling the evidence after the fact" does not take into account contradictory, multiple relations between evidence and conclusions. In decision processes such as those in grocery shopping, it is impossible to specify whether a rational account of choice is constructed before or after the fact. It occurs both before and after different orders of fact; before a unique item is chosen but after the determination that a choice must be made. The multiple relations of evidence and conclusion is not, then, a matter of "domestic thinking" or "unscientific use of evidence" but is characteristic of the constitution of practice.

Quantitative relations are assembled in various forms in grocery shopping, among which are price and quantity comparisons. These occur at the end of largely qualitative decision-making processes when a person-acting faces a dilemma and the elimination of alternative grocery items comes to a halt before a choice has been made. It was pointed out (chapter 5) that if arithmetic is utilized, it is employed when the number of choices still under consideration is not greater than three and rarely greater than two, and precisely at moments when shoppers have no strong qualitative preferences (Murtaugh 1985a). Arithmetic problem solving is both an expression of and a medium for dealing with these stalled decision processes. It is, among other things, a move outside the qualitative characteristics of a product to its characterization in terms of a standard of value, money.

That arithmetic is a common medium of problem solving among shoppers is itself an interesting problem. It returns us to the discussion of relations between math and money in chapter 6: the juxtaposition of money with math in school math lessons strongly implies the technical, value-free, "natural" character of money by disguising it as a form of arithmetic in school. This normative characterization gives arithmetic in the supermarket, still intertwined with money, a rich and specialized meaning. For the terms in which arithmetic is used there to justify choice are just the symbolically powerful images of rationality, utility and objectivity that were earlier argued to pervade the association of math and money in school-based socialization. In the supermarket, calculation may be the most immediate means at hand for asserting the rationality of grocery choices when qualitative criteria of choice have been exhausted. Indeed, a good case can be made that shoppers' commitment to rational decision-making is evidenced by their justificatory calculations and explanations, for the alternative is to declare that choices as constrained as those for which price arithmetic are invoked are arbitrary and hence not worth the effort required to make them. There is only one instance in the shopping transcripts in which someone appeared to recognize this. This shopper, referring to a television commercial in which an animated package of margarine gets in an argument at the dinner table, selected that brand and commented ironically:

Shopper: I'll get the one that talks back.
Observer: Why?
Shopper: Others would have been more trouble.

The location of math in shoppers' decision processes provides persuasive evidence that price arithmetic contributes more to constructing the incorrigibility of "rationality" than to the instrumental elaboration of preference structures.

In sum, it appears that arithmetic is more structured by than structuring of shopping activity. Justifying choices, just before and after the fact, is a more appropriate description of its typical character. And in contrast with its instrumental role, the meanings and values condensed in calculation as an expressive form are played upon with considerable frequency and intensity.

Dialectical arithmetic processes

It is time to reconsider in dialectical terms, as gap–closing processes, the best-buy calculations discussed in earlier chapters. A dialectical account of problem-solving procedures in the supermarket may help to explain two conspicuous puzzles in the grocery shopping data. The first is the virtually error-free arithmetic performance by shoppers who made frequent errors in parallel problems in formal testing situations. Secondly, in arithmetic practice in the supermarket shoppers frequently make more than one attempt to calculate in the course of buying a single grocery item. On average, shoppers carried out 2.5 calculations for each item that served as an occasion for arithmetic activity. Further, while the nearly error-free character of best-buy problem solutions is a remarkably clear finding, intermediate steps in sequences of calculations were often in error. This must be accounted for as well.

It seems likely, given the routine nature of grocery-shopping activity and the location of price arithmetic at the end of decision processes, that shoppers have already assigned rich content and shape to a problem resolution by the time arithmetic becomes an obvious next step. Problem solving under these circumstances is an iterative, transformational process. It involves, on the one hand, what the shopper knows and what the setting holds that might help and, on the other hand, what the solution or resolution looks like. The activity of finding something problematic subsumes a good deal of knowledge about what would constitute a (re)solution, or a method for arriving at one. In the course of grocery shopping many of a problem's parameters are assembled in the process of deciding, up to a point, what to purchase. Consider again the shopper who wanted to find out if the price on a package of cheese was in error. He was relatively certain *which* cheese package was inconsistent with the rest before he established whether there was really an inconsistency or not. The dialectical process in the particular context of everyday arithmetic is one of gap closing between resolution characteristics and information and procedural possibilities.

Thus a change in either resolution shape or resources of information and activity leads to a reconstitution of the other. The act of identifying a problem changes, dialectically, the salience of setting characteristics. These in turn suggest, more powerfully than before, procedures for generating a specific solution. Information and procedural knowledge accessed by eye, hand, or transformed in activity, make possible a move toward the solution or suggest a change in the solution shape that draws it closer to the information at hand. In sum, gap-closing arithmetic involves first establishing a field for generative action (problem and resolution shape) as well as that action itself. "Problem solving" is part of an articulatory phenomenon constituted between persons-acting and the settings of activity.

An extended segment of a grocery-shopping expedition may be used in illustration. But before doing so, it would be useful to reflect on the method used for observing and recording ongoing activity in the supermarket. It illustrates the claim (chapter 5) that forms of inquiry, no matter how unobtrusive, give shape to the activity observed. To begin with, introducing an observer into "ordinary" activity changes the activity whose "ordinariness" recommended it for study. The research can only take form as a resolution, not a solution, to this dilemma. Before entering the supermarket shoppers strapped a tape recorder over their shoulder and were asked to "think out loud" while proceeding through the store. Shoppers were told that the researcher accompanying them was interested in learning about their shopping procedures, whatever they might be. Shoppers felt more comfortable describing their behavior in conversation rather than appearing to talk to themselves as they moved through the store. So as they walked through the store, the researcher talked with the shopper. This arrangement made it possible to clarify shoppers' comments, and to indicate aspects of the shopping situation which would otherwise not be clear on tape. It also made it possible to ask questions about why shoppers rejected various alternatives to the products that were selected. The researcher tried not to interpret the situation for the shopper, but rather to clarify the shopper's ongoing activity where it related to research issues. This did not, of course, eliminate the impact of interaction between actor and observer. Rather than ignore it we have tried to take it into account in the analysis.

It seems probable that interaction between the shopper and the observer in the example gave a special character to the activity segments to be discussed here, perhaps not a difference in kind so much as in emphasis. The shopper may well have thought of the observer as the embodiment and arbiter of normative shopping practices, while the observer believed his own role was to investigate empirically the appropriateness of normative models of rational problem solving. The combined effect of the assumptions each had about the observer's role was to intensify the focus on rational accounting in terms common to folk beliefs and much of consumer economics, at the expense of the qualitative character of decision making which in fact led to most purchase selections in the supermarket (even) during the observational sessions.

In the shopping transcript, a 43-year-old woman with four children discusses the price of noodles, while moving toward the noodle display:

> Shopper: Let me show you something, if I can find it. I mean talk about price. Last week they had that on sale I think for 59 cents.
> Observer: Spaghetti?
> Shopper: [With the vagueness associated with imminent arrival]: Yeah, or 40 – I can't remember . . . That's not the one.

Table 21 *Prices and weights for alternative grocery choices*

Brand	Weight	Price	Price per pound
American Beauty noodles	24 oz.	$1.02	68¢/lb
Perfection noodles	32 oz.	$1.12	56¢/lb
American Beauty noodles	48 oz.	$1.79	$59\frac{2}{3}$¢/lb
American Beauty noodles	64 oz.	$1.98	$49\frac{1}{2}$¢/lb

The shopper shortly found what she was searching for and, transforming an old result into practice, took a package of elbow noodles from the shelf and put it in her cart. It was a 32-ounce package of Perfection brand noodles, costing $1.12. This decision prefigured and shaped the course of the subsequent conversation and calculations. The latter were best-buy problems, comparing price per unit of weight for pairs of packages (Table 21). The other three packages weighed 24 ounces, 48 ounces and 64 ounces. The difference in price per unit was not a linear function of size (the 64–ounce package was clearly the best buy).

> Observer: [Acknowledging the shopper's choice of the 32-ounce package]: Perfection.
> Shopper: Yeah, this is what I usually buy. It's less expensive than – is that American Beauty?
> Observer: Yeah.
> Shopper: That, what I need right now is the elbow macaroni. And I always buy it in two-pound [packages]. I'm out of this.

The statement, "It's less expensive than . . . American Beauty," established the point of reference for comparative calculations. The statement, "I always buy it in two-pound packages," established an initial resolution shape. This statement also provided evidence both that the choice was an old result, a matter of past experience, and that numerical simplification work has occurred, since the weight on the package was printed as "32 ounces" rather than as "2 pounds." The shopper expanded on the qualitative choice criteria that have shaped her purchases in the past:

> Observer: This seems like a big package of elbow noodles, and you add these to the macaroni?
> Shopper: I add some, I just take a handful and add it to the rest, to the other packaged macaroni, 'cause I add macaroni to it. Plus I use that for my goulash.

> Observer: For the goulash. OK. And you like this particular kind? Are there other alternatives here?
>
> Shopper: Yeah. There's large elbow. This is really the too-large economy bag. I don't know if I, probably take me about six months to use this one. And I just, I don't have the storage room for that kind of stuff. I guess if I rearranged my cupboards, maybe I could, but it's a hassle . . . I don't know, I just never bought that huge size like that. I never checked the price, though, on it. But being American Beauty it probably costs more even in that large size.

For qualitative reasons (e.g. the family's customary meals, storage capacity in the kitchen) the shopper has previously avoided purchase of the large size. But she was caught in a public situation in a discussion in which she would like to display her shrewdness as a shopper. And she considered best-buy purchases the best evidence of "rational frugality" in this setting, even though qualitative criteria took precedence for her, as for all shoppers, most of the time.

The next interchange started a process of simplification of the arithmetic comparison. The shopper transformed large numbers of ounces into a small number of pounds:

> Observer: That's what, that's six . . . [probably beginning to say "64 ounces."]
>
> Shopper: It's four pounds, and what did I buy? Two? Oh, there is a big savings. Hmmm, I might think about that next time, figure out where I can keep it. I actually try to look for better prices. I used, I guess I used to, and I was such in the habit of it that some of the products I'm buying now are leftovers from when I was cutting costs. And I usually look. If they have something on sale, you know, a larger package of macaroni or spaghetti or something, I'll buy it.

The shopper's concern with describing her shopping in terms of utilitarian rationality was evident in the preemptive character she attributed to the financial evidence; her decision to reject the large-size package on the basis of kitchen storage capacity (clearly stated earlier), was not sufficient when challenged to override the opposite choice on monetary criteria. She placed a general value on price as a criterion for choice and at the same time emphasized that her current financial state did not require such choices. This had the effect of highlighting the absolute nature of the value. It produced a half-commitment to future action, which did not seem likely to occur once the pressure to produce a rational account for the observer was removed. She also adopted a strategy of, "If I can't be right, at least I can demonstrate my objectivity," both by admitting she was wrong and by accepting quantitative, symbolically objective criteria as overridingly legitimate.

Meanwhile her calculation that four pounds of American Beauty noodles would be cheaper than two pounds of Perfection noodles, was correct.

The next segment follows almost immediately in the transcript. The shopper saw an opportunity to compare packages which offered a counter-example to the conclusion that the large size is generally the better buy. If correct, it would have softened the impression that she had violated a general principle ("bigger is cheaper") in her choice of noodles:

> Shopper: But this one, you don't save a thing. Here's three pounds for a dollar 79, and there's one pound for 59.

However, one of the two packages of American Beauty spaghetti noodles, that she believed to be a one-pound bag, weighed only 12 ounces. She quickly noticed the weight printed on the package and corrected herself:

> Shopper: No, I'm sorry, that's 12 ounces. No, it's a savings.

These two statements involved two calculations. In some form the first was probably one pound is 60 cents so it's 60 cents per pound. Three pounds at 60 cents per pound would be $1.80, so they are almost the same price per pound. Given that the weight of the smaller bag was less than a pound, the equations were no longer equivalent, and the three-pound bag was the better buy. Only a "less than" relation would be required to arrive at this conclusion.

The arithmetic procedures used by the shopper followed a pattern. She started with a probable resolution, but inspection of the evidence and comparison with the expected conclusion led her to reject it. "No, I'm sorry," was her acknowledgment that the initial solution was in error. Pulled up short by the weight information from the package, she recalculated and obtained a new conclusion. This pattern is an example of gap-closing movement between the expected shape of the resolution and the information and calculation devices at hand, all in pursuit of a resolution that is germane to the activity that created its field for action in the first place. The arithmetic would not be as simple in its conventional representation with paper and pencil:

$1.79/48 oz. = $.037/oz.
.037 × 16 = $.59/lb.

It required an active process of simplication to transform the inform-ation on the packages into a form that was easier to manipulate.

Once the shopper concluded that the large bag of noodles was a better buy than the small one, she commented:

> Shopper: They had some on sale there one day, and the large package was like 69 for two pounds, and it was 59 for one pound. And it was just such a difference, I, you know, it was almost an insult to the shopper to have the two on the same shelf side by side.

As if the store assumed that shoppers had so little capacity for rational calculation that they might not notice a difference of such magnitude between the two items.

She concluded with another two-round calculation in gap-closing form. This episode was initiated by the observer, who addressed not the size difference, but the monetary one, emphasizing its magnitude. The observer may have been trying to acknowledge the shopper's amended views, for he repeated her previous conclusion:

> Observer: Well, you seem to think this was a real big difference, then, this four pounds of –
> Shopper: Yeah, that is. That's two dollars for four pounds [*referring to the American Beauty elbow noodles*], this is a dollar [*referring to the Perfection elbow noddles in her cart*]. That's 50 cents a pound and I just bought two pounds for a dollar 12 which is 60. So there is a difference.

That is, the shopper began by simplifying $1.98 to two dollars and $1.12 to one dollar. But the calculation led to the conclusion that both were 50 cents per pounds. This did not fit the established resolution shape, "a big difference" between the smaller and larger bags of noodles. She then transformed the weight from 64 oz. to two pounds, and produced an intermediate solution: four pounds of noodles for two dollars would cost 50 cents per pound. This served two purposes. It was a means to recheck information printed on the package, and it was the first step in the next round of calculation. The second round was a similar price comparison, but with a "more than" relation ($1.12 is more than one dollar). The shopper rounded up from 56¢/pound to 60¢, reiterating her earlier conclusion about the direction of difference in price.

Dialectically ordered problem-solving processes are difficult to analyze, since one characteristic of gap-closing arithmetic is that individual moves serve multiple functions. The dilemma may be resolved by giving up the goal of assigning arithmetic problems to unique locations – in the head or on the shelf – or labeling one element in a problem-solving process as a "calculation procedure," another as a "checking procedure." It may be difficult, even, to distinguish the problem from its resolution.

The problem about cheese and peanut butter sandwiches (chapter 6) led to similar observations about the multiple and mutually constitutive character of problem-solving processes. Another problem posed to new members of Weight Watchers in their kitchens provides a further illustration. As in the exercise concerning peanut butter sandwiches, the dieters were asked to prepare their lunch to meet specifications laid out by the observer. In this case they were to fix a serving of cottage cheese, supposing that the amount allotted for the meal was three-quarters of the two-thirds cup the program allowed. The problem solver in this example began the task muttering that he had taken a calculus course in college (an acknowledgment of the discrepancy between school math prescriptions for practice and his present circumstances).[3] Then after a pause he suddenly announced that he had "got it!" From then on he appeared certain he was correct, even before carrying out the procedure. He filled a measuring cup two-thirds full of cottage cheese, dumped it out on a cutting board, patted it into a circle, marked a cross on it, scooped away one quadrant, and served the rest. Thus, "take three-quarters of two-thirds of a cup of cottage cheese" was not just the problem statement but also the solution to the problem and the procedure for solving it. The setting was part of the calculating process and the solution was simply the problem statement, enacted with the setting. At no time did the Weight Watcher check his procedure against a paper and pencil algorithm, which would have produced $\frac{3}{4}$ cup $\times \frac{2}{3}$ cup $= \frac{1}{2}$ cup. Instead, the coincidence of problem, setting, and enactment was the means by which checking took place.

The calculations made by the shopper in the supermarket were possible because of her active transformation of succeeding versions of them. In order to do the complex work of simplifying problems, she needed a clear grasp of "what she was doing." "Knowing what one is doing" is possible within a field for action, in activity in context. Then, faced with a snag, a partial form of the solution already has been produced. Checking procedures, in this analysis, are an ongoing process of comparing the current state of knowledge of the problem and the current definition of its resolution. The intention is to evaluate the plausibility of both procedure and resolution in relation to previously recognized resolution shapes rather than by comparison of two linear problem-solving procedures.[4]

The shaping of problem resolution activity within ongoing activity and the juxtaposition of various aspects of problem solving makes it relatively easy for the problem solver to appropriate the problem, represent, enact, or transform it into a different problem. People sometimes judge problems too difficult or time consuming to resolve in the context of grocery shopping, however. This is most likely to occur when relations among numbers are intransigent to decomposition or transformation strategies. This is a major factor leading to the abandonment of arithmetic and resolution of snags through other options. In one example, two family members were shopping, a woman, 45, and her 15-year-old daughter. They were in the market with the observers. The mother was intent on buying ketchup but turned to the barbecue sauce next to the ketchup when her daughter called attention to it:

> Daughter: Do you want some Chris and Pits barbecue sauce? We're almost out.
> Shopper: [to the observer]: Heinz has a special [on ketchup]. I have a coupon in here for that. And I was going to make spareribs one night this week, which I didn't mention to you, but that was in my mind now that she mentions the sauce. [Examines her coupons.] I want to see if their price on their barbecue sauce is going to be as – we usually buy Chris and Pits. [Notices a Heinz ketchup coupon.] Now see, this is the one that I was telling you about. But they don't have the 44-ounce ketchup here. [Continues searching through the coupons until she finds the one for the barbecue sauce.] Okay, 25 cents off any size flavor of Kraft Barbecue Sauce, including the new Sweet and Sour, which I would like to try because I'm going to have spareribs. But if you notice they don't have it. Oh, here they do. Hickory.
> Observer: Kraft Hickory Smoked.
> Shopper: Yeah, but they don't have the Sweet and Sour. [To her daughter.] You see it, D? Nope. Okay, see now, in a situation like this it's difficult to figure out which is the better buy. Because this is – I don't have my glasses on, how many ounces is that, D? [Refers to Kraft Hickory Smoked.]
> Daughter: 18.
> Shopper: 18 ounces for 89, and this is? [Refers to Chris and Pits.]
> Daughter: One pound, seven ounces –
> Shopper: 23 ounces for a dollar 17. [Speaks ironically.] That's when I whip out my calculator and see which is the better buy.

The shopper simplified the problem by putting both weights into the same units. But it was difficult to simplify further than 18 ounces for 89 cents compared with 23 ounces for a dollar and 17 cents. Though both prices were near multiples of five, the weights were unwieldy to transform or decompose. The shopper's comment about using a calculator can be interpreted, from the tone of her voice, as a move to abandon the calculation. (She did have a calculator in her purse, which she previously told the observer she used rather frequently in the supermarket, though on this shopping trip it was used in the purchase of just one grocery item.)

She made one more attempt to solve the problem before abandoning it definitely:

Observer: So what are you going to do in this case?
Shopper: In this case what have we got here? I'll try to do it quickly in my head . . .
            They don't have the large, um –
Daughter: Kraft Barbecue Sauce?
Shopper: Yeah, so what I'm going to do is, I'm going to wait and go to another
            store, when I'm at one of the other stores, because I'd like to try this.

Supermarket settings and grocery-shopping activity are rich in options other than price arithmetic (e.g. shop elsewhere, or serve a different meal), and there also appears to be a low penalty level for abandoning calculation in favor of some other criterion of choice.

It seems difficult to address the accuracy and frequency of multiple calculations in the supermarket data with linear templates for solving problems. But explanations follow readily when problem solving is viewed as the resolution of dilemmas through gap-closing activity, that is, as a dialectical relation which seamlessly joins means and ends, resolution shapes and snag repair. Accuracy is partly the result of the structuring of quantitative relations into the ongoing flow of activity. The "logic" of quantitative relations is generated by the person-acting in activity, and if their meaning blurs or is dissolved, the problem would simply cease to exist. When processes of quantitative transformation in everyday activity are self-generated, are an integral part of ongoing activity, often more closely related to other aspects of activity than to each other, reflecting and expressing much more than their literal content, they are not likely to lose their meaning. Correspondingly, they are unlikely to be translated into inappropriate numerical operations, orders of magnitude, or resolution shapes. Also, circumstances that make it feasible to abandon a calculation lead to fewer completed calculations, but more correct ones, than if no option but calculation were available.

The repeated calculations within a single episode may be explained in similar terms. Gap-closing processes of arithmetic require that calculating occurs in dialectically iterative "rounds." Multiple rounds are possible because the problem solver acting in setting generates problem and resolution shape at the same time and each entails the other. Since they are mutually constitutive, they change together. Procedures which operate on both problem and resolution are often juxtaposed, and are enacted with and in the setting. Errors, which are frequent in early rounds, can therefore be recognized and instruct. They are part of the dialectical process of arriving at a resolution.

Arithmetic practice varies and changes within grocery shopping activity-in-setting. The effortful process of snag repair leads to a choice – to the moving of an item from shelf to shopping cart and the resumption of the rhythm of routine activity. Snags are routinely transformed into rationally accountable choices. These choices replace both problem and resolution effort in future grocery-shopping episodes. But such choices create terms for the occurrence of new snags, by becoming baselines for new comparisons or when the criteria invoked in longstanding rational accounts become obsolete (e.g. because of rising prices, changes in relations of price and quantity, changes in family composition or food preferences).

As a whole, grocery-shopping activity changes over time, in a changing arena, in relation to varying activities-in-other-settings, across repeated episodes. Shoppers assume (actively) the routine character of the activity, partially to domesticate this variability. But if they are to shape it effectively there must be scope within it for constructing, transforming, updating, and reflecting changes occurring in the setting and elsewhere. Over time this requires smooth routines partly because they enable shopper-setting interaction to focus on instructive novelties.

Snag repair contrasts with a routine unproblematic choice, an activity-setting relation at its simplest. The shopper's daughter in the last example was part of her mother's setting. The shopper did not initiate a decision process about barbecue sauce. Her daughter pointed it out. That is, the shopper and the setting brought a choice into being. This was reflected in the shopper's comment, "that was in my mind, now that she mentions the sauce." The relevant aspect of the setting is often not a person; a bottle of sauce on the shelf is also part of it, and an equivalent event would be the shopper who does a double-take as she passes a display and backtracks slightly to transfer the (mutually, constitutively) "remembered" barbecue sauce from shelf to cart. Each is a moment in the dialectical constitution of activity and setting.

Conclusions

The accuracy of everyday calculation and its situated assembly within ongoing activities, challenges claims for the hegemony of school-taught math over everyday practice. I have tried to demonstrate that such claims do not hold up under empirical scrutiny. But these claims *are* accepted as valid by the jpfs whose everyday practice invalidates them.

Indeed, we found that the participants in the AMP were unaware of their efficacy at math in nonschool-like settings. This, along with their collusive production of school algorithmic math procedures in test and experimental settings, and their use of math in rational account production (e.g. the noodle buying episode), are major characteristics of the role of everyday math practice in the web of relations which includes schooling and cognitive theory.

The analysis of gap-closing arithmetic is intended to give direct, though only illustrative, evidence of situationally-specific arithmetic practice, and to support the argument (chapter 6) that "problem solving" has been given a misleading preeminence in cognitive theory. The assignment of unwarranted theoretical centrality to problem solving reflects a failure to comprehend these activities as practices *sui generis*. But the reduction of cognition to problem solving *per se* simply cannot grasp the generative nature of arithmetic practice and its constitution as part of ongoing activity in context. In the theoretical terms developed here, persons-acting and settings, in activity, together generate dilemmas and resolution shapes. Moreover, they do so simultaneously. Very often a process of resolution occurs in the setting with the enactment of the problem, and it may transform the problem for the solver. These relations are, finally, generative and dialectical in nature. The implications of this conclusion for everyday practice more generally will be taken up in the final chapter.

8

OUTDOORS: A SOCIAL ANTHROPOLOGY OF COGNITION IN PRACTICE

This expedition to explore the little known territory of everyday activity has been guided by a series of questions: What would happen to theorizing about cognition if investigations were moved to the sites of the activity whose interpretation was under debate? What changes in theoretical orientation would be required in order to make such travels seem sensible and of value in the first place? What further theoretical reformulations would follow from a multi-faceted approach to observation and analysis of everyday activity? The argument has been formulated as a journey from the laboratory into the everyday world. I have tried, chapter by chapter, to move the analysis, and the theory as well, out of the laboratory and the problematic that locates investigation of cognition in that setting (only), and past contradictory positions which attempt to keep one foot in the door. The concept of "context" has been shifted out of "conceptual spaces" and correspondingly, "understanding" appears to belong directly in the experienced world, in activity. The empirical investigation, broadening from laboratory to ethnographic studies and simulation experiments across settings, reached its present limits in the previous chapter, with the analysis of arithmetic practice in the supermarket.

But this analysis was not a closed one. It referred beyond itself to the sociocultural order implicated in the structuring resources that give to, and take their shape from, persons-acting, activity, and context. There is a second reason for concern with a more encompassing theory of sociocultural order, which may be laid out in a chain of interconnected propositions. I have argued against the view that the cognitive holdings of the person are stable, constant and theorizable while their contexts are specific, variable and untheorizable.[1] Instead, persons-acting, arenas, and settings appear to be implicated together in the very constitution of activity. The task here is to delimit their meaning in mutually consistent terms. But if a theory of person and a theory of context presuppose each other, they must be very awkward to invent unless embedded in a more inclusive theory of social order.

Thus, both empirical studies of practice and theoretical critique point to the usefulness of delineating relations between practice and constitutive order. Questions about the framing of practice follow from the problematic developed here, on several different grounds: (1) If the context of activity, however defined, is included in the analysis of activity, then questions about *its* context are also relevant. In the present case, for instance, it is difficult to understand the context of arithmetic practice in the supermarket without considering the constitutive order which shapes both the experienced dilemmas of the shopper and the supermarket as an arena in relation with which setting and, further, activity, are constituted. (2) A critical stance towards conventional premises and analytic questions (e.g. those of conventional cognitive theory) has transformed old assumptions into objects of analysis. This is a practice of reflection on practice, directly concerned with the contexts of practice. (3) To focus on whole-person activity rather than on thinking as separate from doing implies a negation of the conventional division between mind and body. This negation is also reflected in the claim that "cognition" is seamlessly distributed across persons, activity and setting. This in turn implies that thought (embodied and enacted) is situated in socially and culturally structured time and space. This object world, viewed as partially constructed with persons-acting, is an essential aspect of activity. Its constitution is a matter of sociocultural order writ large. (4) Finally, if we claim that activity is situationally specific, it implies that objects of analysis are points of cultural–historical conjuncture, and should be analyzed in those terms.

These four claims represent lines of argument that have been carried through the project as a whole, and they have yet to be resolved. The most general task in bringing the argument to a close is to reformulate relations between the level of analysis of social practice in the everyday world and that of the constitutive order in relations with which experience in the lived-in world is dialectically formed. The first and second claims together suggest an inquiry into how terms and relations whose definitions were fashioned in the course of old debates, for example "culture," fit into a newly formulated theory of practice within a theory of social order. We may also discuss "the person," not as a disembodied mind, but as a person-acting, in setting. The fourth claim, concerning the cultural and historical specificity of situated activity, reopens two issues raised earlier. One is an account of the sources of continuity in everyday activity. For to argue that activity is fashioned in situationally specific forms does change the terms of debate about continuity but does not resolve it. It was suggested earlier that it would be useful to analyze cognitive theory as a manifestation of Western culture. As the analysis has developed, I have discussed a web of cultural meanings concerning "scientific" and "expert" thinking, and the scholastically structured ideology and activity-structured practice of arithmetic pervasively institutionalized in schools, experimental procedures, and everyday life. I have focused on the peculiarities of "problem solving" as a culture-specific vision of mental activity, and on rationality as the overarching cultural preoccupation which gives form to the vision if not to the practice. But arguments about cognitive theory as a cultural practice and as an operationalization of beliefs about rationality, and the alternative to this view posed by the math project, must be brought together. This last problem is addressed first, and leads to a discussion of the theory of social order more generally, followed by a discussion of the person-acting, and finally, the problem of the continuity of activity across settings.

The cultural specificity of "rational problem solving"

It follows from the description of math in everyday practice, from its situational specificity and accuracy, that theoretically charged, unexamined, normative models of thinking lose their descriptive and predictive power when research is moved to everyday settings and relaxes its grip on the structuring of activity. I made two general objections to the normative models ubiquitously applied by cognitive scientists to the interpretation of discontinuities of knowledge and procedure between experimental and everyday situations. First, the norms embodied in these models are culturally and historically specific ones. Secondly, the fashioning of normative models of thinking from particular, "scientific," culturally valued, named bodies of knowledge is a cultural act.

Practices common to both cognitive research and schooling treat arithmetic, logic, and monetary calculations as exemplars of "rational thought." Arithmetic, measurement devices, and the management of money are taught and used as expressions of rational means/ends relations. Math practice is described as general mental exercise. Math in conventional pedagogical guises is presented in the form of capsule puzzles – "problems" – with explicit, prefabricated goals, employing only "factual" information; procedures are construed to be value-free, technical means. Such propositions are based on a concept of problem solving as a series of objective, rational means to pre-specified ends (e.g. Simon 1980).[2]

These taken-for-granted beliefs about relations among higher cognitive functions, problem solving, means/ends relations and rationality have been repeatedly subjected to critical analysis. Social theorists draw attention to connections among means–ends relations, mathematics, the economic locus of the concept of rationality and problem solving as higher cognitive function. Sahlins speaks of rationality as a system of meaning, a product of historical circumstances which have made the economic institutions of Western culture the locus of generation of its symbolic systems (1976: 211). There are widespread critiques of the way in which industrial society commodifies not only labor but also persons (Sohn-Rethel 1978), bodies (Turner 1985) and surely mind as well. "Logic, as Marx has it, is the money of the mind, and no matter how dialectical, it always expresses a reified and alienated mediation of man and reality" (Warren 1984: 50). Adorno argued that there is a special relationship between the commoditization of exchange and labor in capitalist society and the focus on means/ends relations in the social sciences:

> The over-valuation of method is truly a symptom of the consciousness of our time. Sociologically speaking, it is closely related to the general tendency to substitute means for ends. In the last instance, this tendency is related to the nature of the commodity: to the fact that everything is seen as functional, as a being-for-another and no longer as something which exists in itself.   *(Adorno 1977: 131)*

Furthermore:

> The reification of logic . . . "refers back to the commodity form whose identity exists in the 'equivalence' of exchange value."   *(quoted in Jay 1973: 69)*

This is a culture that transforms subjectivity into a physics (Dreyfus 1979), cognitive science into mind/brain relations, and the social construction of mind into "universal cognitive functions." And what else are "cognitive universals" but the very transformation of Western beliefs Sahlins' has claimed as a hallmark of *this* culture; we insist on giving to the cultural the status of "the natural" (see chapter 4).

If rationality is a key *cultural* conception of meaning and value, it calls into question the idea that rationality represents a mode of human thought, an unchallengeable canon of mental processing whose application is sufficient to establish the superiority of its product. More important, if these scholars are correct about its historical and culturally tautological implications, we must finally realize that the concept of rationality has no general scientific power (being ideological) to account for more and less powerful forms of cognition, the efficacy of schooling, or anything else. Instead it must be seen for what it is, a taken-for-granted tenet in terms of which the world is perceived by jpfs and cognitive researchers alike. Under these circumstances it is difficult to defend claims for the universality of "rational" models of good thinking as a scientific yardstick with which to evaluate situated cognitive activities. This may be put more strongly: constructing research in terms of mythological views of scientific thought insures blindness to questions of the structuring of everyday activities themselves.

The rationalist problematic of cognitive research is more than a general program. It transforms beliefs about rational thinking into a literal, detailed, operationalization of those beliefs. It has characteristic forms that should be familiar from earlier discussions: the argument that culture and knowledge are equivalent, and may be treated as if they consist of discrete facts; problem solving as one of a very small number of exemplars of "higher cognitive functions" – those most powerful and valued attributes of human thinking; rational problem solving, in the form of means/ends relations translated into condition/action pairs, i.e. production systems, as a universal form in which any thought can be expressed. Algorithmic problem solving is assumed to be the ideal model for the cognitive procedures employed to solve questions of fact in the service of goals exogenous to the process under study. This view isolates action as technique, and knowledge as "fact" from ends as matters of value, desire, feeling, and judgment. Indeed, the concept of "goals" is merely the obverse of "problem solving procedures." Both result from the single stroke that divides means from ends, fact from value.

Each of these assertions has been challenged by research on everyday math practice, some more strongly than others. The contribution of the research on shopping and cooking is a description of everyday activity in terms other than problem solving and means/ends relations, and with it a challenge to the specific operationalization of rationality in conventional cognitive theory. Problem-solving activity has been reconceptualized in terms of dialectical gap-closing processes. It was argued that what, in subjective terms, is "the same" activity ("arithmetic") takes different forms across situations and occasions, as it unfolds through the articulation of varied structuring resources in varying proportions. The discussion of money management provided demonstrations that arithmetic in practice is never merely that, but is the product and reflection of multiple relations – of value and belief, of people with each other, and of the conditions for producing and reproducing activity over time. Together they structure and are structured in activity, and evidence has been provided for the ideologically motivated uses of math to justify claims for the rationality of activity.

Taken together, these empirically based proposals for how to analyze everyday activity lead to different conceptions of knowledge, situation, and the means/ends form of problem solving. Thus, summed up very briefly: episodes in which a shopper buys apples or looks for enchiladas support the claim that knowledge is not primarily a factual commodity or compendium of facts, nor is an expert knower an encyclopedia. Instead knowledge takes on the character of a process of knowing. It is:

> the active engagement of consciousness in a reciprocal relation with the world and thus is constantly caught up in a simultaneous knowing and changing of the world.
> *(Warren 1984: 67)*

Secondly, I have argued at length that the conception of situation as separate from, and only arbitrarily related to, activity might better be transformed into a concept of dialectically constituted, situated activity. Finally, if relations among activity, setting and processes of dilemma-resolution are dialectically constituted, then it is not possible to separate the means of problem-solving activity from its ends. Gap-closing processes unite means and ends, transforming both in the process into means–ends and ends–means, a distinction without a difference (cf. Warren 1984: 79). This in turn implies that procedures for solving problems, as well as their goals, are inherently value-laden.

Further, if goals are not exogenous to the constitution of problems, then a problem is not structured as an end in itself or by a goal set elsewhere and presented to problem solvers by problem givers. A problem is a dilemma with which the problem solver is emotionally engaged; conflict is the source of dilemmas. Processes for resolving dilemmas are correspondingly deprived of their assumed universalistic, normative, decontextualized nature. As studies of math in practice have demonstrated, problems generated in conflict can be resolved or abandoned as well as solved, and often have no unique or stable resolution. Since quantitative relations, embodying value directly, bear direct relations with aspects of dilemmas that aren't quantitative, most dilemmas which involve relations among quantities are not well-formed arithmetic problems. In short, both theoretical critique and empirical evidence recommend that we recognize the cultural character and historical continuity of the contemporary study of cognition, and act accordingly to broaden the search for alternative conceptualizations that might encompass a richer, less stylized, investigation of the world as is.

Reordering relations between means and ends leaves in question that status and meaning of "rational action." Research on everyday math suggests that it is about as (un)important in practice in the lived-in world as arithmetic in grocery shopping, or as arrangements for the management of money on the basis of its universalistic properties. Calculating activity exists, but formal solutions, boxed products of calculation, are more often built into setting and activity or used as vehicles for the expression of feelings about rationality, than for its implementation. The kinds of quantitative relations observed in the supermarket, structured by ongoing activity, (e.g. "marginal thinking" in difference calculations), generating experience and expectations for the "next time," are pervasive and contribute in substantive ways to ongoing activities. I do not conclude from this that people fail to meet some rational standard of conduct, but rather, that a psychology drawn from an ideology of rationality cannot adequately account for practice. An alternative account of the orderly and (un)remarkably effective character of practice may be found in the complex constitution of structuring resources inventively employed in gap-closing, sense-making processes.

There is still meaning in the practical distinction between rational and irrational action; their cultural politics have been touched not one whit by the current analysis. It makes as good sense as ever to insist that one's own argument is rational while the other person's is not. But people are also concerned with "making sense." And it seems clear that relations among the structuring resources of person, activity and setting, transforming means/ends relations seamlessly through gap-closing processes, lead to action that meets the expectations of self and others efficaciously, most of the time. The ordinary state of persons-acting provides further evidence for the sustained scope of ordered activity in everyday life. People are engaged in ongoing activity far more often than they are paralyzed into suspended action.

Practice theory and constitutive order

The first section of the book concluded with a review of pitfalls engendered by equating culture and mind, and by the strategy of treating "culture" as context – as "that which isn't cognition." Such views, it was argued, deny the cultural character of activity, and thus of cognition also. These have been set aside, along with persistent formulations that in practice create gulfs between minds and their "environments." I have also argued against transmission and internalization as the primary mechanisms by which culture and individual come together. There is a further assumption of functionalist cognitive studies that has been criticized but for which no alternative formulation has yet been proposed. The culture and cognition paradigm assumes that its polar concepts define the limits of analysis beyond which no other theoretical terms and relations are required. But no matter how comprehensive the theory, "culture" by itself cannot provide the underpinnings for a *social* analysis of people acting and their activity. We might now add one more to the general claims with which the chapter began. By arguing that activity, including cognition, is socially organized and quintessentially social in its very existence, its formation, and its ongoing character, we have committed the enterprise to theorizing about the social production of action as well as its cultural character.

This view of the theoretical requirements for the study of everyday cognitive activity is quite different from the position out of which the project emerged. Initially the goal was to turn "culture," "cognition," and their relations from unexamined assumptions into the object of analysis, in order to develop a principled basis for a theory of cognition in culture. But it has become increasingly clear that "culture" and "cognition" are not the analytic units whose relations need clarification in order to proceed. Certainly neither one is an element in "the activity of persons-acting in setting," the unit of analysis adopted here. Nor is the relation between culture and cognition at the core of recent theorizing about practice, which focuses instead on more encompassing terms than either "culture" or "cognition," that is, on relations between sociocultural structure and social practice.

In one such theory, constitutive order is conceived as a different level of analysis than the world as experienced. Constitutive order consists of the mutual entailment of culture, conceived as semiotic systems, and organizational principles of the material and social universe (of political economy and social structure). Neither systems of meaning nor political, material and social structuring have analytic, or any other meaning in isolation from each other. This order, in turn, stands in a dialectical relationship with the experienced, lived-in world (e.g. Comaroff and Roberts 1981, Comaroff 1982, in preparation; also chapter 1).

To make this theoretical approach and its rationale comprehensible in its entirety would venture well beyond the scope of the present project. But the capsule specification here should be sufficient to make the point at hand. However one defines cognition, it surely would be located, in this scheme, in the experiencing of the world and the world experienced, through activity, in context. Culture, on the other hand, is an aspect of the constitutive order. In such a view, culture and cognition belong to *different levels* of the sociocultural order and address each other neither directly, nor in isolation from their entailments with other aspects, respectively, of the constitutive order and the lived-in world. Something like this view of social order must, I think, underlie a theory of persons-acting, engaged in everyday activity in context.

We may reconsider, in the light of this conclusion, the significance of the previous argument about the cultural and historical roots of rationality and cognitive theory. The work of Adorno, especially, and more recently that of Sahlins and Bourdieu, explores what have just been characterized as entailments of meaning and structure within the constitutive order. Their discussions of the foundations of the Western ideology of rationality are not about the nature of cognition, activity or experience as such. Instead, they claim that cultural systems and their structural entailments, *as aspects of a particular constitutive order*, motivate experience and are resources drawn upon in the fashioning of intentional activity in the lived-in world. The same point has been made in the analysis of math in grocery shopping. Math is a resource used to generate claims *about* rationality in the market. (Certainly it would be difficult to argue that calculating in the market provided an objective indicator of the rationality of shoppers' activity, given that shoppers' "choices" were in effect arbitrary at points in the process when price arithmetic was customarily invoked.) Thus "rationality" seemed better described as a cultural resource invoked in the fashioning of action than as the quintessential template for cognitive processing.

Figure 6 provides a summary of analytic relations central to the dialectical problematic of constitutive order and the experienced lived-in world. As a method for the investigation of practice it recommends

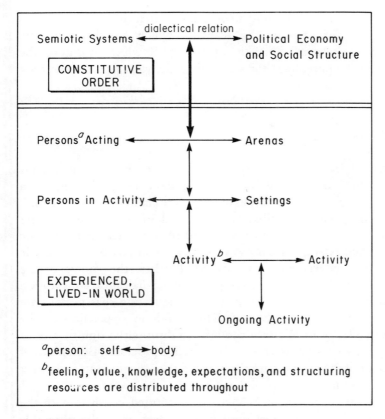

Figure 6 Modes of analysis for a dialectical problematic of practice

three general analytic modes: first, an analysis of semiotic systems *with* their structural entailments. This has been exemplified here in the discussion of relations among systems of belief and social institutions, for example, the meaning of rationality in its relations with commoditization and the institutionalization of cognitive theory in schooling. "Culture" is appropriately brought into analyses of its experienced realization in this complex, entailed form. Secondly, and correspondingly, an analysis of cognition must be constituted as part of a theory of practice, in explorations of the relations among person-acting, setting and activity. The third mode of analysis is one of interlevel, dialectical relations between an experienced world and its constitutive order. It raises questions concerning the effects of practice on structure, and how persons-acting and contexts (in the technical sense developed in chapter 7) are dialectically constituted in relation with semiotic systems and social, political, and economic structuring. These modes of analysis represent inflection points, the ways in which less-than-wholistic analyses are likely to take shape in a problematic which configures the encompassing requirements for a complete analysis of practice as they have been laid out here.

The person-acting

I propose to address cognition and culture and their various entailments at different levels of social analysis. Among other things, this requires a broadening of the terms of analysis to reflect the claim that the "person," including the person thinking, is constituted in relation with other aspects of the lived-in world. An embodied self is entailed with the world and their relations are not completely decomposable for analytic purposes into the elements so entailed. Further, the choice of the experienced, lived-in world as one element in the dialectical constitution of sociocultural order places emphasis on the notion that persons are directly engaged with the world. This stands in opposition to the pervasive tendency in Western thought to dismiss the significance of active experience in the generation of cognitive processes. Both kinds of involvement of the person with the world – their entailments and direct experience – require further discussion.

The claim that the person is socially constituted conflicts with the conventional view in its most fundamental form, with the venerable division of mind from body. For to view the mind as easily and appropriately excised from its social milieu for purposes of study denies the fundamental priority of relatedness among person and setting and activity. The strategy adopted here is to replace dichotomous divisions, especially between the mind and the body, with ones that cross-cut them and reflect what appear to be more fundamental categories of everyday experience. (However, I am aware that this attempt to make explicit some of the issues in a consistent theory of the person-acting overreaches the limits of the empirical research and is thus necessarily both sketchy and speculative.)

The first step is to incorporate the active character of experience into the unit of analysis. The *person-acting* (in setting), as an integral unit of analysis, is quite different from a "person" (Minick 1985: 17ff). Conventional theories of the person, conceived in separation from activity and the object world, may include consideration of the person's activity and context, but only as they are located within the person, as representations to be consulted (Minick 1985: 22–23). In contrast, in a theory of practice, setting and activity connect with mind through their constitutive relations with the person-acting. Further, a description of a person in action includes the person's body. In the Weight Watcher study, for example, self and body are treated as aspects of persons-acting. Both have a social and physical character, and are mutually entailed in one another in multiple and complex ways (de la Rocha 1986; Holland 1981). The person-acting and social world as mutually constituted are not always or exactly divided by the surface of the body. That is, the self has a historical and contingent character, unfolding through the creation of value in action, in relation with other selves, in setting. Its character is thus a relational one. Some of those relations are constituted interactively rather than as internal fixtures of the person, and the social world is partially embodied. Bourdieu has suggested that much of the generative basis of practice is inscribed *in* the person in the form of dispositions – "meaning made body" (1977: 75). Merleau-Ponty argues the conceptual importance of "perspectival privilege," a recognition that the self is without exception embodied, and thus always *located* in the world (Schenck 1985). This constant feature of human subjective experience configures perception of the world into a hierarchy of salience and significance. This view implies that priority, perspective and value are continuously and inescapably generated in activity. The "acting self" so constituted has quite different implications for the nature of the activity-in-setting with which it is engaged, than the simultaneously less social *and* less physical psychologist's "person" who for the most part merely consults the world-as-internalized or constructs it through other persons' knowledge.[3]

The obverse side of the social character of the body is the partially physical character of cognitive activity. People act most commonly and most effectively in the world when employing all of their embodied senses. "Common sensibilities" as de la Rocha has coined the term, extends the idea of "sense" to include kinesthetic sense, embodied and mentally constructed and reconstituted experience, that is, all active channels in the biographically rich, actively concerted character of experience.

> The most important aspect of a category of common sensibilities is that it refocuses attention away from perceptual modalities per se and onto their coordinated use. As such common sensibilities permit a view of engagement as the simultaneous and coordinated application of an *infinitely variable* combination of sensibilities which are usually named in natural language, not for the perceptual system involved – there may be several – but for their specific combination or momentary emphasis . . .
> *(de la Rocha 1986: 34, 36. Italics in the original)*

They might include "digging" a Grateful Dead concert, "getting the point" in a lecture, "catching the eye" of someone across the room, "searching" the frozen food shelves for enchiladas. Both the richness and ambiguity of these expressions for modes of experiencing the world confirm the characterization of sensibilities as specific syntheses.

I have described several related challenges to mind and body conceived as separate entities. There are the concepts of a relational self, the body as socially constructed and part of the social world, and cognition as partially physically constituted in common sensibilities. Cognition in action is by nature fused with feeling since it cannot be separated from the expression and creation of value. There are a number of reasons, it seems, to give up categorizing knowledge, thinking and feeling in the image of a person and world stringently divided.

Direct experience

The theory of sociocultural order discussed here encourages a rethinking of the nature of direct experience as well as of the relations of entailment implicated in the constitution of person, activity and setting. For dichotomous mind/body schemes assign emotions to the negatively valued body as part of the devaluation of immediate, sensuous experience. Correspondingly, higher cognitive functions are presumed to be further away from the body and from "intuitive, concrete, context-embedded" experience. Chapter 2 described this cognitivist view. The only "good" experience was distanced and generalized, removed from the debilitating influence of immediate time and place in the form of abstract accounts of action. The central role given to explicit verbal instruction in functionalist cognitive theory, depends on this view of experience. The common remedy cognitivists have proposed for "cognitive deficiencies" has been to increase the conscious, verbally explicit strategies available to problem solvers. Indeed, these suggestions for improving puzzle-solving techniques recommend changes *in discursive practices – only*.

But social theorists have recently raised serious objections to the idea that verbal discursive processes constitute the exclusive condition for efficacious action (e.g. Giddens 1984: 22) and have argued that in practice, activity appears to be routinely efficacious and reflexively intentional without knowing the conditions of its own production (Bourdieu 1977). Examples to support this view are not difficult to find:

AMP members were unaware of the efficacy of their math practice in the supermarket, and some did not know, even, that they used arithmetic procedures there. Or, contrast experiments on knowledge of physics in which jpfs, asked to explain the trajectory of water emerging from a coiled hose, guessed that it would continue in a curved line (McCloskey 1983), with an experiment which demonstrated that even small children can indicate which motions of water from a hose are "natural" and "unnatural" (diSessa 1985). What has been conventionally interpreted as the absence of correct knowledge raises instead the question of what circumstances surround the construction of verbal descriptions of embodied knowledge.

Discursive commentaries about experience as these are conceptualized unreflexively in "cultural transmission" models, are believed to be necessary conditions for *learning* abstract and general notions, but there is an alternative to this view, when direct experience is taken to be the more basic condition of learning. For example, the culturally ordered spaces of the house or school may be thought of as constituting forms of signification. As such they are fields for action, including the learning of values and symbolic relations as embodied postures, gestures, expectations, common sensibilities and dispositions. AMP research suggests that the classroom, with its authoritative program of knowledge to be transmitted and separation from the aspects of life it purports to prepare pupils for, with its discipline and tests, has a powerful impact on embodied knowledge even as this is constructed in grocery-shopping activity in the supermarket many years later. It signifies the ideology that jpfs act upon — school math is different in kind from activities in other everyday settings, great value is attributed to "real" math, they believe it "*should* be used," and it has a key role in building rational accounts. By contrast, the algorithmic forms of "real math" which were discursively transmitted in the school setting seem far less powerfully embodied in practice.

Reformulating the role of direct experience raises the question of how activity is made accountable while ongoing. An analytic focus on direct experience in the lived-in world leads to emphasis on a reflexive view of the constitution of goals in activity and to the proposition that goals are *constructed*, often in verbal interpretation (as in the apple-buying episode or the conversation about barbecue sauce). This retrospective and reflexive character is not compatible with a linear view of action as directed towards established goals. It suggests that action is not "goal directed" nor are goals a condition for action.

The 'rule-following' which Wittgenstein identifies designates practices which express the recursive character of social life, and which are constituted only in and through those practices; such rules are therefore never fixed or given presences.

It is just through this recursiveness that we can grasp the nature of social practices as in a continual process of production and reproduction. Social practices from this standpoint do not 'express' the intentions of social actors; nor on the other hand do they 'determine' them. *Intentions are only constituted within the reflexive monitoring of action, which however in turn only operates in conjunction with unacknowledged conditions and outcomes of action.*   *(Giddens 1979: 41–42)*

If the meaning of activity is constructed in action, if activity is not motivated by or towards specific targets, from whence comes its intentional character, and indeed, its meaningful basis? I argued earlier (chapter 6) that contradictory principles governing the organization of the family motivated the management of money, creating fields for action. The locus of motivation for such activity was found in complex relations between structural contradictions in the constitutive order and conflicting values and experience in everyday activity. Comaroff argues that:

The organizational principles which compose constitutive orders will be seen, by their very nature, to be inherently contradictory. As a result, they not only impinge on subjective experience as an assemblage of conflicting values, but also demand action upon the world. In short, they *motivate* social practice and, by virtue of their simultaneously semiotic character, impart meaning to it; to be sure, it is in terms of such meaning that intentional activity is contrived and ideologies constructed. Social practice, in turn, fashions concrete relations among living individuals, groups and classes. As such, it becomes the vehicle through which the manifest arrangements of the lived-in world are realized; arrangements which, demonstrably, either reproduce or, under specifiable conditions, transform the constitutive order itself. Herein lies the historical, the internal dialectic, of local systems: in so far as their underlying structures motivate – in the double sense of 'impelling motion' and 'attributing meaning to' individual experience and social practice, they shape the realization of relations in the "real" world . . .   *(In preparation: 16–17)*

In this perspective, motivation is neither merely internal to the person nor to be found exclusively in the environment. That is, even as goals are not "needs" (hunger or sexual desire are socially constituted in the world), they are not prefabricated by the person-acting or some other goal-giver as a precondition for action. And activity and its values are generated simultaneously, given that action is constituted in circumstances which both impel and give meaning to it. Motivation for activity thus appears to be a complex phenomenon deriving from constitutive order in relation with experience.

Settings, persons-acting, and activity intersect in the construction and playing out of what might be called *expectations* rather than goals. They may be thought of as potential resolution shapes embodied in experienced activity in setting. Expectations, dialectically constituted in gap-closing processes, enable activity while they change in the course of activity, backward and forward *in* time at the *same* time. People act inventively in terms of expectations about what has happened, is happening and may happen. And these in turn affect what does happen. Expectations are also structuring resources employed in shaping activity as a whole. Thus, a cook who uses a whole package of noodles while fixing a goulash dinner generates expectations about grocery shopping – again. In the supermarket, the shopper-acting and setting generate shopping activity partly on the basis of expectations about how the activity unfolds. And shopping activity leads to expectations about what dinners will consist of, how consistently, over the time until the next shopping expedition.[4] This view of the unfolding, experiential and multiple character of peoples' sense of what they are doing draws attention to, and offers an explanation for why the "everyday" character of any sustained form of activity is so important to its structuring. But to develop this idea requires a discussion of routine and continuity in activity, questions to be pursued in the next section.

One further observation may serve to draw this discussion to a close. The view that activity is dialectically constituted and the significance attached here to direct experience are closely related to each other and to the method of close, observational research *in situ*. Thus, it has been argued that the roots of the view that activity is rule-governed are to be found in the stance researchers take in relation to the objects of their studies – anthropologists in relation to "the natives" and psychologists to "subjects." That stance emphasizes for psychologists the virtue of objectivity which is assumed to result from "conducting" experiments so that social relations are standardized and the experimenter is not part of the social organization of activity but the giver of a task. Ethnographers are nonmembers of the cultures they study, being observant strangers whose ignorance they themselves take to be a condition for eliciting from informants explicit accounts of the obvious and basic aspects of culture and everyday practice. An alternative might lie in initiating the ethnographer into practice, but this is antithetical to research goals concerning objectivity (Favret-Saada 1980). But by asking for accounts of the taken-for-granted from informants, the ethnographer insures that what are produced are rule-like guides for the uninitiated. This suggests that even the practice of keeping a judicious distance from the object of study is caught in dilemmas that lead to systematically distorted analyses of practice.

Bourdieu has made this argument in a critique of the practice of anthropology:

> Exaltation of the virtues of the distance secured by externality simply transmutes into an epistemological choice the anthropologist's objective situation, that of the "impartial spectator," as Husserl puts it, condemned to see all practice as a spectacle.
> *(1977: 1)*

The critique readily applies to cognitive psychology as well. For it appears that the epistemological choice – the distance-that-distorts – leads cognitivists to project normative models of good thinking on subjects as assumptions about how they solve problems (or don't).

If the stance of the observer is an epistemological choice projected onto natives and subjects through assumptions about the rule-governed nature of their activity, we may ask of what that projection consists. For that we must look to the value placed on direct and distanced experience in different theoretical positions. Where emphasis is strong on the importance (to both researcher and jpf) of distance as a condition for generalization, a view of activity follows which emphasizes abstracted, normatively formulated rules. Conversely, where direct experience is taken to be the more fundamental character of activity, its construction in practice is not conditioned on abstractive formulation of rules, but is taken to be constituted in nondeterminant forms of activity.

The sources and limits of continuity in activity

The question of continuity in activity across settings was initially posed in terms of learning transfer. This is far enough removed from the question as presently conceived to warrant a review of the argument that connects them. First, the concept of transfer appeared inadequate to account for continuity of activity across contexts. The comparison of math practice across shopping, simulation experiment, and tests gave evidence of the situated structuring of activity. "Situated structuring" being only a description of this state of affairs, we sought its explanation, in spite of fears and suspicions that a theory of situational specificity might be a contradiction in terms. I argued that fear of being forced onto theoretical "low ground" by claims for the specificity of activity has inhibited attempts to theorize. But there were more serious barriers to a general approach to situational specificity, most especially several misconceptions about relations between culture and cognition: by taking culture and cognition to be the central terms of the theory; by treating their relations as an empirical question to be decided after treating each separately first; and by not recognizing the need for a general theory of sociocultural order within which to develop a dialectical conception of each crucial analytic term in relation with the rest. To raise the question here, "wherein lies the continuity of activity across situations" presupposes both that learning transfer is not the central source of continuity, and that it is possible to propose an alternative. The question, more precisely, is how situated activity is organized so as to be "the same" from occasion to occasion.

Continuity of situationally specific activity across occasions and contexts in this view is a matter of social reproduction, and thus of dialectical relations between the constitutive order and the experienced world. Continuity may be thought of as an active production of the reproduction of settings, activities and selves. It is achieved through change and improvisation, partly subjectively and partly through the reproduction of the constitutive order (Giddens 1979: 216ff.). That is, continuity of activity over occasions and settings depends on consistently flexible variability in the structuring of activity.

Persons-acting, arenas and settings contribute in different ways to what is reproduced and what varies flexibly in the process. Arenas are constructed "to last," some of them in concrete. But even arenas for grocery shopping instantiate common transformations of grocery shopping activity. There are express checkout lanes within the supermarket, and small neighborhood convenience markets as well. Both are used on quick trips rather than for major shopping expeditions. Such features of the arena are incorporated in activity when time is important and price minimally so (see Murtaugh 1985a for these and other broad transformational dimensions of markets). Arenas – realizations of dialectical relations among semiotic systems, social structure and political economy – are affected by practice indirectly and with considerable inertia. It is not inertia, however, which distinguishes arenas from persons-acting, but rather the sources of that inertia. Persons-acting have a good deal at stake in their own continuity, both as bodies and as selves, (while being required to act inventively to achieve this effect). They also have much to gain from the routine expectability of what they take to be cycles of activity. Operating with rich working expectations, broad resolution shapes for roughly repeated segments of social life are protected by fancy footwork and fiat.

For example, smooth progress through the supermarket is enhanced if calculations made on past trips apply to purchases made on more recent trips. Leaving work by five o'clock makes it possible to expect to generate a weekly, routine grocery shop, but by six o'clock it is too late to shop and still get dinner on the table on time. The production of one "weekly grocery shopping" with particular purchases, in a given length of time, is a condition for reproducing this form of grocery shopping over time, for if not purchased all at once, shopping must occur every day or two instead. Some dieting cooks produced "the same" breakfast every morning: (i.e. the same person cooked in the same kitchen, at the same time of day and made roughly the same meal). But one morning a dieter turned on the kitchen light because it was dark, took a knife out of the dishwasher rather than the drawer, and moved lettuce bought the previous day in order to find the oranges, after stopping first to wonder what had happened to them. If the production of routine is inter-dependent with the production of other routine activities and easy to disrupt, its production is surely a constructed accomplishment and especially when successful, a fiction.

I used the term "continuity by fiat." Processes and products of activity are "the same" partly because they are regarded that way. The variation in light, location of food, and utensils did not challenge the routine definition of the situation for the cook, though the process of preparing breakfast was patently different from one occasion to the next. It is a matter of interpretation whether some variant is encompassed by or interrupts routine; if breakfast included frozen rather than fresh orange juice, one cook might view it as "breakfast as usual," while another would see it as a violation of routine and expect a trip to the market to buy oranges.

Continuity in activity is quintessentially a distributive phenomenon. Neither persons nor arenas, and certainly not cognitive strategies nor contexts for thinking, are by themselves the locus of continuity in experience over time and across situations. There is a dialectically constituted gap-closing operation, between "shopping – again" (the resolution shape) and the experience of producing it. Inevitably, the person-acting, activity and setting each vary more than the product of the production (groceries) and than the production as a product ("grocery shopping as usual").

The constitutive order and everyday practice together reflect and constitute the distribution of power and interest such that, in general, reproduction of activity in setting is much more likely than its transformation or change. There are other limitations on variability as well. Resolutions to contradictions normally take a small number of culturally generated forms that are better described as partially appropriated and partially invented by persons-acting, across occasions. (The buyer of noodles was caught between two familiar resolutions to a common dilemma: whether to be frugal with food or money. The Weight Watchers used different measurement strategies depending on their long term, culturally shaped resolutions to dieting dilemmas.) And because persons-acting act with attention and expectations, in synomorphically and routinely structured settings and activities, there is almost without exception a central activity-in-setting and some personal ordering that inevitably gives priority or *point* of view to the activity of persons-acting.

It is not at the level of activity, but at the level of a set of transformations of articulated structuring resources that activity may be said to be "the same" from one occasion to the next. This helps to explain why transformational relations which are part of "intentionless but knowledgeable inventions," can be anticipated and expectable without having literally been experienced as the resolution shapes in relation with which experience is constituted. Expectations about the structure of ongoing activity have a rich basis because activity differs from one occasion to another mainly by shadings of difference in the proportional articulation of common structuring resources. Certainly, the ease with which AMP participants in the unfamiliar simulation experiment generated best-buy resolution processes closely resembling those in the market supports this view. In short, transformations of activity do not form a closed set of logical possibilities, but are open-ended and contingent. There is nothing to guarantee that the same multiple realities converge, nor that the arena, the person, or the setting as constituted are the same, nor that the immediate convergence of all of these will lead to one rather than another articulation of structuring resources. They nonetheless form a field for action, one held in expectations. Familiarity and routine are experienced in just this sense by persons-acting-in-setting.

Conclusions

I have tried to move the investigation of "cognition" outdoors in several senses: out of the laboratory, out of the head, out of a confusion with a rationalistic "culture," out of conflation with conventional "knowledge structures," and out of the role of order-producing, primary constraint on activity in the world. In the first chapter I suggested that everyday activity might be conceived in terms of its routine character, rich expectations generated over time about its shape, and settings designed for those activities and organized by them. The units of analysis and analytic questions developed here reflect a move away from the idea that the everyday is to be found in the domestic settings of jpfs, and towards the idea that all synomorphically structured, routine activity, for which fields for action are held in settings and in expectations, have much in common. In such a world it should be relatively easy to imagine, and generate in activity, new variants on old articulations of structuring resources, including novel configurations that enable the production of continuity across occasions. And it should be relatively difficult to generate new configurations of persons-acting, activities and contexts.

There may well be no polar category – a way of thinking or type of activity – to contrast with "everyday activity." This approach to the study of practice does not divide the construction of routine activity from the manufacture of change. Processes of reproduction, transformation, *and* change are implicated in the reproduction *or* transformation or change of activity in all settings and on all occasions. This implies that it is not at the level of cognitive processes that the unique, the nonroutine, the crisis, the exception, the creative novelty, the scientific discovery, major contributions to knowledge, ideal modes of thought, the expert and the powerful, are brought into being and given significance and experienced as such. These are all matters of constitutive order in the broadest and most complex sense, and they are constructed in dialectical relations between the experienced lived-in world and its constitutive order – in practice. If everyday practices are powerful it is because they are ubiquitous. If ubiquitous, they are synomorphically organized and sites of the direct, persistent and deep experience of whole-persons acting. These seem to be crucial conditions for efficacious human activity.

NOTES

1 Introduction: psychology and anthropology I

1 The term "just plain folks" (jpfs) will be used throughout the text. A double irony is intended: on the colonialist's distance and condescension that plagues psychology only slightly more subtly than anthropology (see Gifford and Marcus 1986; Said 1978; Bourdieu 1977, 1984; chapters 4 and 8), and on the belief of jpfs that the rubric is appropriate.

2 Murdock has described his version of the division of labor between psychology and anthropology at the turn of the century.

> "Spencer, Tylor and Durkheim understood psychology as the science which had undertaken the study of the behavior of the human individual. With the individual pre-empted as an object of investigation, they felt compelled to search elsewhere for an appropriate subject matter." . . . In the search for some viable "supra-individual realm of phenomena," the anthropological solution took two forms: the reification of the concepts of "culture" and of "social system," both of which required simplifying assumptions of intra-societal behavioral homogeneities.
>
> *(1975: 8)*

3 I shall use the term "functionalist" for the core theoretical formulations of cognitive psychology though I have seldom heard it used as a self-designation (but see Flanagan 1984). For the contemporary conceptualization of mind is, arguably, a direct analogue of the conception of society in functionalist theory; both are conceived as self-perpetuating, closed, input/output systems. Many other parallels follow from this. But I have chosen to characterize their commonalities for present purposes at a less profound level, where substantive propositions about the functioning of mind and society are caught up in relations with methods for investigating these same propositions.

"Functionalist" explanation has a variety of meanings within anthropology and a clarification seems in order. It includes both Malinowski's genre of functionalism and the "structural-functionalism" introduced into British anthropology in Radcliffe-Brown's reading of Durkheim. They share crucial properties: "that societies are being conceived of as coherent and consistent wholes, 'seamless,'" (Jarvie 1968: 199), and the notion that these seamless wholes are composed of parts whose relations may be used to explain each other. These common theoretical tenets

191

lead to a method – it is assumed that observation of a cross section of society at a point in time should reveal the structure, the unchanging basic form of a society.

> The appeal of functionalism undoubtedly consisted partly in that it prescribed explanations which required only the known and observable facts. Conjectures and history, both of which went beyond the observable facts, were unnecessary. All the parts of society could be explained by reference to their relations to other parts. What could be more appealing to the empiricist conscience?
> *(Jarvie 1968: 210)*

I take the same description to apply to the method of psychological experimentation as well, since it too looks for evidence of stable (mental) structures at a moment in time, and values the ability of experimental methods to keep history and past experience from "contaminating" the investigation of that structure. Jarvie ends by characterizing functionalism as more ideology than theory. In this spirit I am proposing that the institutional forms of schooling have taken shape, along with cultural visions of the meaning of mathematics and the working of the mind, in the ambience of a 150-year-old functionalist ideology fashioned more recently into the theory and method of both anthropology and psychology.

4 The duality of person is reflected in polarized categories of scientific thought versus collective beliefs, culture, emotions, and the body. It pervades the thinking of jpfs and scientists alike when they think about their relations with culture. Traweek, an anthropologist of science, reports the view of a physicist interviewed during extensive fieldwork at the SLAC accelerator laboratory at Stanford. The physicist argued, "culture is like a Poisson distribution. You have to understand that scientists are drawn from out here in the tail of the distribution where cultures have very little impact." Traweek comments, "in other words, he saw culture, and reason as standing in inverse relation to each other" (in press: 5). (See Turkle 1984, especially chapter 6 for startling descriptions of the strength of these beliefs and their cost to computer hackers.)

5 LCHC argues that:

> Berry offers analyses at both the individual and cultural levels of analysis. Or so it appears. However, when one considers the nature of the independent variables it is quickly apparent that with two exceptions, *the same independent variable codes must apply to all subjects within a cultural group.*
> *(1981: 59. Emphasis added)*

Another example of the cultural uniformity posited in functionalist psychology is provided by Bronfenbrenner:

> The macrosystem [society at its broadest] refers to *the consistency observed within a given culture* or subculture in the form and content of its constituent [sub]-systems, *as well as any belief systems or ideology underlying such consistencies.*
> *(1979: 258. Emphasis added)*

6 Its feasibility is of course, under challenge. Smart (1982: 121) argues that "the most significant central problems of sociology are inevitable," first and foremost subject/object dualism. Subject/object distinctions constitute "necessary features of the epistemological configuration within which the human sciences are located"

(1982: 140). He bases this view on Foucault's attempts to locate the human sciences within a specific epistemological configuration and set of historical preconditions. Both insist on the specifically historical character of subject/object relations that underlie, and make possible the social sciences.

It seems to me, however, that a dialectical theory, such as that proposed here, does *not* overcome subject/object dualism, but rather shifts the focus of attention from relations internal to subject and to object, to relations between them, and from deterministic monist to historically contingent and open dualistic theory (see Warren 1984: 57).

The views of Foucault and Smart have obvious implications for cross-cultural cognitive studies. If the social sciences are the product of a particular historical episteme based on a particular relation between subject and object, this implies that there is a historically specific, circumscribed and local character to all thought. Cognitive theory would thereby lose credibility as a yardstick of truth with which to measure and evaluate forms of thought in cultures with other histories. Were this recognized, it would lead, logically, to recognition of the *specific* character of those systems of belief and action for which hegemonic legitimacy is conventionally assumed. It would also lead to a recognition of equivalent specificity of "scientific thought" and thought traditionally claimed to be, by contrast, culture-bound (primitive, ethnic, lower class, or female, for instance).

7 The characteristic focus of practice theory on individuals in activity in social interaction suggests strong ties with ethnomethodological or other phenomenologically-based theories. But practice theory focuses on everyday activity in human-scale institutional realizations of sociocultural order. Principles of production and political organization are incorporated through the analysis of how they present themselves to the experience of individuals in the arenas of everyday action in the world. Practice theory, which treats macrostructural systems as fundamental, and focuses on relations between structure and action, is thus not to be confused with a phenomenological view, which treats social systems as (only) epiphenomena of intersubjectively constituted experience. That both focus analysis on the details of everyday practice should not obscure the essential differences between them.

8 Giddens argues that:

> both the 'normative functionalism' of Parsons and the 'structuralist Marxism' of Althusser exaggerates the degree to which normative obligations are 'internalized' by the members of societies. Neither standpoint incorporates a theory of action which recognizes human beings as knowledgeable agents, reflexively monitoring the flow of interaction with one another.
>
> *(1984: 30)*

That is, it prevents consideration of the ways in which social practices are produced and reproduced in activity in the world, dialectically, rather than exclusively within or between persons.

It should be added, that treating peoples' relations with the external world as theoretically central is not intended as an individualistic reduction of the problem of social relations to individual action. Such a reductionist argument would be incompatible with claims for the integral relations of persons with their activities and

194 Notes to pages 18–50

settings. Rather I wish to avoid, respectively, functionalist and phenomenological reductions of the constitutive order and lived-in world to internal representations and inter-subjectively constructed ones.

9 His discussion of alternative views of memory does provide useful arguments for rejecting literal recall in favor of more active constructive processes of remembering (1984: 45ff.). But this is not reconciled with the schemas and stocks of knowledge that seem to reside solidly in the memory in other aspects of his theoretical formulation.

2 Missionaries and cannibals (indoors)

1 *Time*, in its education section (24 December 1984: 61), discusses a flourishing movement to teach Latin in the public schools. They quote a teacher who explains its value: "Latin helps students become more disciplined . . . It's a good means of training the memory."

2 Both this paper and Hayes and Simon (1977) treat differences in solution time (controlling for order of presentation) as their central criterion of transfer. Ginsburg (1977) argues that this is not adequate evidence for transfer: to demonstrate transfer requires evidence that similar procedures are used across situations. His criticism is timely, adding further doubts about transfer research to those expressed throughout the chapter.

3 Foucault argues that the eighteenth century brought into play a view, still prevalent, that language is a privileged, transparent, value-neutral vehicle for the scientific description of the world – a different order of phenomenon from the objects which it describes. In *The Order of Things* (1970) he argues strongly against this view – language is part of the world's stuff, and obscures and values as it goes. It seems to me that the psychologist's laboratory, the psychoanalyst's office and the school classroom have been accorded the same privileged, lucid power of demonstration as language, through the simplifying assumption that, being out-of-context with respect to the "real" sites of the activity and knowledge addressed within them, they are not themselves contexts of activity (White 1973).

4 Even Dreyfus (1979) whose critique of artificial intelligence and cognitive simulation leads to a proposal that contextual analysis is key to a new approach, in the end treats the context of activity as a conceptual space.

3 Life after school

1 Here is another link between schooling and cognitive experimentation. If years of schooling is the only variable deemed necessary in order to control for subjects' past experience with the tasks given in the experiments, the tasks, or the skills they instantiate, must be assumed to be influenced only by schooling.

2 Participants were recruited in slightly unorthodox ways. For example, given the amount of time asked of each participant and our intrusion into their homes and customary routines, we could not recruit people through completely impersonal sampling techniques. For the supermarket study we therefore decided on a network sample, using peripheral acquaintances in our own lives as intermediaries who

vouched for us to peripheral acquaintances of theirs as a means of recruiting the first participants. Subsequently we pursued other peripheral two-step links of the same kind and also asked participants to serve as intermediaries.

For the Weight Watchers study an advertisement was placed in local weekly advertising circulars in communities varying in class/income characteristics. All participants recruited by this means were planning to join a dieting organization in the immediate future, but were not currently members. Participants in both studies were paid $100 for 30–40 hours of their time. Care was taken not to introduce AMP interest in arithmetic into the initial negotiations, for we were afraid of biasing the acceptance pattern toward those who were exceptionally at ease with math; or possibly uneasily obsessed with it, but in any event away from the diversity of views and attitudes we were seeking.

3 The participants spoke English as their first language, and had attended US public schools. We thought these factors might affect spoken and written number systems and the form of basic arithmetic operations (Reed and Lave 1979) and the form of school-taught arithmetic algorithms. No attempt was made, however, to control for historical or regional differences in US public school approaches to the teaching of arithmetic.

4 There is a significant association of income with participants' higher math classes beyond minimal public school requirements, and (reported) high involvement with math on the job, raising the issue under debate in the sociology and economics of education as to whether relations like these are a product of credentialing or of skill acquisition in school. The general import of AMP research, as we shall see, is to support the position that relations between schooling and position in the workforce are more a matter of credentials than skill. But the issue is too central in other academic arenas to approach here in a superficial way, and too peripheral here to warrant concentrated treatment. It will be set aside at this point (*see* Lave 1986).

5 The total number of best-buy calculations was derived from all those cases in which an outcome was reached by the informant. As in the arithmetic test, not all problems initiated in the supermarket were completed. In order to compare them, the number of problems completed is used as a baseline in both cases.

6 Each participant was given the following instructions:

> We have some arithmetic problems that we would like you to work out. This is not a test in the usual sense, since we are not particularly interested in how many questions you get right and wrong, but rather how you do the problems and what *kind* of mistakes you make, not how many. There is no time limit for working these problems and you will not be timed so work at the pace which is most comfortable for you. Feel free to skip any problem and return to it later but please at least try to work out all of the problems. If you want to change something that you have written, please cross it out neatly, using only one or two lines, so that it is still readable. After you have finished all of the problems, we will go over some of them and talk about how you got your answer.

7 I am grateful for the generous help of the TORQUE Project at MIT for making their tests available to us.

8 Each problem was rated for comparative ease of solution by fraction and by decimal methods. 18 of 24 participants varied their methods accordingly. Two others

translated all of the problems into fractions while five used decimals exclusively. Here is anecdotal evidence for the ability of participants to assess the mathematical properties of the problems they were asked to solve. Rigid single-method approaches versus flexible ones did not correlate with anything else.

9 Data on 34 of the 35 participants are used here. One of the shoppers had had a stroke and showed a quite extreme pattern of everyday/test differences. These are of interest in their own right, but in this context would distort the analysis (albeit in the direction of its conclusion). The data on this person have therefore been omitted.

10 Virtually error-free performance in the supermarket creates a methodological embarassment, for there is so little variance in this variable that it must be discarded for purposes of statistical analysis. Although the frequency with which a shopper carries out calculations in the market is only an indirect measure of problem-solving success, it is the most adequate substitute available. It is used in the next table.

11 There is a little more evidence to add to the picture of accurate calculation in the supermarket. We asked shoppers to estimate the total cost of the groceries in their cart while they stood in the checkout line at the market before reaching the checker. The most erroneous estimate differed from the actual grocery bill by 35%. However, this is the exception to estimates half of which were within 10% of the total on the bill. Such accuracy is of some interest, given the large number of items purchased and the substantial size of the average bill. We also asked shoppers to estimate the number of items in their grocery cart, something we suspected they had no routine occasion to do. The inaccuracy of these estimates was quite pronounced; many were off by as much as 50%. The contrast in accuracy between the cost estimate and the estimate of number of items purchased suggests that the former is a complex accomplishment.

12 I am indebted to Katherine Faust for her work on error analysis and to her and Oliva de la Rocha for the suggestion that problem transformation is a common factor in many errors on the test.

13 This section draws from J. Lave, Experiments, tests, jobs and chores: How we learn what we do. In K. Borman and J. Reisman (eds.), *Becoming a worker*. Norwood, NJ: Ablex. 1986.

14 This suggests a second problem concerning subjectivity, that when a given problem is presented to two people they may both recognize it as a problem while its meaning may be subjectively different. This is clearly an appropriate complication (de la Rocha 1986). But here the discussion concerns "what is a problem" rather than "what does a particular problem mean?"

15 Scribner has examined arithmetic organized in response to problem-solving processes where problems are experienced as external and objectively given by the experiencing actor, while in the supermarket control of problem-solving processes is experienced as subjective. Our explanations for situation-specific activity tend to be weighted in the direction of our (situationally specific) research experience, it appears, as Scribner (*et al.* 1982) places theoretical emphasis on the objective, and I on the generative, character of problem construction. This recommends the broadest possible empirical base when theorizing about situated studies of math.

4 Psychology and anthropology II

1 This chapter draws on a wide range of sources, across time and across subdisciplines

within psychology and anthropology. There is not space, nor am I prepared, to present the argument in finely drawn historical terms. But the scope of the discussion is nonetheless intentional. I believe the issues under critical examination here are enduring commonalities in the study of thinking since it began the transition "from its long past to its short history" (Danziger, 1979: 28).

2 Horton (Horton and Finnegan 1973: 253–254) also calls attention to this lacuna in Levy-Bruhl's work.

3 The scientific/primitive and scientific/everyday dichotomies dissolved in the work of Boas (e.g. 1911) when he moved to a position that people use their cognitive capacities primarily (and merely) to rationalize existing social custom, after the fact. That these two changes occur together supports the claim made here concerning their mutual dependence.

4 As Bourdieu (1984: 567) puts it: "idealization . . . is . . . a form of refusal."

5 The idea is not new. "Each occupation . . . constitutes a milieu *sui generis* which requires particular aptitudes and specialized knowledge, in which certain ideas, certain practices, certain modes of viewing things, prevail; and as the child must be prepared for the function that he will be called upon to fulfill, education, beyond a certain age, can no longer remain the same for all those to whom it applies." (Durkheim 1956: 68, originally lectures delivered about 1905).

6 It may be noted that the project has now come full circle, since the anthropologist Mary Douglas has applied (1973) Bernstein's taxonomy of elaborated and restricted speech codes to differences in cosmology and ritual *between* cultures.

7 Consider both Bartlett and Simon in this regard: the first half of Bartlett's treatise on thinking (1958) provides detailed reports on a handful of puzzle-solving tasks in the laboratory. The second half covers enormous territory – everyday thinking, experimental science, and artistic thinking, with topic and data in inverse proportions to those of the first half of the book, as Bartlett was well aware. "All I can attempt is to select a few illustrations, and to put forward in a general way, and without detailed evidence, certain conclusions which may help to establish some important relations . . . between the tactics and aim of everyday thinking and those characteristic of thinking in the closed system, and in experiment" (1958: 166). Simon (1976: 264) likewise recognizes "how little direct evidence is available about the second-by-second, or even hour-by-hour, course of the decision process," and advocates descriptive studies of the complex practice of cognition in the everyday world. But he refuses the challenge to address these questions either descriptively or experimentally, on feasibility grounds: "I am in no position to cast the first, or even the second, stone at social psychologists who have retreated to the 'social psychology of one,' for I have retreated even a step further into individual cognitive psychology. I have rationalized that retreat with . . . two arguments . . .: the greater cost-effectiveness of individual studies and the reductionist argument that nothing more may be needed" (1976: 265).

8 The uniformity of society in its relationship with the individual posited in the functionalist view should be evident. Bronfenbrenner provided us with an example earlier (chapter 1, note 5), with his micro-, meso-, and exosystems (1979: 258). Social roles, preestablished bundles of rights and expectations which people move through, are also central to his "ecology of human development" (see especially 1979 chapter 5).

9 It is unfair, in one sense, to hold cognitive studies to a theory of culture, for psychologists certainly do not consider this one of their theoretical responsibilities. Indeed, the division of labor between the disciplines discourages their consideration of culture theory. But those concerned with cognition must live with the limitations that incidental enabling assumptions impose on their studies, and as such the concept of culture deserves careful examination.

10 D'Andrade (1981) does not critique the information pool view of culture, though in the same paper he presents an alternative to the cognitivist equation of computer and human learning in very interesting terms, to wit: cultural (as opposed to computer) programs are general fields for action rather than algorithms, learned mainly through apprenticelike relations, slowly, and by guided discovery; they involve a content-based, rather than formal, logic, and feelings play an integral role in sustaining activity. It is difficult to reconcile these two views of culture.

11 That knowledge domains or problem spaces are taken to be the "context" of cognitive activity (see chapter 2), is consistent with a further common cognitivist view: that the world "around" the task is a natural "environment" rather than a social situation in relation with which activity is concerted. This transformation of the sociocultural into the natural illustrates Sahlins' argument concerning the "naturalization" of culture in Western society (see below).

12 As Samelson notes, in his critique of positivist psychology, "To reject metaphysics does not guarantee the non-metaphysical nature of one's position; to proclaim the end of ideology may itself be an ideological move" (1974: 228).

13 This is not the only possible temporal framework for a theory of memory (cf. Giddens 1984: 45ff.). Kvale (1977) equates memory with consciousness by locating the process of remembering *in the present*. Memory, then is a process of refraction, through present experience, of continually transformed versions of past experience. Overlaid on conventional metaphorical models of the "memory as toolkit" variety, it would follow that remembering must continually distort the objective content of (past) experience. Treated as an activity in the present, remembering becomes a set of relations among experiential processes, and relations among those relations, integrally shaped and motivated in the present. This concept of memory locates the articulation of cognition and culture in complex relations between the individual and the world in relation with which experience is constituted, challenging dichotomies which are unavoidable when culture is construed as "something that happened in the past" and mental representations are conceived of as subsequently abstracted and generalized.

14 Frankfort School critical theorists have pointed out that a tendency to devalue direct experience has a long history, rooted in modern political economy. Adorno argued that it was "related to advanced bourgeois society's destruction of . . . experience and its replacement by administered, lifeless concepts. The disappearance of true experience, which Benjamin had also stressed as a characteristic of modern life corresponded to the growing helplessness of modern man" (Jay 1973: 70). Jay adds, "In his article on the decline of story-telling . . . Benjamin wrote: 'Experience has fallen in value . . . Never has experience been contradicted more thoroughly than strategic experience by tactical warfare, economic experience by inflation, bodily experience by mechanical warfare, moral experience by those in power.'" (1973:

313–314). Bourdieu, more recently, identifies distance from experience as a defining characteristic of bourgeois class culture (1984: 53ff.). These views suggest some of the ideological roots of contemporary cognitive theory.

15 The argument is a general one, but can be given a quite specific interpretation in terms of the "many chunks" theory of culture. If the unit of culture in this theory were objective "*bits*" of information, knowledge would reside "out there" in the world, independent of the individuals who have it stored in their minds; culture and cognition would have different bases of existence. But the unit in this theory is the *chunk* of information, a subjective unit (Jeeves and Greer 1983; see also Norman 1980). To characterize some portion of culture as 50,000 chunks is, to begin with, a contradiction in terms, since no chunk has a fixed definition. Yet the numbers make it sound as though each had a countable existence. Further, if chunks are subjective units, then indeed culture and cognition fit the diagnosis proposed here.

16 Bronfenbrenner (1979; LCHC 1981) frequently employs phrases such as "the culture selects contexts . . ." Indeed, the unitary view of cultures goes back at least to Wundt (see Leach, 1957: 121, 126).

5 Inside the supermarket (outdoors) and from the veranda

1 Whether there is "a lot" or "a little" calculation persists as a question within and about the AMP. In AMP research it appeared that neither the shoppers nor adept Weight Watchers calculated nearly as often as the dieting cooks at the beginning of the new diet. But most shoppers had, in the past, made price comparisons for essentially all the staple items they currently purchased and many others as well. They had a large, readily available stock of outcomes of these calculations. Thus, a single trip through the supermarket with a 16% calculation "rate" underestimates the degree to which current activity is "calculationally-informed."

There are several virtually insurmountable difficulties in making the judgments suggested above. One of them is the problem of establishing units of analysis. The "grocery purchase" served reasonably well in the supermarket. But what constitutes such a unit in the kitchen? Attempts to analyze cooking activity, for example, the preparation of a complicated casserole, suggested that cooking has a more complex structure of activity-person-setting relations than grocery shopping and would be very hard to reduce, other than mechanically through some standardized measure of time, to a series of comparable units. Another difficulty stems from the comparative character of the original question. The implied referent is professional mathematics, a mathematical knowledge domain, or rates of math problem solving in school, unfortunately. So many arguments against this kind of inquiry have been reviewed that further comment seems superfluous.

What *doesn't* transfer from school has already been discussed in part; essentially no problem in store or kitchen was solved in school algorithmic form. Transformational rules (which eliminate algorithmic approaches to fractions and decimals), do not travel, nor does place holding notation, since paper and pencil are not used, calculus, trigonometry, analytic geometry, algebra, etc., etc. The question really should be, "is there anything that *does* transfer?" The question will be taken up in chapter 7.

2 Capon and Kuhn's experiments are described in two br ef research reports. The second experiment is slightly more elaborate than the first, but basically a replication. What recommends an extensive analysis of this circumscribed body of work is its similarity to the AMP experiment. Issues concerning structuring resources and validity are so strongly thrown in relief by the comparison that it seemed worthwhile to discuss them at length.

3 Four problems were presented on cards to all participants. The remaining eight items were divided into four "bottles and jars" problems and four problems for which the information about prices and quantities was written on cards. The original idea was to compare responses to more and less realistic and fam liar presentations of the problems. Participants were divided so that half were given one set of problems on cards and the rest the remaining set. Within each group half worked problems from cards first and half problems from the grocery items themselves. The theoretical motivation for these elaborations was minimal, and on analyzing the data the form of presentation made no difference in success at problem solving. This aspect of the experiment is not discussed further, therefore.

4 In the latter cases the actual unit price difference was, variously, four-tenths of a cent per ounce, three-tenths, one-half cent and one cent per ounce. There were similarly small differences in unit price for other problems however, where shoppers did conclude that one item was a better buy than another. The judgment that two products were of equal value seemed to be a genuine one, not an attempt to avoid calculating, for it occurred with equal frequency on problems of varying difficulty.

5 I have indicated without special comment a number of ways in which Capon and Kuhn's research shares attributes with the experiments examined in chapter 2. The reverse argument may also be made – the central critique of Capon and Kuhn is applicable to the transfer experiments. That is, they all begin with a univocal, normative, mathematico–scholastic myth about how the lived-in world should be, and interpret in just these terms an everyday practice whose values, priorities, dilemmas, structuring resources and concerns are on *a priori* grounds deemed irrelevant to the practice of arithmetic.

6 Further, best-buy calculations are more efficient than unit-price calculations because they begin with two items the shopper wishes to compare This comparison can be carried out in two steps (see Figure 3) while a *universal* unit-price procedure is less efficient, requiring three steps – two ratio solutions and then a comparison of the results. This suggests that "universal" procedures may have some specific characteristics that make them less generally useful than a strictly mathematical viewpoint would suppose.

6 Out of trees of knowledge into fields for action

1 Money is argued to be, most especially by Marxist scholars, the central symbol of capitalist societies. In *Capital* (1887) Marx carried out a sustained analysis of the nature of money, its symbolic properties and material implications. Simmel (1907) has also treated the issue at length and there is now an extensive literature on the subject. The present discussion does not attempt to encompass this work.

2 Ten participants began the Weight Watchers study. Nine completed the process.

3 Lest the structuring of math into and by ongoing activity appear to be a domestic specialty ("everyday" in the functionalist sense), there is evidence that this description also applies to high technology activity-in-setting as well. Hutchins' recent fieldwork on the process of navigating an aircraft carrier reveals special purpose measuring and calculating devices – gyrocompasses with built-in correction factors, special-purpose slide rules, charts and tables in which old (some centuries old) calculations are stored. Navy personnel use these in a way that fits smoothly into the flow of (everyday) ongoing activity as six people coordinate sightings and plot the ship's position but do very little formal calculation in the process. (Hutchins personal communication.)

4 It should not be surprising to find that measurement activities likewise are expressive and situationally specific and that special-purpose "stashes" (to borrow a metaphor) of numerical information are embodied in measuring instruments. A survey of the local dimestore produced the following list of over 80 different measuring and calculating devices intended for home use.

Stationery department
 month at a glance calendar
 school tools: books with drawing and stenciling aids, tables of weight and
  volume, and metric/British conversions, postal scales with sensitivity adjust-
  ments, in ounces; for first and third class mail and airmail
 a metric conversion rule: fluid ounces to mililiters and gallons to liters
 six sided rulers with various scales
 compasses
 protractors
 various rulers
 slide rules
 special rulers with metric equivalents
 pencil boxes with multiplication tables and rulers
 personal telephone books with area codes, time zones, three years of calendars,
  metric conversion tables and credit card records
 personal month planning books
 perpetual diaries – (about $2\frac{1}{2}'' \times 3\frac{1}{2}''$) including demographic information,
  personal auto description, states and their capitals, population of principal
  cities, for '50, '60, '70, presidents, birthstones, wedding anniversaries, weights
  and measures, desirable body weights, cash accounts, addresses, memoranda
  household property inventory forms
  various home budgeting guides
  budget and tax files
  daily expense records

Clock and watch department
 24-hour clocks marked on 12-hour watch
 clocks with times in different cities
 digital clocks and watches, with many varieties of time marking features
 calendars

Camera department
 darkroom thermometer 10°–120°F, 68° marked
 calculators

Pet shop
  fish tank thermometers
  floating glass 10°–110°F marked in 2°'s, and colored green at proper range
  thermometers 30°–100°F
  suction cup circular thermometers, 30°–120°, marked between 70°–80°

Toys
  dart board
  play clock
  alphabet and number printing set
  math/coloring books
  play money

Kitchen
  blender jars, mostly in cups and ounces
  coffee pots, marked in cups
  egg timers
  baster syringes, marked in ounces, from $\frac{1}{4}$ to $1\frac{1}{2}$ cups
  measuring spoons, in tablespoons, teaspoons and metric
  measuring cups in graduated sizes, all with both British and metric scales
  diet scales in ounces and grams to one lb.
  oven thermometers, 100°–500° (warm-100–250°, slow 250–350°, moderate
      350–400°, hot 400–450°)
  outdoor thermometers with metric −60°F to 120°F
  indoor digital thermometers in C and F 64°–84°
  candy thermometers, 75°to 400°F with special markings
  indoor/outdoor themometers C and F
  freezer–refrigerator thermometers −30° to 70°F (deep freeze −10, freeze −10
      to +30, refrigerate 30 to 40, defrost 70+)
  meat thermometers F and C in 10's of degrees, poultry, lamb, beef; rare, medium
      and well-done
  candy thermometers 150–400° (jelly, softball, hard ball, crack, hard crack,
      doughnuts, fish, potatoes. A cooking chart on back)
  cocktail shaker with recipe book (whiskey sour, manhattan, etc.), multiply
  ingredients by number of drinks, recipes in mls and ounces
  jigger glass – double, $\frac{3}{4}$ and $1\frac{1}{4}$ ozs
  pocket adder four columns ($10 dollars, dimes, cents; instructions for use on back)
  sifters marked in cups
  hand mixers marked in mls, ounces, cups
  choppers marked in mls, ounces, cups
  juice containers, one gallon; marked in ounces, pints, quarts, gallon

Hardware
  carpenter's levels with rulers
  different size wrenches
  L–rule with level and ruler in inches
  extension rulers

Auto accessories
  compasses (three types)

liquid thermometers with "comfort mark"
suction cup thermometers
dashboard clocks

Sporting goods
racquet ball inflation kits (pounds per square inch)
bike speedometers with odometer in miles and kilometers
fishing lure weights

Notions
sewing gauges in inches and centimeters
hemming markers using fold (looks like a paper clip)
folding yard sticks
tape measures

All of these devices were designed, produced, and sold in a mass market, with emphasis on the substantive particularity of their intended uses. Thermometers provide an example of their variety and specificity. There were indoor and outdoor air-temperature devices, oven thermometers, temperature regulators in refrigerators, candy thermometers, and fever thermometers as well as even more specialized ones for automobiles, fish tanks, pools and darkrooms. These instruments supported activities such as monitoring a child's illness, making candy, and cooking a roast. Each was marked in standard units, but truncated to a limited range of values. Each was specialized for a particular use and was rarely adaptable to other purposes. Further, most were designed so that specially marked points rather than the structural properties of the regular scale markings, were the salient focus for "reading" the instruments. These allowed easy assignment of qualitative meaning to a point or region – 98.6° on a fever thermometer, "soft-ball" stage on a candy thermometer, "rare," "medium," and "well-done" on the meat thermometer, and warm, slow, medium, and hot on the oven thermometer.

5 A semiotic study on the communicability of cursive writing argues that the structure of handwriting is a product of just such contradictory principles; in the limit it is easiest to produce a straight, horizontal line. However, the more distinctive the characters, the clearer the communication. Any given resolution to the contradiction is a specific compromise between ease of production and decipherability (Watt 1979). It will be argued here that particular resolutions to such contradictions depend on relative pressures in the situation toward getting the job done and talking about it. A revaluation of Bernstein's elaborated and restricted codes (see chapter 4) is clearly implied.

6 Recent work by sociologists (e.g. Boltanski 1984; Thevenot 1984) provide other examples. Boltanski shows how moves toward universalization of the parties and issues involved in letters of denunciation written to a Paris newspaper enhance the legitimacy of the author's claims, or when absurd or otherwise inappropriate, brand their writer as a crank.

7 Through the supermarket

1 This chapter is a revised version of Lave, Murtaugh and de la Rocha (1984). I especially wish to thank my collaborators, Murtaugh and de la Rocha for permission to incorporate our collective efforts into the book.

2 The logic of Barker's index of setting interdependence is as follows:

> The operations for determining the interdependence index K of pairs of synomorphs [similarly structured behavior pattern–milieu combinations] are based upon two sets of assumptions: (1) that interdependence between synomorphs occurs (*a*) via behavior, which has effects across synomorphs, (*b*) via inhabitants, who migrate between synomorphs, and (*c*) via leaders, who are common to synomorphs; and (2) that the amount of interdependence that occurs via these channels is a direct function of (*a*) the amount of behavior, the number of inhabitants, and the number of leaders that span the synomorphs, (*b*) the closeness of the synomorphs in space and time, and (*c*) the similarity of the synomorphs with respect to behavior objects and behavior mechanisms.
> *(Barker 1968: 40)*

3 This example is from a pilot participant in the Weight Watchers study.
4 Though gap-closing processes have been described here in the context of domestic chores, it may be worth reiterating that "everyday activity" crosscuts conventional categories of social differentiation. Thus, scientific practice has been described by the well-known physicist Richard Feynman (on a NOVA television program) in terms strongly suggesting that there, too, problem solving is conceptualized as a gap-closing process. While he talked about his research he was facing the (TV) camera, gesturing with his hands which were about a foot apart, at chest level.

> I spent a few years trying to invent mathematical things [wiggling his right hand] that would permit me to solve the equations, but I didn't get anywhere. And then I decided that in order to do that, I must first understand more or less how the answer [gestures with left hand] probably looks. Its hard to explain this very well, but I had to get a qualitative idea of how the phenomena works rather before I can get a good quantitative idea . . . [brings hands together] we need to compare the theory to experiment by seeing what the consequences are. And checking it, we're stuck in seeing what the consequences are.
> *(NOVA, Jan. 25, 1983)*

8 Outdoors: a social anthropology of cognition in practice

1 In fact, cognitive theory is not silent on the subject of regularities of activity in the social world; limited processing capacity, or limitations of cognitive developmental stages, or the stable, tool like, character of knowledge as transferred, are invoked in conventional views to account for the uniformity of cognitive performances, and for the uniformity of culture and the social world. Processing constraints are appealing as a form of explanation for this assumed uniformity, perhaps because they may be couched in formal rather than substantive terms and attributed to the mind rather than to the lived-in world. Limitations of memory undoubtedly do have a role to play in the shaping of activity (though not nearly so large a role as cognitivists are forced to claim when the only locus of relevant knowledge they allow themselves for explanatory purposes lies in the head of a problem solver). But as an explanation for the structured regularities of activity, occasion and context, such limitations are insufficient to specify what, whom, when, where (and what not and whom not) and their relations. Any such limitations, it might also be noted, are sources of the creation of choice, priority, indeed value, given that resources of attention must be

allocated to some but not other aspects of ongoing activity. But the limitations cannot explain or account for the value created or choices made, nor explain how they are made.

2 Cognitivists do not stand alone in their notion that the social sciences are somehow a project in comparative rationality. Anthropologists and philosophers with widely varied interests have assumed that this was their mission when comparing cultures, religions, magical practices, genders and social classes (e.g. Wilson 1970). Intellectualist theories of culture hinge on the presumption of a natural rationality; it enters into science as "theory" *because* its cultural character is not treated as an object of speculation.

3 Giddens (1984) takes the view that bodies constrain the nature of social life. Two bodies cannot occupy the same place at the same moment; it is difficult to speak and listen at the same time so conversation requires linearization of communication. And he treats front/back zones and "face" as crucial to the organization of copresence and social interaction. His emphasis on embodied action leads him to emphasize time–space contextualization as fundamental to activity as well. Foucault's work has had a major impact on rethinking the social nature of the body. Lash (1984) contrasts Foucault's conception of the body – passive, inscribed by knowledge in power; Merleau-Ponty's – a lived body with unity, coherence and intentionality; and Deleuze's – a body without organs, a desiring machine, a surface of intersection between the libidinal forces and external social forces. Turner (1984) and Falk (1985) have analyzed the historical, political fashioning of the body in Western culture. Turner adopts Nietzche's argument that "our corporeal existence does not pre-date our classificatory systems of knowledge and thus the body is nothing more and nothing less than a social construct." Both body and mind are "a product of classificatory knowledge and of power." (Turner 1984: 5). This analysis may be applied to laboratory studies of cognition. Thus, experimental categories code cognitive functions and varieties of cognitive performances as lower and higher. Subjects are classified as male/female, black/white, middle class/lower class. They are, by this analysis, thus subjugated (made subject, conjugated) in political terms.

   This discussion is intended to suggest that there are theoretical debates concerning the body in close parallel to those discussed here about the mind. Their correspondences would repay further study, for elaborating the implications of these theories of the body would generate as many different theories of practice.

4 Expectations and activity generate each other across situations, in ways that reflect relations between those situated activities. We observed that shoppers often "have their heads in the kitchen" while they shop. They talk about the storage characteristics of their kitchen cabinets and existing inventory in refrigerator and cupboards; they anticipate what they are going to cook, who will eat which meals, and what each family member likes to eat. In the kitchen the pattern of activity and expectations is quite different; when coordinating and timing meal preparation, cooks tend to stop talking. While doing mainly physical, repetitive tasks like chopping vegetables, however, they talk about one or more of the multiple realities of which their activity-in-setting is a part. Cooking talk rarely conjures up the supermarket and shopping activity, though it may generate items on grocery lists and create an expectation about shopping. The expectations about cooking generated in the supermarket are, in short, much richer than the other way around, as the expected activities in the kitchen are much more directly entailed in shopping than the process of shopping is entailed in cooking.

REFERENCES

Acioly, N. M. and A. D. Schliemann. 1985. Intuitive mathematics and schooling in understanding a lottery game, unpublished paper on file at Recife, Brazil: Universidade Federal de Pernambuco.

Apple, M. 1979. *Ideology and curriculum*. London: Routledge and Kegan Paul.

Adorno, T. W. 1977. 'Goldman and Adorno: To describe understand and explain' in L. Goldman (ed.), *Cultural creation in modern society*, p. 131. St Louis: Telos Press.

Barker, R. G. (ed.). 1963a. *The stream of behavior*. New York: Appleton, Century, Crofts.

1963b. On the nature of the environment: Kurt Lewin memorial award address – 1963. *Journal of Social Issues* 19: 17–38.

1968. *Ecological psychology: concepts and methods for studying the environment of human behavior*. Stanford University Press.

Barker, R. G., and H. F. Wright. 1954. *Midwest and its children: the psychological ecology of an American town*. Evanston, Illinois: Row, Peterson and Company.

Barnes, B. 1973. 'The comparison of belief-systems: anomaly versus falsehood' in R. Horton and R. Finnegan (eds.), *Modes of thought*. London: Faber and Faber.

Bartlett, F. C. 1923. *Psychology and primitive culture*. Cambridge University Press (Reprinted 1970, Greenwood Press).

1932. *Remembering: A study in experimental and social psychology*. Cambridge University Press.

1937. Psychological methods and anthropological problems. *Africa* 10: 401–420.

1958. *Thinking: An experimental and social study*. New York: Basic Books.

Bernstein, B. 1972. 'Social class, language and socialization' in P. P. Giglioli (ed.), *Language and social context*. Harmondsworth, Middlesex, England: Penguin Books, Ltd. (Reprinted from *Class, codes and control*, Vol. 1, *Theoretical studies towards a sociology of language*. Routledge and Kegan Paul, 1970).

Boas, F. 1910. Psychological problems in anthropology. *American Journal of Psychology* 21: 371–384.

1911. *The mind of primitive man*. New York: Free Press.

Bohannon, P. 1955. Some principles of exchange and investment among the Tiv. *American Anthropologist* 57: 60–70.

Boltanski, L. 1984. La Denonciation. *Actes de la recherche en sciences sociales* 51: 3–40.

Bourdieu, P. 1973. 'Cultural reproduction and social reproduction' in Richard Brown (ed.), *Knowledge, education and cultural change*, pp. 71–112. London: Tavistock.

206

1977. *Outline of a theory of practice.* Cambridge University Press.

1984. *Distinction: a social critique of the judgment of taste.* Cambridge, MA: Harvard University Press.

Bowles, B., and H. Gintis. 1976. *Schooling in capitalist America: educational reforms and the contradictions of economic life.* New York: Basic Books.

Brenner, M. 1985. Arithmetic and classroom interaction as cultural practices among the Vai of Liberia. Unpublished doctoral dissertation. University of California, Irvine.

Bronfenbrenner, U. 1979. *The ecology of human development: experiments by nature and design.* Cambridge, MA: Harvard University Press.

Bronfenbrenner, U., and M. A. Mahoney (eds.), 1975. *Influences on human development* (Second edition). Hinsdale, Illinois: The Dryden Press.

Bruner, J. S., R. R. Olver, and P. M. Greenfield. 1966. *Studies in cognitive growth.* New York: Wiley.

1974. 'The organization of early skilled action' in Martin P. Richards (ed.), *The integration of the child into a social world.* Cambridge University Press.

Burling, R., 1964. Cognition and componential analysis: God's truth or hocus-pocus? *American Anthropologist* 66: 20–28.

Campbell, D. T. 1961. 'The mutual methodological relevance of anthropology and psychology' in F. L. K. Hsu (ed.), *Psychological anthropology.* Homewood, Illinois: The Dorsey Press.

Capon, N., and D. Kuhn. 1979. Logical reasoning in the supermarket: adult females' use of a proportional reasoning strategy in an everyday context. *Developmental Psychology* 15(4): 450–452.

1982. Can consumers calculate best buys? *Journal of Consumers Research* 8: 449–453.

Carraher, T., D. Carraher, and A. Schliemann. 1982. Na vida dez, na escola, zero: Os contextos culturais da aprendizagem da matimatica. Sao Paulo, Brazil. *Caderna da Pesquisa* 42: 79–86.

1983. Mathematics in the streets and schools, unpublished manuscript on file at Recife, Brazil: Universidade Federal de Pernambuco.

Carraher and Schliemann. 1982. Computation routines prescribed by schools: Help or hindrance?, paper presented at NATO conference on the acquisition of symbolic skills. Keele, England.

Chamberlain, A. F. 1917. *The child: a study in the evolution of man.* New York: Charles Scribner's Sons. Second edition 1917 (First edition, 1901).

Cohen, P. C. 1982. *A calculating people: the spread of numeracy in early America.* University of Chicago Press.

Cole, M. 1981. Society, mind and development. Paper delivered at the Houston Symposium IV on Psychology and Society: the Child and other Cultural Inventions. (To appear in a book by that title, F. Kessel (ed.).)

Cole, M., J. Gay, J. Glick, and D. Sharp. 1971. *The cultural context of learning and thinking.* New York: Basic Books.

Cole, M., L. Hood, and R. McDermott. 1978. Ecological niche picking: ecological invalidity as an axiom of experimental cognitive psychology, unpublished manuscript on file at University of California, San Diego and the Rockefeller University.

Collins, R. 1979. *The credential society: a historical sociology of education and stratification.* New York: Academic Press.

Comaroff, J. L. 1982. Dialectical systems, history and anthropology: units of study and questions of theory. *The Journal of South African Studies* 8(2): 143–172.

In preparation. *Capitalism and culture in an African chiefdom: a study in anthropological dialectics.*

Comaroff, J. L. and S. Roberts. 1981. *Rules and processes: the cultural logic of dispute in an African context.* University of Chicago Press.

Cooter, R. 1979. 'The power of the body: The early nineteenth century' in B. Barnes and S. Shapin (eds.), *Natural order: historical studies of scientific culture.* Beverly Hills, CA: Sage Publications.

D'Andrade, R. G. 1974. 'Memory and assessment of behavior' in H. M. Blalock, Jr. (ed.), *Measurement in the social sciences.* Chicago: Aldine.

1981. The cultural part of cognition. *Cognitive Science* 5: 179–195.

1982. Reason versus logic. Talk for Symposium on the ecology of cognition: biological, cultural, and historical perspectives. Greensboro, North Carolina.

Dannefer, D. 1984. Adult development and social theory: a paradigmatic reappraisal. *American Sociological Review* 49: 100–116.

Danziger, K. 1979. 'The social origins of modern psychology' in A. R. Buss (ed.), *Psychology in social context.* New York: Irvington Publishers, Inc.

Datan, N., and H. W. Reese (eds.). 1977. *Life-span developmental psychology: dialectical perspectives on experimental research.* New York: Academic Press.

de la Rocha, O. 1986. Problems of Sense and Problems of Scale: an ethnographic study of arithmetic in everyday life, unpublished doctoral dissertation. University of California, Irvine.

DiSessa, A. 1985. Final report on intuition as knowledge, pp. 14–15. For the Spender Foundation.

Dougherty, J., and C. M. Keller. 1982. Taskonomy: a practical approach to knowledge structures. *American Ethnologist* 9: 763–774.

Douglas, M. 1966. *Purity and danger: an analysis of concepts of pollution and taboo.* New York: Praeger.

1967. 'Primitive rationing' in R. Firth (ed.), *Themes in economic anthropology.* A.S.A. Monographs 6, pp. 119–147. London: Tavistock.

1970. *Natural symbols. Explorations in cosmology.* New York: Pantheon Books.

1973. *Natural symbols.* New York. Vintage Books.

Dreyfus, H. 1979. *What computers can't do: the limits of artificial intelligence* (revised edition). New York: Harper Colophon Books.

Duncker, K. 1945. On problem solving. *Psychological Monographs* 58 No. 270.

Durkheim, E. 1956. *Education and sociology.* Translated and with an introduction by S. D. Fox. Glencoe, IL: The Free Press.

1915. *The elementary forms of the religious life.* New York: The Free Press.

Durkheim, E., and M. Mauss. 1963. *Primitive classification.* R. Needham (ed. and trans.). University of Chicago Press.

Edgerton, R. B. 1974. Cross-cultural psychology and psychological anthropology: one paradigm or two? *Reviews in Anthropology* 52–64.

Ellis, H. C. 1969. 'Transfer: nature, measurement, and fundamental processes' in M. H. Marx (ed.), *Learning processes*, pp. 381–478. New York: Macmillan Co.

Falk, P. 1985. Corporeality and its fates in history. *Acta Sociologica* 28 (2): 115–136.

Favret-Saada, J. 1980. *Deadly words.* Cambridge University Press (Translation of *Les mots, la mort, les sorts.* Paris: Editions Gallimard, 1977).

Feynman, R. 1983. The pleasure of finding things out. *NOVA.* Boston: WGBH Educational Foundation. No. 1002, January 25.

Flanagan, O. 1984. *The Science of the mind*. Boston: Bradford Books, MIT Press.

Foucault, M. 1970. *The order of things: Introduction to the archaeology of the human sciences*. New York: Pantheon Books.

Gay, J., and M. Cole. 1967. *The new mathematics and an old culture*. New York: Holt, Rinehart and Winston.

Geertz, C. 1983. *Local knowledge: further essays in interpretative anthropology*. New York: Basic Books.

Gentner, D., and D. R. Gentner. 1983. 'Flowing waters or teeming crowds: mental models of electricity' in D. Gentner and A. Stevens (eds.), *Mental models*. Hillsdale, NJ: Erlbaum.

Gentner, D., and A. Stevens. 1983. *Mental models*. Hillsdale, NJ: Erlbaum.

Gick, M. L., and K. J. Holyoak 1980. Analogic problem solving. *Cognitive Psychology* 12: 306–355.

Giddens, A. 1979. *Central problems in social theory: action, structure and contradiction in social analysis*. Berkeley: University of California Press.

1976. *New rules of sociological method*. London: Hutchinson. New York: Basic Books.

1984. *The constitution of society*. Berkeley: University of California Press.

Gifford, J., and G. Marcus (eds.). 1986. *Writing culture. The poetics and politics of ethnography*. Berkeley: University of California Press.

Ginsburg, H. 1977. Some problems in the study of schooling and cognition. *Quarterly Newsletter of the Institute for Comparative Human Development*, 1: 7–10. New York: The Rockefeller University.

Giroux, H. 1981. *Ideology, culture and the process of schooling*. Philadelphia, PA: Temple University Press.

Gladwin, C. 1975. 'A model of the supply of smoked fish from Cape Coast to Kumasi' in S. Plattner (ed.), *Formal methods in economic anthropology*, pp. 77–127. American Anthropological Association. Special publication.

Gladwin, H., and C. Gladwin. 1971. 'Estimating market conditions and profit expectations of fish sellers at Cape Coast, Ghana' in George Dalton (ed.), *Studies in Economic Anthropology*. Anthropological Studies No. 7, pp. 122–143. Washington, DC: American Anthropological Association.

Goffman, E. 1964. The neglected situation. *American Anthropologist* 66 (no. 6 pt 2): 133–136.

Goody, J. 1977. *The domestication of the savage mind*. Cambridge University Press.

Hallpike, C. R. 1979. *The foundations of primitive thought*. Oxford: Clarendon Press.

Hayes, J. R., and H. A. Simon. 1977. 'Psychological differences among problem isomorphs' in N. J. Castellan, D. B. Pisoni, and G. R. Potts (eds.), *Cognitive Theory*, Vol. 2, pp. 21–41. Hillsdale, NJ: Erlbaum.

Henriques, J., W. Hollway, C. Urwin, C. Venn, and V. Walkerdine. 1984. *Changing the subject: psychology, social regulation and subjectivity*. London: Methuen.

Herndon, J. 1971. *How to survive in your native land*. New York: Simon and Schuster, Inc.

Holland, D. 1981. An American folk theory of the person-in-the-social world: imagery and metaphor in talk about insults and compliments, paper presented at American Anthropological Association Meetings, 1981.

Horton, R., and R. Finnegan (eds.). 1973. *Modes of thought: essays on thinking in Western and non-Western societies*. London: Faber and Faber.

Hospers, J. 1968. 'On explanation' in R. A. Manners and D. Kaplan (eds.), *Theory in anthropology: a sourcebook*, pp. 69–79. London: Routledge and Kegan Paul.

210   *References*

Hurn, C. 1978. *The limits and possibilities of schooling: an introduction to the sociology of education*. Boston: Allyn and Bacon, Inc.

Hutchins, E. 1980. *Culture and inference: a Trobriand case study*. Cambridge, Massachusetts: Harvard University Press.

Jay, M. 1973. *The dialectical imagination*. Boston: Little, Brown and Co.

Jeeves, M., and G. Greer. 1983. *Analysis of structural learning*. London: Academic Press.

Judd, C. H., 1908. The relation of special training and general intelligence. *Educational Review* 36: 42–48.

Kintsch, W., and T. Van Dijk. 1978. Toward a model of text comprehension and production. *Psychological Review* 85: 363–394.

Knorr-Cetina, K. 1981a. Time and context in practical action. *Knowledge* 3(2): 143–165.

1981b. *The manufacture of knowledge: an essay on the constructivist and contextual nature of science*. Oxford: Pergamon Press.

Knorr-Cetina, K., and M. Mulkay. 1983. *Science observed: perspectives on the social study of science*. London: Sage Publications.

Kohler, W. 1937. Psychological remarks on some questions of anthropology. *American Journal of Psychology* 50: 271–288.

Kozulin, A. 1984. *Psychology in Utopia: toward a social history of Soviet psychology*. Cambridge, MA: The MIT Press.

Kramer, D. A. 1981. Logic in action: a 'not-so-logical' approach to daily problem solving. Symposium on adaptation and competence: perspective for the 80s. Biennial Meeting of the Society for Research on Child Development. Boston.

Kvale, S. 1977. 'Dialectics and research on remembering' in N. Datan and H. W. Reese (eds.), *Life-span developmental psychology: dialectical perspectives on experimental research*. New York: Academic Press.

Laboratory of Comparative Human Cognition. 1978. Cognition as a residual category in anthropology. *Annual Reviews in Anthropology* 7: 51–69.

1979. What's cultural about cross-cultural cognitive psychology? *Annual Reviews in Psychology* 30: 145–72.

1981. *Culture and cognitive development*. University of California, San Diego: CHIP Report 107 (To appear in J. V. Wertsch (ed.), *Culture, cognition and communication*. New York: Cambridge University Press).

Lakoff, G. V., and M. Johnson, 1980. *Metaphors we live by*. University of Chicago Press.

Larkin, K. M. 1978. An analysis of adult procedure synthesis in fraction problems. Boston: Bolt Beranek and Newman ICAI Working Paper 1.

Lash, S. 1984. Genealogy and the body: Foucault/Deleuze/Nietzsche. *Theory, culture and society* 2(2): 1–17.

Latour, B., and S. Woolgar. 1979. *Laboratory life: the social construction of scientific facts*. Beverly Hills, CA: Sage.

Lave, J. 1977. Cognitive consequences of traditional apprenticeship training in West Africa. *Anthropology and Education Quarterly* 8(3): 177–180.

1980. What's special about experiments as contexts for thinking. *The Quarterly Newsletter of the Laboratory of Comparative Human Cognition* 2(4): 86–91.

1982. A comparative approach to educational forms and learning processes. *Anthropology and Education Quarterly* 13(2): 181–187.

1986. 'Experiments, tests, jobs and chores: how we learn what we do' in K. Borman and J. Reisman (eds.), *Becoming a worker*. Norwood, NJ: Ablex.

In preparation. *Tailored learning: apprenticeship and everyday practice among craftsmen in West Africa*.

Lave, J., M. Murtaugh, and O. de la Rocha. 1984. 'The dialectic of arithmetic in grocery shopping' in B. Rogoff and J. Lave (eds.), *Everyday cognition: Its development in social context*. Cambridge, MA: Harvard University Press.

Leach, E. R. 1957. 'The epistemological background to Malinowski's empiricism' in R. Firth (ed.), *Man and culture. An evaluation of the work of Bronislaw Malinowski*. (Reprinted, London: Routledge and Kegan Paul, 1970.)

Levy-Bruhl, L. 1910. *How natives think* (Reprinted, New York: Washington Square Press, 1966).

Lynch, M. 1982. *Art and Artefacts in Laboratory Science*. London: Routledge and Kegan Paul.

Marx, K. 1957 (1887). *Capital*. Dona Torr (ed. and trans.). London: Allen & Unwin.

McCloskey, M. (1983). 'Naive theories of motion' in D. Gentner and A. L. Stevens (eds.), *Mental models*. Hillsdale, NJ: Erlbaum.

McDermott, R. P., and S. V. Goldman. 1983. 'Teaching in multicultural settings' in L. van de Berg-Elderling, *Multicultural education*, pp. 145–163. Dortrecht: Foris.

Mehan, H. B. in press. 'Oracular reasoning in a psychiatric exam: the resolution of conflict in language' in A. D. Grimshaw (ed.), *Conflict talk: sociolinguistic investigations of arguments in conversations*. Cambridge University Press.

Minick, N. J. 1985. *L. S. Vygotsky and Soviet activity theory: new perspectives on the relationship between mind and society*. PhD dissertation. Evanston, Ill: Northwestern University.

Morris, M., and P. Patton. 1979. *Michel Foucault: power, truth, strategy*. Sydney: Feral Publications.

Murtaugh, M. 1985a. A hierarchical decision process model of American grocery shopping. PhD dissertation. University of California, Irvine.

  1985b. The practice of arithmetic by American grocery shoppers. *Anthropology and Education Quarterly* 16(3): 186–192.

Nadel, S. F. 1937. Experiments on cultural psychology. *Africa* 10: 421–435.

Neisser, U. 1976. *Cognition and reality: principles and implications of cognitive psychology*. San Francisco: W. H. Freeman and Company.

Newman, D., P. Griffin, and M. Cole. 1984. 'Laboratory and classroom tasks: Social constraints and the evaluation of children's performance' in B. Rogoff and J. Lave (eds.), *Everyday cognition: its development in social context*. Cambridge, MA: Harvard University Press.

Norman, D. 1980. 'Cognitive Engineering and Education' in D. T. Tuma and F. Reif (eds.), *Problem solving and education: issues in teaching and research*, pp. 97–107. Hillsdale, NJ: Erlbaum.

Ortner, S. B. 1984. Theory in anthropology since the sixties. *Comparative Studies in Society and History* 26(1): 126–166.

Parkin, D. 1980. 'Kind bridewealth and hard cash: Eventing a structure' in J. L. Comaroff (ed.), *The meaning of marriage payments*. New York: Academic Press.

Parsons, T. 1957. 'Malinowski and the theory of social systems' in R. Firth (ed.), *Man and culture: an evaluation of the work of Bronislaw Malinowski*. London: Routledge and Kegan Paul.

Pelto, P., and G. Pelto. 1975. Intracultural variation. Special issue. *American Ethnologist* 2(1).

Petitto, A. 1979. Knowledge of arithmetic among schooled and unschooled African tailors and cloth-merchants. PhD dissertation. Ithaca, NY: Cornell University.

Polanyi, M. 1958. The stability of scientific theories against experience. Excerpts from Michael Polanyi, *Personal knowledge*, pp. 286–294. University of Chicago Press. (In *Witchcraft and sorcery*, ed. M. Marwick. Harmondsworth, Middlesex, England: Penguin Editions, 1970.)

Polanyi, K., C. M. Arensberg, and H. W. Pearson (eds.). 1957. *Trade and market in the early empires; economies in history and theory*. Glencoe, Ill: Free Press.

Pollner, M. 1974. Mundane reasoning. *Philosophy of the Social Science*. 4: 35–54.

Posner, J. 1978. The development of mathematical knowledge among Baoule and Dioula children in Ivory Coast. PhD dissertation. Ithaca, NY: Cornell University.

Price-Williams, D. 1980. 'Anthropological approaches to cognition and their relevance to psychology' in H. C. Triandis and W. J. Lonner (eds.), *Handbook of cross-cultural psychology*, vol. 3. Boston: Allyn and Bacon.

Quinn, N. 1975. Decision models of social structure. *American Ethnologist* 2(1): 19–46.
  1976. A natural system used in Mfantse litigation settlement. *American Ethnologist* 3: 331–351. Revised and reprinted in R. Casson (ed.), *Language, culture, and cognition*. New York: Macmillan.
  1982. 'Commitment' in American marriage: A cultural analysis. *American Ethnologist*. 5 (2): 206–226.

Reed, H. J., and J. Lave, 1979. Arithmetic as a tool for investigating relations between culture and cognition. *American Ethnologist* 6 (3): 568–582.

Reed, S., G. Ernst, and R. Banerji. 1974. The role of analogy in transfer between similar problem states. *Cognitive Psychology* 6(3): 436–450.

Rivers, W. H. R. 1926. *Psychology and ethnology*. London: Kegan Paul, Trench, Trübner.

Roberts, J. M. 1964. 'The Self-management of cultures' in W. H. Goodenough (ed.), *Explorations in cultural anthropology*, pp. 433–454. New York: McGraw-Hill.

Rogoff, B., and J. Lave (eds.). 1984. *Everyday Cognition: its development in social context*. Cambridge, MA: Harvard University Press.

Romney, A. and R. G. D'Andrade, 1964. Cognitive aspects of English kin terms. *American Anthropologist* 66 (3) part 2: 146–170.

Romney, A. K., R. N. Shepard, and S. B. Nerlove. *Multidimensional scaling*, Vol. 2, *Applications*. New York: Seminar Press.

Romney, A. K., S. Weller, and W. Batchelder. 1986. Culture as consensus: a theory of culture and informant accuracy. *American Anthropologist* 88(2): 313–338.

Sahlins, M. 1976. *Culture and practical reason*. University of Chicago Press.
  1981. *Historical metaphors and mythical realities*. Ann Arbor: University of Michigan Press.

Said, E. 1978. *Orientalism*. New York, NY: Random House.

Samelson, F. 1974. History, origin, myth and ideology: Comte's "discovery" of social psychology. *Journal for the Theory of Social Behavior* 4: 217–231.

Sampson, E. 1977. Psychology and the American ideal. *Journal of Personality and Social Psychology* 35(1): 767–782.

Schenck, D. 1985. Merleau-Ponty on perspectivism, with references to Nietzsche. *Philosophy and Phenomenological Research* 46(2): 307–314.

Schliemann, A. 1985. Schooling versus practice in problem solving: a study on mathematics among carpenters and carpentry apprentices, unpublished paper on file at Recife, Brazil: Universidade Federal de Pernambuco.

Scribner, S. 1977. 'Modes of thinking and ways of speaking: Culture and logic reconsidered' in P. N. Johnson-Laird and P. C. Wason (eds.), *Thinking: readings in cognitive science*, pp. 483–500. Cambridge University Press.

1984a. (ed.). Cognitive studies of work. Special issue of the *Quarterly Newsletter of the Laboratory of Comparative Human Cognition*. 6(1 and 2).

1984b. 'Studying working intelligence' in B. Rogoff and J. Lave (eds.), *Everyday cognition: its development in social context*. Cambridge, MA: Harvard University Press.

Scribner, S., and M. Cole. 1973. Formal and informal education. *Science* 182(4112): 553–559.

1981. *The psychology of literacy*. Cambridge, MA: Harvard University Press.

Scribner, S., and E. Fahrmeier. 1982. Practical and theoretical arithmetic: some preliminary findings. Industrial Literacy Project, Working Paper No. 3. Graduate Center, CUNY.

Shepard, R. N., A. K. Romney, and S. B. Nerlove. 1972. *Multidimensional scaling*, Vol. 1, *Theory*. New York: Seminar Press.

Shweder, R. A. 1977. Likeness and likelihood in everyday thought: magical thinking in judgments about personality. *Current Anthropology* 18: 637–648.

Siegel, A. W. 1977. '"Remembering" is alive and well (and even thriving) in empiricism' in N. Datan and H. W. Reese (eds.), *Life-span developmental psychology: dialectical perspectives on experimental research*. New York: Academic Press.

Simmel, Georg. 1978 (1907). *The philosophy of money*. T. Bottomore and D. Frisby (trans.). London, Boston: Routledge and Kegan Paul.

Simon, H. A. 1969. *The sciences of the artificial*. Cambridge, MA: The MIT Press.

1976. 'Cognition and social behavior' in J. S. Carroll and J. W. Payne (eds.), *Cognition and social behavior*. Hillsdale, NJ: Lawrence Erlbaum.

1980. 'Problem solving and education' in D. T. Tuma and F. Reif (eds.), *Problem solving and education: issues in teaching and research*, pp. 81–96. Hillsdale, NJ: Erlbaum.

Simon, H. A., and M. Barenfeld. 1969. Information processing analysis of perceptual processes in problem solving. *Psychological Review* 76: 473–483.

Slovic, P., B. Fischoff, and S. Lichtenstein. 1976. 'Cognitive processes and societal risk taking' in J. S. Carroll and J. W. Payne (eds.), *Cognition and social behavior*. Hillsdale, NJ: Erlbaum.

Smart, B. 1982. Foucault, sociology, and the problem of human agency. *Theory and Society* 11(2): 121–141.

Sohn-Rethel, A. 1978. *Intellectual and manual labor: a critique of epistemology*. Atlantic City, NJ: Humanities Press.

Stevens, A. L., and D. Gentner. 1983. 'Introduction' in D. Gentner and A. Stevens (eds.), *Mental Models*. Hillsdale, NJ: Erlbaum.

Suchman, L. A. 1980. Office procedures as political action: organization theory and system design, unpublished paper on file at Palo Alto: Xerox Research Center.

Thevenot, L. 1984. Rules and implements: investment in forms. *Social Science Information* 23(1): 1–45.

Thorndike, E. L. 1913. *Educational psychology*, Vol. 2, *The psychology of learning*. New York: Columbia University Press.

Traweek, S. In press. 'Discovering machines: Nature in the age of its mechanical reproduction' in F. A. Dubinskas, (ed.), *Chronos' children: anthropologies of time in science and high technology organizations*. Philadelphia: Temple University Press.

Turkle, S. 1984. *The second self: computers and the human spiri*. New York: Simon and Schuster.

Turner, B. S. 1984. *The body and society*. Oxford: Basil Blackwell Publisher.

Varenne, H., and M. Kelly. 1976. Friendship and fairness: ideological tensions in an American high school. *Teachers College Record* 77: 601–614.

Wallace, A., and J. Atkins. 1960. The meaning of kinship terms. *American Anthropologist* 62: 58–80.

Warren, S. 1984. *The emergence of dialectical theory*. University of Chicago Press.

Watt, W. 1979. Iconic equilibrium. *Semiotica* 28: 31–62.

Wexler, K., and A. K. Romney. 1972. 'Individual variation in cognitive structures' in R. N. Shepard, A. K. Romney and S. Nerlove (eds.), *Multidimensional scaling: theory and application in the behavioral sciences*, Vol. 2, pp. 73–92. New York: Seminar Press.

White, H. 1973. Foucault decoded: notes from underground. *History and Theory* 12(1): 223–254.

White, L. 1949. *The science of culture*. New York: Wiley.

Williamson, M. D., J. D. Hollan, and A. L. Stevens. 1983. 'Human reasoning about a simple physical system' in D. Gentner, and A. L. Stevens (eds.), *Mental models*. Hillsdale, NJ: Erlbaum.

Willis, P. E. 1977. *Learning to labour*. Farnborough, England Saxon House.

Wilson, B. (ed.). 1970. *Rationality: key concepts in the social sciences*. Oxford: Basil Blackwell.